THE COMIC
TRADITION
IN IRISH
WOMEN
WRITERS

Edited by
THERESA O'CONNOR

UNIVERSITY PRESS OF FLORIDA

Gainesville Tallahassee Tampa Boca Raton Pensacola Orlando Miami Jacksonville

Chapter 1, "What Foremothers?" by Nuala Ní Dhomhnaill, is reprinted by permission of *Poetry Ireland Review*.
Chapter 4, "'Humor with a Gender': Somerville and Ross and *The Irish R.M.*," by James M. Cahalan, copyright 1993 by the Irish American Cultural Institute of St. Paul, Minnesota, is reprinted by permission of the editors of *Éire-Ireland* and the Irish American Cultural Institute.
In chapter 9, lines from "Cathleen" (translated by Paul Muldoon) from *The Astrakhan Cloak*, by Nuala Ní Dhomhnaill, and from "The Race" (translated by Derek Mahon), "The Broken Doll" (translated by John Montague), "Blodewedd" (translated by John Montague), "The Unfaithful Wife" (translated by Paul Muldoon), and "Oriental Morning" (translated by Michael Hartnett) from *Pharaoh's Daughter*, by Nuala Ní Dhomhnaill, are reprinted by permission of Wake Forest University Press. Lines from "Dúil," "Bradáin," "Máthair," "Labhrann Medb," "Cú Chulainn I," "Cú Chulainn II," "Agallamh," and "Labhrann an Mhór-Rion" are reprinted by permission of Nuala Ní Dhomhnaill.

01 00 99 98 97 96   6 5 4 3 2 1

LIBRARY OF CONGRESS CATALOGING-IN-PUBLICATION DATA
The comic tradition in Irish women writers / [edited by] Theresa O'Connor.
p. cm.
Includes bibliographical references (p.) and index.
ISBN 0-8130-1457-3 (cloth: alk. paper)
1. English literature—Irish authors—History and criticism. 2. Humorous stories, English—Women authors—History and criticism. 3. Humorous stories, English—Irish authors—History and criticism. 4. English wit and humor—Irish authors—History and criticism. 5. English literature—Women authors—History and criticism. 6. Women and literature—Ireland—History. 7. Comic, The, in literature. 8. Ireland—In literature. I. O'Connor, Theresa.
PR8733.C66 1996
823'.0099287—dc20   96-22957

The University Press of Florida is the scholarly publishing agency for the State University System of Florida, comprised of Florida A & M University, Florida Atlantic University, Florida International University, Florida State University, University of Central Florida, University of Florida, University of North Florida, University of South Florida, and University of West Florida.

University Press of Florida, 15 Northwest 15th Street, Gainesville, FL 32611

for my mother, Catherine O'Connor,
and my father, James L. O'Connor

Contents

Acknowledgments

This book had its earliest beginnings in a conversation with Vivian Mercier and Eilís Dillon at a Joyce conference on the island of San Giorgio Maggiore in Venice in 1988. I benefited greatly from the encouragement I received from this wise, generous, and formidably learned pair.

I would like to thank my parents, my sisters, Jo, Jula, Anne, and Noirìn, my brother, James, Ché (a Swiftian satirist), and my neighbors in Brosna, County Kerry, for giving me the gift of a comic faith, a faith that is deep inside me forever. I also wish to thank Mary Cunningham Shallow for her *bon vivant* encouragement over the past decade. I am indebted too to the Knox *Finnegans Wake* reading group—Zali Gurevitch, Jon Berry, Holly Montague, Lance Factor, and Bill Young, for reminding me of the value and importance of comedy, and to Bridget McCarthy (Roscam), Mary Ann English, Lee Jacobus, and Margaret Higonnet for their generosity and practical assistance.

I owe thanks too to David Wasser and Susan Abbotson for reading this manuscript, acting as editorial assistants, and providing invaluable advice. I wish to acknowledge my deep gratitude to Rose Quiello; I profited enormously from her kindness and expertise. I also wish to acknowledge my gratitude to Deidre Bryan of the University Press of Florida, Brendan Teeling of the Dublin Public Libraries, and the International James Joyce Foundation, whose award of a graduate student fellowship helped me to begin the work that finds its completion here.

My greatest debt is to James McCarthy, whose wisdom, irreverence, and creative imagination enabled me to complete this book.

Introduction
Tradition and the Signifying Monkey

THERESA O'CONNOR

Tradition is the practice of ceaselessly excavating, safeguarding, violating, discarding and reinscribing the past. . . . history is not a fair copy, but a palimpsest, whose deleted layers must be thrust to light.
TERRY EAGLETON

In *The Signifying Monkey,* Henry Louis Gates draws on a Yoruba tale entitled "The Two Friends" to illustrate the bifocal hermeneutic impulse at the heart of the African (and African-American) comic tradition. The story, which has at its center the dual-gendered trickster figure Esu-Elegbara, tells of two friends who had vowed eternal friendship to one another without taking Esu into account. In order to teach them a lesson, Esu donned a black and white hat and rode between them as they worked in the fields. Thus, while one man saw only the black side of the hat, the other saw only the white side. Later, a violent argument arose between the friends as to the color of the stranger's hat. In the midst of the uproar Esu returned, and, admonishing the friends for their base and foolish conduct, s/he showed them the two-colored hat. As Gates notes, this story "ascribes to Esu his principal function of the indeterminacy of interpretation. . . . The folly depicted here is to insist—to the point of rupture of the always fragile bond of a human institution—on one determinate meaning, itself determined by vantage point and the mode one employs to see" (35). Gates goes on to argue that

"The metaphor of a double-voiced Esu-Elegbara corresponds to the double-voiced nature of the Signifyin(g) utterance. . . . Signi-fyin(g), then, is a metaphor for textual revision" (88). Signifyin(g), the trope that Gates finds in black texts as "explicit theme, implicit rhetorical strategy, and as a principle of literary history" (89), is also indigenous to Ireland. In fact, this Yoruba tale might serve as a model for the form of critical attention appropriate to the comic tradition of Ireland—a nation whose early links with Africa are attested to in the *Geography* of Ptolemy of Alexandria (A.D. c. 100–178)—a tradition that has at its center a dual-gendered trickster figure who bears a striking resemblance to Esu.

Vivian Mercier's *The Irish Comic Tradition* (1962) significantly paved the way for this book. Mercier's groundbreaking work claims the comic as the central tradition in Irish literature; however, in characterizing this tradition, he has tended to exclude or ignore women's literary expression. In other words, his interpretative frame of reference is one-sided. While Mercier acknowledges his debt to Maria Edgeworth's *Essay on Irish Bulls* (a work she coauthored with her father), he makes only a brief mention of her comic novels, works in which the comedy, as Eiléan Ní Chuilleanáin observes in "The Voices of Maria Edgeworth's Comedy," often comes "from the suppression of [women's] protesting voices." The works of Edith Somerville, Martin Ross, and Lady Gregory are mentioned only in passing. What emerges, ultimately, from his classic work is a vision of a nation where men—among them Swift, Congreve, Farquhar, Goldsmith, Sheridan, Wilde, Shaw, Beckett, and Joyce—are conspicuously witty and women are conspicuous only by their absence.

The goal of this collection is to address the absence of the female in the Irish comic tradition and, indeed, in the canonical Irish literary tradition. According to the authors of *Tradisiun Liteartha na nGael*, a historical survey of the Irish literary tradition, as Nuala Ní Dhomhnaill notes in chapter 1 of this volume, "Is beag rian a d'fhag na mna ar thraidisiun litheartha na Gaeilge" [Women have left little mark on the Irish literary tradition]. Similarly, *The Field Day Anthology of Irish Writing* mentions few women.

It is the occulted comic voices of women that this work represents, bringing them back to disturb and interrupt the writing of the Irish canon. I have two broad aims. First, I want to make clear the role played by nine Irish women writers in shaping the Irish comic tradition: Maria Edgeworth (1767–1849), Lady Gregory (1852–1932), Edith Somerville

(1858–1949), Violet Martin/Martin Ross (1862–1915), Molly Keane (1904–), Iris Murdoch (1919–), Edna O'Brien (1930–), Julia O'Faolain (1932–), and Nuala Ní Dhomhnaill (1952–). Second, I want to suggest that the notion of ethical dialogue dramatized in the Yoruba story of Esu, but also indigenously Irish, might serve as a frame for a revisionist reading of Ireland's comic heritage.

Among the most influential studies of Ireland's comic tradition to date are Mercier's work and David Krause's *The Profane Book of Irish Comedy* (1982). While Mercier traces the roots of Ireland's comic tradition to what Michael Patrick Gillespie describes in his essay in this volume as "a legacy of sardonic, polemic critiques of society," Krause's study has as its focus the tradition of subversive humor that informs the Ossianic dialogues. "The main thrust of Krause's argument," James MacKillop points out, "is that the Ossianic dialogues form a vast literature, much largely lost, which celebrates the joys of the pagan world of nature and berates the repressions of foreign Christianity. He sees Oisín as the first subversive against the strictures of Holy Ireland, the ancestor of a figure who runs through Irish culture and literature down to modern times" (*Celtic Myth*, 126).

I would like to suggest a third frame of reference for discussing Ireland's comic tradition: the notion of ethical dialogue that informs the African hermeneutic system Gates describes in *The Signifying Monkey* and early Irish mythic tales. "Ethical dialogue," as Simon Critchley states, "should not result in the annulment of alterity, but in respect for it" (*Deconstruction*, 13). It is precisely this ideal that comprises the crux of the comedy of shifting perspectives we find in the stories of the young poet Finn (a Janus-faced seer who sees, like Esu, from two perspectives simultaneously). These stories, particularly *Machniomhartha Finn* (The boyhood deeds of Fionn), show a culture trying to devise strategies to mediate between self and other, male and female, the world of being and nonbeing. At the heart of *Machniomhartha Finn* (a story that served as a prototype for the Perceval myth, the work in which Cixous's theory of *écriture féminine* is rooted) is a quest for a language of the essentially other in the Otherworld of women.

In Ireland, as in Africa, the trickster figure became increasingly masculinized. Eventually its female aspect was suppressed. The ideal of ethical dialogue survived in the cultural unconscious, as it were, and it eventually found a (doubled) voice in the African-American cultural system bound up with the "signifying monkey" (Gates, 1–50) and in works such as *Finnegans Wake*. It survived too in Irish women's writing. The women whose work is discussed in this volume bring widely different perspectives to their work, but transcending these differences are certain commonalties, most notably a focus on boundaries and a hybridizing vision that engages in witty negotiation with established patriarchal, colonial, and nationalist orthodoxies.

I turn now, very briefly, to the specifics that inform each essay. The essay/letter that serves as chapter 1 of this volume, Nuala Ní Dhomhnaill's "What Foremothers?," is a bitingly funny response to a critic who argues that Irish women poets have "a long healthy chain of foremothers." Ní Dhomhnaill paints a blunt yet witty portrait of the struggle of the Irish woman poet to gain "even a precarious toehold" in the Irish literary tradition, a tradition in which "there hasn't been mention of even as much as one woman poet . . . for over a thousand years."

Just as the *Book of Kells* serves as kind of "contact zone"—to use Mary Louise Pratt's phrase—between the Christian worldview and the worldview of pagan Celtic Ireland, the work of the eighteenth-century essayist and novelist Maria Edgeworth serves as a contact zone between colonial Anglo-Irish culture and the indigenous Gaelic cultural tradition. Eiléan Ní Chuilleanáin's "The Voices of Maria Edgeworth's Comedy" examines the links between the theory of comedy developed in Edgeworth's *Essay on Irish Bulls* and the comic vision that informs her many novels, among them *Castle Rackrent, Almeira, Belinda, Patronage, Vivian,* and *Helen.* What appears to be missing in the criticism of Edgeworth, Ní Chuilleanáin points out, is a frame of reference that might supply a connection between the comic vision of her Irish characters, her moral-social commentary on women's lives, and the philosophical/educational interests she shared with her father.

With Edgeworth, Lady Gregory is one of the Irish women writers whose work best represents the hybridizing vision in Ireland's comic intellectual heritage. Mary Lowe-Evans's "Hyacinth and the Wise Man: Lady Gregory's Comic Enterprise" examines the influence of Lady Gregory's comic vision—a vision shaped by the work of writers such as Molière—on the Abbey playwrights and in particular on the work of Yeats. She argues that Lady Gregory's "Kiltartan Molière" pieces—such works as *Twenty Five, The Poorhouse, Spreading the News,* and *Hyacinth Halvey*—set out to open "the discourse of the National Theater to carnival, forcing the polemic of identity construction to become communal rather than autocratic."

James M. Cahalan's "'Humor with a Gender': Somerville and Ross and *The Irish R.M"* looks at the careers of two cousins, Edith Somerville

(1858–1949) and Violet Martin/Martin Ross (1862–1915). Cahalan's essay, a feminist rewriting of the history of their collaboration, focuses on their interrelations with the cultural world of their time as reflected in the history of their work's reception. Drawing on Langston Hughes's insights into the comedy of the oppressed in *The Book of Negro Humor*, he argues that the comic vision that informs the work of these women has been repeatedly misunderstood: they were not victimizers but the victims of the Irish.

In "The Crumbling Fortress: Molly Keane's Comedies of Anglo-Irish Manners," Rachael Jane Lynch examines Molly Keane's tragicomic portraits of Anglo-Irish society in its death throes. Keane's work, she points out, "dances at the crossroads where two comic traditions meet." Equally concerned with imperialist politics and sexual politics, with the Anglo-Irish "Big House" tradition and patriarchy, Keane's "viciously funny novels," Lynch argues, might be read through the lens of contemporary feminist comic theory and the comic theories of Mercier and Krause.

How do we distinguish an "authentic" from an "inauthentic" Irish writer? Flora Alexander's essay, "Iris Murdoch's Moral Comedy," responds to the present need for a reevaluation of the complex issue of identity in the work of Murdoch, a writer born—like Joyce and Beckett—in Dublin. Alexander examines the Irish element in the work of this writer/philosopher who views herself as a kind of exile. While Murdoch's "moral comedy" is crucially influenced by the comic melancholia of Beckett, Alexander points out that her "comedy of human relations" is interwoven with a satiric treatment of prejudiced attitudes to Ireland and the Irish.

The influence of Joyce—a man dismissed by many feminist readers as "a chauvinist author, a misogynist, a pornographer, and a champion of patriarchal privilege" (Henke, "Re-Visioning," 138)—on Edna O'Brien and Julia O'Faolain is the subject of the next two essays in this collection. In "(S)he Was Too Scrupulous Always: Edna O'Brien and the Comic Tradition," Michael Patrick Gillespie looks at the writings of Edna O'Brien in the context of two disparate Irish traditions: "the convention of sardonic social commentary that has formed an integral part of the Irish comic tradition" and the work of Joyce. What distinguishes O'Brien's satiric vision from that of the majority of her Irish male contemporaries, he points out, is her distinctly Joycean "partiality for ambiguities."

In my own "History, Gender, and the Postcolonial Condition: Julia O'Faolain's Comic Rewriting of *Finnegans Wake*," I make a similar argument. My basic thesis is that O'Faolain's *No Country For Young Men* is an intertextual tale rooted in the *Wake*, Joyce's comic history of history. Both works have at their center a traumatized dreamer haunted by a black "bogey." A key difference between O'Faolain's story and that of Joyce, I argue, lies in the gender of the dreamer: whereas Joyce presents a man as a model for the split psyche of history, O'Faolain uses a woman.

In "Lashings of the Mother Tongue: Nuala Ní Dhomhnaill's Anarchic Laughter," Mary O'Connor situates Ní Dhomhnaill's work simultaneously in the Gaelic Irish comic tradition and in the tradition of those Third World writers engaged in the process of cultural decolonization. Ní Dhomhnaill, she argues, is creating and becoming part of what Frantz Fanon calls a "national literature." Even as she lashes out at the repressive pieties of contemporary Ireland, she searches for a "healing balm" that might make whole the wounds of Ireland's nightmarish history. In the work of Ní Dhomhnaill, the Gaelic-language poet whose West Kerry ancestors numbered among their foremothers the daughter of a pharaoh, the doubled vision of a Gaelic-speaking people whose archaic comic tradition celebrates what Salman Rushdie terms "hybridity, impurity, intermingling, the transformation that comes of new and unexpected combinations of human beings, cultures, ideas, politics" ("Pen," 482). Nowhere is the continuity of this tradition more readily apparent in Ní Dhomhnaill's work than in the title she chose for a recently published bilingual collection of poems, *Pharaoh's Daughter*.

"All of a sudden Alice heard her father's voice; Father, who had been dead for years! His light tenor was muffled and weighted as if it clawed through the layers of earth which encased his body, to get to her." This passage from Clare Boylan's *Black Baby* describes the struggle of Boylan's central character, Alice, to exhume her mother tongue, represented here as the spirit of her father. The nurturing father figure (entombed in a gramophone) who haunts Boylan's work might be Joyce. In "Joyce and Boylan's *Black Baby*: 'Swiftly and Silently'" Jean-Louis Giovannangeli traces the links between Joyce's work—in particular, his deconstruction of whiteness in the *Wake*—and Boylan's. Like Joyce, he argues, Boylan struggles to exhume Ireland's occulted mother tongue by deconstructing the racism and sexism in which the father tongue is buried. If the secular angel of epiphany who calls for the resurrection of Erse (Irish) in the *Wake* is a black "bogey" bound up with the Egyptian *Book of the Dead* and the *Book of Kells*, the dark other who resurrects Alice's mother tongue in *Black Baby* is a black woman: "Dark

Dinah, high in her spreading patch of light." "Dark Dinah," who paints Alice's decaying house and the rotting plaster angel that adorns its wall a brilliant yellow, is Boylan's dark angel of epiphany; she is the repressed "bogey" buried in the subconscious of the Alice in Wonderland, the Sleeping Beauty, that is contemporary Ireland.

I would like to conclude my discussion here by turning to T. S. Eliot's often-quoted "Tradition and the Individual Talent." "The existing monuments [of a literary tradition]," Eliot argues, "form an ideal order among themselves, which is modified by the introduction of the new (the really new) work of art among them. . . . the *whole* existing order must be, if ever so slightly, altered" (761). Similarly, our vision of the Irish comic tradition is modified when we include in the existing "ideal order" the outlawed texts of Irish women. A revisionist reading of Ireland's comic tradition, in other words, a reading from the perspective of two genders, demands a new kind of double optic, a new kind of interpretative frame of reference capable of grappling with difference. As Homi K. Bhabha states, "it is by living on the borderlines of history and language, on the limits of race and gender, that we are in a position to translate the differences between them into a kind of solidarity" ("DissemiNation," 320).

WORKS CITED

Bhabha, Homi K. "DissemiNation." In *Nation and Narration*, edited by Homi K. Bhabha, 320. London: Routledge, 1990.

Critchley, Simon. *The Ethics of Deconstruction: Derrida and Levinas.* Oxford: Blackwell, 1992.

Eliot, T. S. "Tradition and the Individual Talent." In *Critical Theory Since Plato*, edited by Hazard Adams, 761. New York: Harcourt Brace Jovanovich, 1992.

Gates, Henry Louis, Jr. *The Signifying Monkey: A Theory of African-American Literary Criticism.* Oxford: Oxford University Press, 1988.

Henke, Suzette. "Re-Visioning Joyce's Masculine Signature." In *Joyce in Context*, edited by Vincent J. Cheng and Timothy Martin, 138. Cambridge: Cambridge University Press, 1992.

MacKillop, James. *Fionn mac Cumhaill: Celtic Myth in English Literature.* Syracuse, N.Y.: Syracuse University Press, 1986.

Rushdie, Salman. "A Pen Against the Sword." In *One World, Many Cultures*, edited by Stuart Hirschberg, 482. New York: Macmillan, 1992.

What Foremothers?

Nuala Ní Dhomhnaill

In a recent issue of the *PN Review,* the American poet Anne Stevenson (living in England) responded to Eavan Boland's essay "Outside History," which had previously appeared in the *Review* and was also printed in Ireland as a LIP pamphlet from the Attic Press under the name *A Kind of Scar: The Woman Poet in a National Tradition* (1989).[1] In her contribution, Stevenson berates Boland for being polemical and for not appealing to the "long healthy chain of foremothers" that seemingly are available to her as a woman poet in Ireland. "Why is her imagination not excited by these vivid figures of the past," she asks, "but set off instead by the defeated image of the Achill woman?" As an Irish woman poet who writes in Irish, not out of any specifically conscious agenda but because I have no choice (I can write prose in English no bother, and even jingles and verse, but *never* poetry), I confess to finding myself at a bit of a loss. Long healthy chain of foremothers? Does Anne Stevenson have access to some latest scholarship that I, not attached to any academic institution, know nothing about? Have the canonical precepts of accepted criticism been so thoroughly debunked that all is changed utterly? Maybe it is high time they should be, but how could all this have gone on completely unbeknownst to me, who am, after all, passionately and totally interested in this subject? The whole article and especially this claim about foremothers deserves closer scrutiny.

Anne Stevenson confesses to being "at most, an enthusiastic amateur in Irish Studies." There is nothing intrinsically wrong with that; in fact, enthusiastic amateurs are very much to be welcomed in an area that has long been nearly invisible in the cultural context of these islands. We, the colonized, have always had to know much more about the other island than they have ever taken the slightest effort to know about us. Nevertheless, some of the claims that Stevenson makes on our behalf are, to say the very least, alarming. It seems that her main authority for the "long healthy chain of foremothers" is a verbal statement of John Montague's to the effect that "women poets had never been discriminated against in Ireland. Many of the greatest poets in Irish had been women." Now, though in one noted case (that of Eibhlín Dubh Ní Chonaill) the second part of this statement may be true, it does not necessarily follow from the first part. Make no mistake about it, women poets in Irish were always highly discriminated against and still are (more on which anon). Now, either John Montague was having a joke at Anne Stevenson's expense, or there was something infinitely more subtle and sinister going on, that is, the lavish overpraising of mythical women poets of some great prelapsarian past as an excuse for not taking proper cognizance of living women poets of our own day. (We are just not good enough; we don't measure up to the women who have gone before us.) Either way the statement is just arrant nonsense. In any case, as Anne Stevenson says, she disbelieved him. Sensible woman. Millions would.

But then something peculiar happens. She subsequently comes across *The Faber Book of Irish Verse* edited by Montague and undergoes a conversion to his viewpoint. Again this Damascene revelation and its aftereffects deserve a little closer scrutiny, because it is at this point that inaccuracy and wishful thinking disintegrate into downright falsehoods. In what I admit is a quick paraphrase of Montague's introduction, Stevenson says that "pagan classics like *The Great Tain* and *Cúchulain* survived, ironically enough, in the monasteries." Now, at the risk of being pedantic, I feel obliged to point out that there are no such texts as *The Great Tain* and *Cúchulain.* Cúchulainn is a character in the Ulster Cycle, and one of the main texts of his exploits, though not by far the only one, is the *Táin Bó Cuailnge.* A small point, I know, but I am only working up to it.

Farther down the text, Stevenson announces that Giolla Brighde Mac Namee, a thirteenth-century poet who is praying for a child, is a woman.

How she can have come to that extraordinary conclusion, I do not know, except through a misunderstanding of the poet's own line: "Brigid after whom they named me / Beg a son for my reward." Even much later it is not unusual for Irish men to be named after female saints (Joseph Mary Plunkett, for instance), the saint's name following the word *giolla*, which according to *Contributions to a Dictionary of the Irish Language*, published by the Royal Irish Academy, is "commonly used from the close of the 10th century as the first element of masc. proper names." At no time could this name be taken as anything other than masculine, and even a cursory glance by Stevenson at Montague's introduction would have saved her from this mistake: "Though Giolla Brighde Mac Namee prays for a son, he is also hoping for an intellectual heir." And that is not all.

Later on in the article, a poem called "The Snoring Bedfellow" is at-tributed by Stevenson to, again, a woman. The original of this transla-tion by John V. Kelleher is the poem that starts, "Ní binn do thorann rem thaoibh, a mhacaoimh shaoir na bhfonn ngarbhl," published by T. O Rathaille in *Meascra Dánta 1*. The various stanzas translated are not attributed to any author, though another version of only four qua-trains followed by two stanzas in stress meter is ascribed to Aindrias Mac Craith. That version, however, was obviously written later than was the poem Kelleher translated. There is no evidence whatsoever to make out that the poet was a woman; on the contrary, the bedfellow is very obviously a male.

To be the bedfellow of the chieftain was at the time a great favor bitterly fought over by professional (male) poets and was considered especially by those who were *ollaimh flatha* (chieftain's poets) to be their legal right. A poet of the time could tell his patron that it was no act of adultery against his wife to "lie with me and my kind." Indeed, one of the commonest tropes for the relationship of the poet to his chief was that of a woman to her lover; many poems were written on that subject, the most famous of which perhaps is the poem beginning, "Feach féin an obair-se, a Aodh," which features in T. O Rathaille's *Dánta Grá*. No less a scholar than Robin Flower himself, influenced perhaps by the sexual mores of his time, describes this poem in his introduction to the book as a picture of a woman swaying between two lovers. James Carney, in a chapter of his *Studies in Irish Literature and History* de-voted to what had become known as the "Féach Féin Controversy," de-molishes this theory for good and proves that the poem is a (not en-tirely) conventional eulogy written by a professional poet: "The poet visiting O'Rourke's household where Costello, possibly O'Rourke's son-in-law, is a guest, is called to exercise his profession and to praise both. As a kind of *tour de force* he praises the two men in a single poem, dividing his praise so equally that it is hard to say—like all his caste he is a professional diplomat—where his better affection lies." So much for another insomniac woman poet.

Peppered throughout the Stevenson article are references to early woman poets such as Liadán of Corcaguiney or the Hag of Bere [*sic*]. She speaks of the recognizable voice of Emer and notes that the earliest mention of all of a woman poet, that of Fidelm, *banfhaidh* (the prophetess), is described in the *Táin* (not to mention the fact that Déirdre speaks great poetry). It is true that we have a long tradition of poems beginning "Grania, Derbhorgilla etc. . . . cecinit," even way back to one spoken by the very earliest foremother of us all, "Mé Éabha." But here we have to make a very important distinction between (a) a woman poet producing a text, (b) a woman character described in a text written by a man, and (c) a woman described as a poet in a text written by a man. Medhbh, Liadán, the Hag of Beare, and so on, wonderfully powerful and enabling as they may be, and even when described as *banfhile* (woman poet), *banfháidh* (woman soothsayer), and *bancháinteach* (woman satirist), *are all fictions of the imaginations of men*. Not one of them holds up as what Eavan Boland is looking for: "the lived vocation, the craft witnessed by a human life."

The Classical Irish period, from the twelfth century onward, is even worse from the point of view of women poets. Apart from Isibeul Ni Mhic Cailín, Countess of Argyll, to whom at least one poem is attributed in *Dánta Grá*, no other woman is mentioned as writing a poetic text of this period. (And she was Scottish anyway, writing before the common literary language of the two countries broke up along geographic lines as the social fabric underlying it disintegrated.) The poets at this time were rigidly jealous in safeguarding the status quo. As Donnchadh O Corráin says, "this caste of hereditary/quasi-hereditary scholars quite self-consciously held themselves in the highest esteem and discharged duties of very considerable political and social importance. . . . Their powers as arbiters of good custom, as provers of pedigree (and thus of claim to role and property), as panegyrists of the great, and above all, as makers of the past who reshaped it to accord with the pretensions and ambitions of the contemporary holders of power, were extensively and jealously guarded."[2] As we know from other professions, such as medicine and gynecology, whose practitioners jealously guard their acquired status and power, there was fat chance of women getting a look in. Out go the banfhilí (women poets) with the *mná luibheanna* (herb women) and the *mná cabhartha* (midwives). In come the poets (male only) with the physicians and obstetricians.

Things haven't changed much since then. Even after the great shipwreck of the native tradition, when all that was left of aboriginal literary activity was a few lonely scribes working by rushlight in smoky cabins to transcribe the rather paltry oral compositions of the day, women were not allowed into the canon. As Seán O Coileán has pointed out in *The Irish Lament: An Oral Genre*, "even when the paper manuscripts which received it were poor affairs indeed, transcribed by every common sort, the literary canon, such as it was, still found no place for the keen."

Because the fact of the matter was, though the literary canon was drawn up without them, there *were* women poets. The extensive keening tradition, or *caoineadh* was their prerogative, and the very excellence of Eibhlín Dubh Ní Chonaill's lament for her husband in "Caoineadh Airt Uí Laoghaire" is proof that this was a highly intricate and extensive tradition, capable of producing enormously effective poetic compositions.

As Angela Bourke has argued in a recent article, the skill of the traditional keener was to express powerful emotion with discipline and rhythm and to convey the immediacy of grief without disintegrating into tears.[3] Eibhlín Dubh's composition is not a fluke; it just happens to be one of the very few (almost) complete keens that is extant. That it survives at all *is* very much a fluke, which owes more to the accident of her high birth, to her youth, and to its appeal to Victorian romanticism than it does to any great effusion of male generosity. There is no reason to believe that Eibhlín Dubh was even literate in Irish, but that does not matter one whit as she did not actually write this poem but rather composed it in a spontaneous oral performance on two separate occasions.

We owe the two most complete texts to transcripts taken, with an interval of some seventy years between them, from a single informant, a West Cork woman by the name of Norry Singleton. Norry Singleton herself was a keener and is more typical of the traditional keener described by Crofton Croker in *Researches in the South of Ireland* as poor, old, and often living alone. As Angela Bourke argues, "Irish women lament-poets were doubly colonised; they belonged to a society and composed in a language considered inferior and barbarian to those in power, but even in their own society they were an underclass, not taught to write, not admitted to the academy of serious poets, rarely named as authors of their own compositions." (The only woman poet who may have been literate is Máire Bhuí Ní Laoghaire, but she has left no written manuscript in her hand, and so we have no way of knowing if her highly ornate compositions were not also entirely oral performances.) There may have been hundreds, even thousands of them, and yet with the one exception of Eibhlín Dubh, none of them has made it into the canon. Healthy line of foremothers indeed!

In his very comprehensive book on the role of the poet in Irish, Daithí O hOgáin notes that there hasn't been mention of even as much as one woman poet in the Irish literary tradition for over one thousand years. Seán O Tuama, in an essay on my own work, remarks what little help the Irish literary tradition is to women poets. Gearóid O Crualaoich, in his controversial essay "Dearcadh Dána," notes how the writing of poetry is considered a manly act in the Irish tradition. Indeed, there is a consensus on this idea, which is expressed most succinctly, perhaps, by Seán O Ríordáin in his poem "Banfhile," in which he repeats again and again with a sense of ever-increasing hysteria, "Ní file ach filíocht í an bhean" [Woman is not poet but poetry]. Caerwyn Williams and Máirín Ní Mhuiriosa's *Tradisiún Liteartha na nGael* (1979), which Máirín Nic Eoin calls "our most substantial historical survey of the Irish literary tradition," mentions by name something like twenty-five women from history, but, he observes, "most of these are the daughters or wives of famous men whose lives and work are discussed in the book." The authors themselves state quite baldly, "Is beag rian a d'fhág na mná ar thraidisiún litheartha na Gaeilge" [Women have left little mark on the Irish literary tradition]. Nowhere in the Irish tradition can I find anything but confirmation of Eavan Boland's claim that women have been nothing else but the "fictive queens and national sibyls" of which Anne Stevenson, going by her enumeration of the great deeds of Gráinne Mhaol, seems to be enamoured.

That is the literary tradition in Irish. The position of the woman poet in the oral tradition outside of the caoineadh is not much better. From scattered references throughout the folklore collections we know that they existed, but that is about all. The very concept of a woman poet was inherently threatening, as witnessed by the extreme hostility that surrounds the subject. I was brought up amid a welter of proverbs and formulaic phrases of the likes of: "Na trí rudaí is measa i mbaile— tuíodóir fluich, síoladóir tiubh, file mná" [The three worst curses that

could befall a village—a wet thatcher, a heavy sower, a woman poet].
No explanation for why a woman poet was a curse was needed; that
was considered as self-evident as the misfortune of having a thatcher
who let in the rain or a sower who broadcast his seed too densely.

There was a widespread belief that if poetry, which was a hereditary
gift [*féith nó tréith dúchais*], fell into the female line, then it was gone
from that particular family for seven generations to come. There is a
story about the poet Giúistí from *An Leitriúch,* who, mindful that some
such calamity had occurred, asked his daughter for a glass of ale in a
spontaneous *leathrann* (half quatrain). When she equally spontaneously
and deftly finished the quatrain while handing him back the beer, he
knew that the poetry in the family was finished.

A similar taboo existed against women telling Fenian tales: "tráthaire
circe nó Fiannaí mná" [a crowing hen or a woman telling Fenian tales],
but that did not stop women being storytellers or *filiúil* (poetic), though
a better translation of this word might perhaps be "witty" or "quick at
repartee." Some of the best storytellers in West Kerry were women,
notably Peig Sayers, who had an active vocabulary of about thirty thousand words and knew how to use them, and the two sisters from
Ardamore married in Dunquin, Cáit and Máire Ruiséal. Máire Ruiséal,
also known as Cú and Tobair because of Tobair Chéirín near where she
lived, was renowned as a wise woman and a healer and was consulted
once even by De Valera when he toured the area.

This is the canon, as I know it. It is "hedged with taboos, mined with
false meanings" (Rich). That it will be greatly modified in the near future I have no doubt, as Old Irish scholars such as Máirín Ní
Dhonnchadha, Muirean Ní Bhrolcháin, and Máire Herbert edit a lot of
medieval texts that have as yet never seen the light, and as literary critics such as Máirín Nic Eoin, Angela Bourke, and Bríona Nic Dhiarmada
bring a feminist perspective to bear on what is already available. But
such an enabling network is already too late for the likes of me. When I
came back to boarding school from the first Scoil Gheimhridh Merriman
in 1969, my ears still ringing with the stunning impromptu (and mag-
netically unrecorded) riposte that Seán O Ríordáin gave to O Cadháin's
Pápéirí Bána, Pápéirí Breaca and looking for all the world, as a
schoolfriend remarked years later, "like someone who had found her
vocation," there was precious little in the line of role models to look
up to.

Perhaps I was luckier than Eavan Boland, in that Cáitlín Maude was
already on the Leaving Certificate course and that Máire Mhac an tSaoi

was already enshrined as one of the great trinity of poets who had dragged Irish poetry, screaming and kicking, into the twentieth century by their stunning achievements back in the fifties. There was no question about Mhac an tSaoi and Maude not being banfhilí, or women poets, as their subject matter and technical strategies were very definitely different from those of men poets. There was also no question of their not being very good poets, though Cáitlín Maude's untimely death greatly reduced her output. But that was about it.

The usual catalogue of indignities dogged the steps of any poem I tried to see into print. Editors chipped and chopped with no by-your-leave. Totally outmoded ideas of *an caighdéan* (the standard) were brought to bear on what was purporting to be, after all, something other than civil service jargon. One poem ("An Cuairteoir") was refused publication because it was deemed to be blasphemous (I only meant it as a description of a possible female reaction to the presence of the Divine). When I first experimented with the long line it was deemed unprintable, and the poem "An Casadh" was reorganized to suit the editor. You name it, I've suffered it: the lack of freedom, the lack of adequate critical reaction, the lack of reviews.

It has been a long and tedious struggle for us women writing in Irish to get even a precarious toehold in visibility. Like the boy in the magic cloak in the fairy story, you've got to keep saying to the ship of culture, "seol seol, a bháidin, táimse leis ann" [Sail, sail, little boat, I'm there too]. The unkindest cut of all was the total lack of support or comprehension or even acknowledgment of our existence by women writing in English. Thanks mostly to Ailbhe Smyth's inclusion of six women writing in Irish in her anthology *Wildish Things*,[4] this has improved slightly, but many of the reviews of that book left out the Irish altogether or took a rather arch and superior view of it. Many people are embarrassed by their own lack of Irish and are not woman enough to admit that it has a legitimate place on the cultural menu and a significant role to play in the life of this country. As Máirín Nic Eoin says in *Graph*, "The relationship between women writing in Irish and their peers who write in English is still problematic, in my opinion, and will continue to be so as long as the present unequal power relationship between English and Irish exists in this country."

But ultimately none of this really matters. The publicity, the recognition, the literary round, all these are ultimately just distractions. The only thing that matters is the work. Important work, first and foremost, is produced in solitude, far from the noise of the world. Work requires retreat, and at least momentary indifference to the social, even where an institution is needed for the work's financing or publishing. It's not easy. *Ars est longissima via.* But then any of us who have chosen to write in Irish have made our decision in full awareness of what it entails. I still remember when I had an audience I could count on the fingers of one hand. I was perfectly prepared for that. I still am. If, as Máirín Nic Eoin's recent article in *Graph* suggests, the main postcolonial strategy that we employ—the use of the precolonial language as a creative medium—is beginning to be appreciated for the revolutionary and subversive act that it undoubtedly is, then, who knows, we may be in for a brief period of being fashionable. That too will pass. These are all temporary aberrations and weaknesses. The long haul is what matters.

But to return to the Stevenson article, where she questions Eavan Boland's engaging "with the virulence and necessity of the idea of a nation." She wonders if it is her own American background that makes her pause. I agree that it is. Coming from America, where the chthonian aboriginal earth energies have more or less been wiped out with the Amerindians, their bearers, and where the colonizing planter Calvinist ethos is so strong that later immigrants—no matter what their race or their incoming cultural baggage—become subsumed in it, she can have no hint of a tint of a clue of what it is like to live in a country such as Ireland where the myth of sovereignty envisaged as a woman (Éire, Banba, Fodhla, etcetera) sweeps through the ages from untold millennia, gathering momentum all the way through the "aisling" poems or turn-of-the century nationalist rhetoric: "'Did you see an old woman go down the path?' 'I did not, but I saw a young girl, and she had the walk of a queen.'" This image galvanized a whole population at the beginning of this century and is still shockingly alive in the collective psyche, for all that an unholy alliance of Marxist-Freudian reductionist intellectuals may seek to deny it. Eavan Boland is dead right to engage polemically with this image because, as Marina Warner has shown most comprehensively in her book *Monuments and Maidens,* there is a psychotic splitting involved where, the more the image of woman comes to stand for abstract concepts like justice, liberty, or national sovereignty, the more real women are denigrated and consigned barefoot and pregnant to the kitchen. We are all of us—men and women—as Eavan Boland points out, existing in "a mesh, a web, a labyrinth of associations. . . . We ourselves are constructed by the construct."

Freud's biographer, the English psychoanalyst Ernest Jones, gave a memorable address to the British Psychoanalytic Society in the late twenties about why the nationalist image of Ireland as a woman was so potent. This purely from an outsider's point of view, without any knowledge of the long line of cultural vehicles for this imagery, from medieval myths through aisling poems to contemporary come-all-ye's. As Eavan Boland quite rightly states, "Images are not ornaments; they are truths." If nothing else, the practice of poetry has taught me that there is a psycho-emotio-imagistic dimension to our being, a feeling soul, which has fallen through the interstices of the mind/body polarities of the dominant discourse so that it has become quite literally unspeakable. A whole realm of powerful images exist within us, overlooked by, and cut off from, rational consciousness. This is very dangerous because, if Freud has taught us anything, it foreshadows the inevitable return of the repressed. If these images are not engaged with in playful dialogue, if we do not take them seriously, then they will wreak a terrible revenge by manifesting somatically as illnesses or by being acted out blindly and irrationally, as we see them being acted out at this very moment in the sack of Sarajevo, as ethnic and historic tensions, long brushed under the carpet of a monolithic Marxism, explode to the surface. Anne Stevenson wonders if an Irish poet "in a republic secure in the Economic Community, whose changing mood is now reflected in the election of a woman president" should deal in such currencies. She forgets that we live in a republic in the name of which hapless human beings are dragged nightly from their beds and murdered or used as human bombs to murder others. The fact that the other side is every bit as bad doesn't change anything.

I think in the long run, though, that we are lucky that for one reason or another on this island the door between the rational and this other world or dimension has never been locked tight shut. There was always someone—the bard in the hall, the *seanchai* by the fireside, or the ballader in the pub—who kept his foot in the door. Walter Ong calls it our "high degree of residual orality," and the spoken word, by its very nature and spontaneity has a plumbline into the subconscious that, except for the very best fiction and poetry, literary activity almost never has. I love this aspect of our culture. It is one of the main things that drew me back to live here, after seven years on the shaughrawn. It is infinitely more exciting and much more of a human challenge to live in a country that is even just intermittently in touch with the irrational than to live in one that has set its face resolutely against it.

But this gift of ours is not without its inherent dangers, one of which is that in the absence of a responsible intelligentsia, this permeability of the collective ego-boundaries can be maneuvered and choreographed for very dubious purposes. The moving statues are a case in point. So too is the recent procession through the streets of Dublin of the image of Our Lady of Guadeloupe, on which, or so it is widely noised abroad, rose petals descended (presumably from whatever level of the stratosphere that Heaven keeps them conveniently frozen). These potent images are nevertheless something that we deny at our peril, and it is not the credulous many who are at the most danger of being manipulated by them but the very same rationalists who most deny their existence. Let me give an example. A few years ago I saw a very interesting video called *Mother Ireland*. The only woman in that video recording who denied utterly the existence of that image in her psychic make-up, and who hotly protested that it had no hold on her at all was, yes, you may have guessed it, Máiréad Farrell. I hardly need to add that it came as no great surprise, though it was no less painful, to hear of her subsequent murder in Gibraltar. On active service for the IRA, she was acting out the impulse fueled by the image she consciously denied. No doubt she continued to deny it to the end, substituting instead the pseudorationalist (though really utopian) Marxist cant that the IRA has taken to spouting in these latter times. And so I highly commend Eavan Boland on her skillful and unevasive tackling of this issue. It is a highly important and ethical matter. Poetry is the delineation of the human soul, and the human soul is a fuming abyss. Sarajevo is just down the road.

A penultimate point: there is something else in the Anne Stevenson article that disturbs and bothers me. It is not the obvious mistakes. Anyone can make a mistake. But it seems that she is swayed by some underlying agenda that causes her to make these mistakes. There is a subtle sneering tone that pervades the whole piece, surfacing here and there in lines such as, "Do I hear faint feminist complaints that all their women were treated as 'sex objects' and that their verse only confirms that men have exploited women since history began"—and finally culminating at the end in the extraordinary statement: "Only contemporary self-consciousness and a feminist piety far more inhibiting than healthy Catholicism seems to be snuffing out the truly Pagan spirit of the Irish past, substituting ideology for mythology and pity for energy and wit." Now this year alone in Ireland we have seen the incarceration of a fourteen-year-old female rape victim by the full powers of the state and the revelation that a hapless woman in the height of vulnerability at the end of pregnancy and shortly after parturition was emotionally bludgeoned and harangued by a senior episcopal figure to give up her (and his) baby, even though such an act would be equivalent to psychic and emotional murder for her, so please don't talk to me about an uninhibited and healthy Catholicism. There is no such thing. Not in present-day Ireland there isn't.

Admittedly, Catholicism does allow at least for a female presence in the Blessed Virgin and a whole plethora of female saints, and that is marginally more woman-friendly than Calvinism, where the female image is entirely abhorred. But as Marina Warner has admirably and comprehensively documented in her book on the Virgin Mary, *Alone of All Her Sex*, what Catholicism presents to women in the image of the Virgin Mary is a classical example of a spiritual double-bind. The more the Virgin is revered as a spotless and shining example, the more ordinary human women are made to feel guilty for not being simultaneously virginal and motherly (forget the biological impossibility), masochistic, and above all producers of suicidal sons.

I admit also that there does exist a certain radical fringe of feminism that seems hell-bent on outdoing the traditional patriarchy in its rigid adherence to dogma and PC piousness. Nevertheless, the feminist movement is pluralist and heterogeneous enough to be able to take all shapes and sizes of women's issues in its stride. To hold Catholicism up as inherently more healthy and less inhibiting to women than feminism seems at the very least a very dubious gesture.

And now should I deliver my final cudgel? It also seems to me that there runs through the whole of Anne Stevenson's article an attitude rather akin to the orientalizing tendencies of the West that Edward Said has so expertly commented on. There is a fetishing of the Other ("Ancient Irish Women Poets") as both sexually free and exotic, etcetera, etcetera, ... but no! Enough! This postcolonial thing is getting out of hand and anyway it seems too easy: everyone is doing it.

Eavan Boland has produced an essay that addresses very real and pertinent subjects: the dearth of women poets in the Irish literary tradition; how the two concepts of "woman" and "poet" seem incapable of being entertained simultaneously by the tiny little minds of the literati of this island; how a diagrammatic and dehumanized image of woman has been used by Irish male poets as a kind of literary shorthand long after its historical moment has passed; and how the image of woman in the national tradition is a very real dragon that every Irish woman poet has to fight every time she opens her literary door. Though I

might quibble with some of the details (for instance, I think she unfairly overlooks Paul Muldoon's constant attempts to deconstruct the
literary *spéirbhean*, I find her arguments necessary and compelling.
Anne Stevenson, in her reply, does an extremely competent job of fudg-
ing the main issues. I consider her article as prime an example of obscur-
antism as I wish ever to read in a lifetime.

NOTES

1. Anne Stevenson, "Inside and Outside History," *PN Review* 18, no. 3 (Janu-
ary-February 1992): 34–38; Eavan Boland, "A Kind of Scar: The Woman Poet in
the National Tradition," *LIP* pamphlet (Dublin: Attic Press, 1989). Boland's essay
has been reprinted in her book *Object Lessons: The Life of the Woman and the
Poet in Our Time* (Manchester: Carcanet Press, 1955): 123–53.

2. Donnchadh O Corráin, "Women in Early Irish Society," in *Women in Irish
Society: The Historical Dimension,* ed. Donnchadh O Corráin and M MacCurtain
(Dublin: Arlen House, 1978).

3. Angela Bourke, "Working and Weeping: Women's Oral Poetry in Irish and
Scottish Gaelic Poetry," *Women's Studies Working Papers,* no. 7 (Dublin: UCD
Women's Studies Forum, 1988). For a discussion of the oral lament-poet, see also
Eiléan Ní Chuilleanáin's "Women as Writers," in *Irish Women: Image and
Achievement,* ed. Eiléan Ní Chuilleanáin (Dublin: Arlen House, 1985), 120.

4. Ailbhe Smyth, ed., *Wildish Things: An Anthology of New Irish Women's
Writing* (Dublin: Attic Press, 1989).

2

The Voices of
Maria Edgeworth's Comedy

Eiléan Ní Chuilleanáin

Maria Edgeworth is not merely a major comic novelist and ancestress of the regional novel. She also evolved a theoretical and practical approach to comedy that was opposed to traditional definitions of the absurd and that made space for the suppressed voices of those who traditionally had been the objects of derision: women, servants, speakers of a nonstandard idiom. A couple of facts about her theory are notable: she developed it as part of the criticism of the literary and educational stereotypes of her day, which she undertook in collaboration with her father; she and he stress the authenticity of the examples of popular speech that they present as evidence, and thus the admission of real voices that clash and conflict with each other.

In this essay I will draw attention to elements of both theory and practice in Edgeworth's comic writing that recall the "heteroglossia" of Bakhtin, the comic juxtaposition of "almost all the levels of literary language, both conversational and written, that were current at the time." But it is the "individualization of the narrator," which Bakhtin defines as an alternative to the "parodic stylization of generic, professional and other languages," that is Edgeworth's special strength (*Dialogic*, 301–2). In her version of the comic tradition of the novel, the violent suppression of certain voices is a recurring feature of her most successful writing.

Edgeworth's literary career was marked by both the experience of collaboration and the effect of censorship (on later editions of *Belinda*, where an interracial marriage and some shocking expressions in the letters of a worldly aunt to the heroine were omitted on the insistence of an editor). Her creation of a multiplicity of speakers and her calling attention to the silencing of some voices thus reflect her actual writing experience.

One of Edgeworth's lesser-known works, the short novel *Almeria*, was published in 1809 as part of the first series of *Tales of Fashionable Life*. Its theme is satiric; it mocks social climbing through the story of Almeria, who wishes to rise in the world. She is the stepdaughter of a rich grazier, John Hodgkinson. The document that makes her the heiress to his estate is an informal will, written on the first leaf of his late wife's cookery book and the last of her prayer book. The author uses this legal instrument to perpetrate a comic explosion, not simply of conflicting voices but a struggle of competing scribal hands overwriting each other and themselves in a bewildering variety of nonliterary modes of writing. In this feverish palimpsest, the testator's dispositions, *"it is my* intention to make my will and to leave," are interrupted by *"a receipt in a diminutive female hand, seemingly written some years before"* for "Mrs Turnbull's recipe, infallible for all aches bruises and strains." The ingredients include: "Half a handful of Red Earthworms, two ounces of Cummin-seeds, Deasy-roots, Columbine, Sweet Marjoram, Dandylion, Devil's bit, six pound of May butter. . . . It will be better if you add a dozen of Swallows, and pound all their Feathers, Gizzards, and Heads before boiling." The will resumes at this point, "All I am worth in the world real or personal," to be interrupted again by a recipe for collared pig, followed by: "to my step-daughter Almeria . . . but if she disoblige me, by marriage or otherwise, I hereby revoke the same." Then: *"[Written diagonally in red ink.]* Memm—Weight of the Big Bullock, 90 score, besides offal. *[The value was so pale it could not be deciphered.]*" Further provisions on the prayer book leaf frame, but do not quite erase, the dead mother's identity:

Hodgkinson late
Hannah Turnbull (my wife)
her prayer book
born Decr 5th 1700,
died Jany 4th, 1760;
leaving only behind her, in this world,

Almeria Turnbull (my step daughter)
(*Tales and Novels,* vii, 248–51; Edgeworth's emphasis)

In this farcically distorted text, the reader of Edgeworth is confronted with two kinds of authenticity. The recipe with the earthworms and swallows in it is, we are not surprised to learn from one of her characteristic footnotes, "Literally copied from a family receipt-book in the author's possession." Reality and history are stranger than invention. The other kind of authenticity is that of a fictional document that apes the peculiarities of a historical manuscript but in so doing draws our attention to the character and interests of the scribe. Character, which appears here as relentless idiosyncrasy, emerges via the role of a narrator—it is through John Hodgkinson's document and its role in the story of Almeria's fortunes that we are made aware of his dead wife—who imposes his own projections on the lives of others. The will is a babel of conflicting voices, where the preoccupations of the dead woman are drowned by her husband's egotism. Two originally separate books, each carefully kept through several years by its owner, are cannibalized to form the background for one document. The power of the testator over his estate is also that of the writer over words and inherited paper, and the typography forces our attention, as readers, to concentrate on the act of writing. Comedy comes from the overwriting, the suppression of a life that is simply erased by the man who controls, by his control of inheritance and narration, the traffic between the generations. If, as I shall argue, Edgeworth's comedy is the comedy of history, it is so by virtue not only of her acute sense of historical reality but also of her awareness of the prejudices of the narrators of history and of those of their readers. This awareness lies behind her ability to defeat and mock the expectations of readers and to expose the blindness of narrators and editors.

Edgeworth is known to the twentieth-century reader especially as the author of *Castle Rackrent.* This first novel is relished for its anarchic humor, while the moral seriousness of her later work has been conventionally deprecated. This does not mean that the later novels have not had a public. Irish readers have always found much to interest them in *Ormond* and *The Absentee.* Feminist critics too have more recently discovered the acuteness of her satire as it applies to social roles and individual motivation, particularly—but not only—of the women characters in *Belinda, Patronage, Vivian,* and *Helen,* all novels with a wide range and a marked preoccupation with work, class, power, and politics.

Almeria, on the whole far from equal to her best work, shows, as the passage I have quoted demonstrates, an awareness of women's history, a sense of the suppression of that history, and the comic power to sum up the silent struggle in a memorable fiction.

What is missing in the criticism of Edgeworth of which I am aware is a sense of the totality of Edgeworth's outlook that might supply a connection between the energetic wit of her Irish characters, her moral-social commentary on women's lives, and the educational interests she shared with her father. Richard Lovell Edgeworth traditionally was accused of having corrupted his daughter's natural comic genius, though in recent years Marilyn Butler's account of the evidence for the part he played in her writing has shown him rather as a sympathetic critic and editor, not as a censor demanding morality at the expense of wit. I shall argue for a close connection between her individual comic vision and her view of human, and female, potential, which can be explored through the works she wrote in collaboration. I am not setting out here to supply the comprehensive view that her work demands but rather to suggest that one element in such a view would be an account of her attitude toward laughter and of the links between laughter, narration, and power in historical situations—in short, an account of the politics of laughter in the culture of Ireland and of Britain.

Of the works Edgeworth wrote with her father, one, *Practical Education* (hereafter PE), is an assault on the central cultural stronghold of their society, while another, *An Essay on Irish Bulls* (hereafter *Bulls*), is a critique of a kind of racist humor that still flourishes in Britain (and still fuels political prejudice). In *Bulls* they develop a theory of the absurd that challenges standard critical assumptions and indicates their close connection with political attitudes. The thoroughness of the Edgeworths' rejection of the cultural and political traditions of the English establishment has perhaps not been sufficiently appreciated; Marilyn Butler records their "progressive" connections, but, I think, underplays their own revolutionary contribution.

Practical Education has tended to be dismissed as an example of the Edgeworths' notorious faddishness or to be ignored by literary critics. In arguing against the traditional curriculum for the education of males in single-sex institutions and in favor of a family-based upbringing that could be shared by both sexes, the authors are taking on a whole system of social and cultural values. The subjects that they suggest should be central to the education of the governing class are those that up to now had been studied by women (modern languages and literatures, natural science) and by younger sons not destined for the church but for a trade or profession (mathematics, mechanics). Their attitude to the traditionally central position of the classics, and to the custom of dispatching boys automatically to the great public schools, is distinctly cool: "there are many circumstances in the management of public education which might be condemned with reason . . . too much time is sacrificed to the study of the learned languages . . . too little attention is paid to the general improvement of the understanding and formation of the moral character" (PE, 147).

While the study of the classics has its preeminent place in the culture by convention, the subjects the Edgeworths favor are praised because children take naturally to them: chemistry makes the child observant (PE, 43), while of mechanics they write, "no species of knowledge is better suited to the taste and capacity of youth, and yet it seldom forms a part of early instruction" (PE, 89).

If we compare the Edgeworths' outlook with, for example, Edmund Burke's in his *Reflections on the Revolution in France*, written in the same decade, we find that he defends the "Gothic and monkish education" of the ancient schools and colleges in terms that show how closely this is linked to the established order of precedence affecting class, gender, and religion. He continues: "Our education is in a manner wholly in the hands of ecclesiastics, and in all stages from infancy to manhood. . . . By this connexion we conceive that we attach our gentlemen to the church" (198–99).

The Edgeworths' plan for a new curriculum gives prominence to science and modern literature, both regarded in progressive circles as especially suitable pursuits for females. Already in 1795, Maria's *Letters for Literary Ladies* had treated the theme of women's education and observed that, "Botany has become fashionable. . . . Chemistry will follow botany. Chemistry is a science well suited to the talents and situation of women" (*Tales and Novels,* xiii, 302, 294). On the other hand, as the Edgeworths tell us in *Practical Education,* males are ill-prepared for life in mixed society by merely "conning their Greek and Latin. . . . At the tea-table he now seldom hears even the name of Plato, and he often blushes for not knowing a line from a popular English poet, whilst he could repeat a cento from Horace, Virgil and Homer" (164). Women do not have this problem: "From the study of the learned languages women by custom, fortunately for them, are exempted" (213). The emphasis on modern languages, history, and science permits a reintegration of the education of the two sexes. If segregation and the tradition of confining each sex to certain traditional subjects are a poor preparation for life in a society where men and women are to meet, converse, and cooperate, the Edgeworths' comments are also a criticism of the actual divisions in the culture in which they live: between males and females, between home and the masculine public institutions (of government, religion, and professions as well as education), between the classicizing culture of the eighteenth century and the romantic, revolutionary outlook that was to challenge and in part succeed it.

While both Maria Edgeworth and her father reacted to the events of 1793 in France and of 1798 in Ireland by moving in some respects in a conservative direction, she writes in her published work throughout her life with a sense of emancipation from the prejudices of the past, one so deeply grounded that it seems as if it is essential to the act of writing itself, as an act that is essentially a new beginning every time. This past can be very recent; *Rackrent*, we are assured on the title page, depicts the habits of the Irish gentry "before 1782," that is, before Ireland's legislative independence was achieved; the picture of French society in *Ormond* shows life in France in the bad old days of Louis XV, "during the reign of Madame du Barré" (293). In *Belinda*, the author added a note to a late edition defending her repetition of the atrocious swearing of Sir Philip Baddely but consigning it to history: "Swearing has gone out of fashion" (1810, 79).

In *Bulls*, the belief in progress is elaborated in historical and political terms. In the peroration to the work, the authors draw on a quotation from an unnamed editor of Voltaire's *Age of Louis XIV*. (Voltaire had originally written, "Some nations seem made to be subject to others. The English have always had over the Irish the superiority of genius, wealth and arms. The superiority which the whites have over the negroes.") The editor noted that the last sentence had been erased by Voltaire in subsequent editions and that since "religious hatreds are appeased . . . the Irish no longer yield to the English, either in industry or in information" (*Bulls*, 135). The Edgeworths hail this tribute and go on to dismiss the Gaelic past with cheerful enumeration of the names dear to "rusty antiquaries": "We moreover candidly confess, that we are more interested in the fate of the present race of its inhabitants, than in the historian of St. Patrick, St. Facharis, St. Cormuc, the renowned Brien Boru, Tireldach, King of Connaught; M'Murrough, king of Leinster; Diarmod, Righ—Damhna" (*Bulls*, 136).

History has replaced nature as scapegoat for Ireland's ills, which can then be seen as capable of, as indeed inevitably yielding to, enlightenment. But as we shall see, enlightenment is far from synonymous with the acceptance of English ways. In Maria Edgeworth's determined optimism, she is the intellectual offspring of revolutionary philosophers, while in her sense of tradition and historical process she belongs to the romantic movement.

The striking feature of her best-known novels is their handling of cultural diversity. In *Rackrent,* the reader is delighted by the "natural" wit of Thady Quirk but not allowed to be merely delighted. At all points in the book Thady's peculiar idiom—his distinctive voice—is presented as the product of his culture rather than as just an individual's eccentricity. More subtly, it becomes evident from Thady's narrative that a folk hero like his patron, Sir Condy Rackrent, is as much a prisoner of convention, as arbitrarily constrained and indulged, as the most rigidly brought-up young lady. And the reader is not permitted simply to patronize these buffoons. The enthusiasm and the depth of analysis with which a "barbarous" society and its chief protagonists, the chieftain and the storyteller, are presented are connected, I shall argue, with a revolt against "classical" standards in literature that is of a piece with their refusal to accept those standards in education and philosophy. *Bulls* illuminates her rejection of such standards.

The value of the commentary on the absurd in *Bulls* by an accomplished comic novelist and her influential mentor has not, I think, been fully appreciated. Cóilín Owens has dismissed it as "heavy-handed and pedantic" (*Chronicles,* 74), and G. R. Neilson calls it "censorious—even ill-natured" (*Bulls,* vi). Marilyn Butler has observed, more acutely, that *Bulls* is a kind of "atonement" (*Biography,* 360). In *Rackrent,* by displaying the humor of Irish characteristics, Maria Edgeworth might be thought to have questioned the fitness of the Irish for self-government. *Bulls* is not merely a work on the nature of comedy: rather it constructs a context, political as well as critical, for our definitions of the comic and the absurd.

In 1800, the Act of Union had abolished the Irish Parliament and thus disabled Dublin as a political center. The comedy of *Rackrent* could be read in the context of this event as exhibiting the absurdity and childish incompetence of a subject people for the delight and reassurance of their governors in the metropolis. Such a reading was not to be allowed to pass unchallenged; the irony in the studiously reassuring voice is cool but implacable: "we need not apprehend that to ridicule our Hibernian neighbours unmercifully is unfriendly or ungenerous. . . . It would indeed be an intolerable restraint upon social intercourse if every man were subject to be taxed for each inaccuracy of language—if he were compelled to talk upon all occasions as if he were amenable to a Star Chamber of criticism and surrounded by informers" (*Bulls*, 23–24).

The political implications of laughter are given extra point, and the ironic appeal to the shibboleths of British political liberty (the bugbears of the Star Chamber and arbitrary taxation) prepares the way for a declaration of artistic independence. *Bulls* is, throughout, formally addressed to the English reader, as was *Rackrent*. But such a reader is not supposed to be without prejudice or interest. Edgeworth is aware that any expectation of impartiality from outsiders is ill-founded; in her fiction, the "visitor" to Ireland is not a disinterested spectator—Lord Glenthorn in *Ennui* and Lord Colambre in *The Absentee* have their own agendas and their own emotional perspectives when they set out from London to discover their Irish inheritance.

In the "Glossary" prefaced to *Rackrent*, the fallacy of expecting objectivity from the educated is exposed, as the voice of "the Editor" is heard learnedly commenting on the prejudices of Thady, for example, in favor of beginning a new piece of work on Monday morning: "'Oh, please God we live till Monday morning, we'll set the slater to mend the roof of the house.' . . . All the intervening days . . . are wasted, and when Monday morning comes it is ten to one that the business is deferred to the *next* Monday morning. The Editor knew a gentleman who, to counteract this prejudice, made his workmen and laborers begin all new pieces of work on a Saturday" (xv-xvi). The Editor's impatience is that of an employer irritated by the resistance of the Irish worker; the reader is assumed to belong to the same class and thus to share his exasperation. But the employer's power over his laborers is simultaneously called into question by the absurdity of beginning work on the *last* day of the week and the tyranny of the authority that demands it.

In the same way, the first purpose of *Bulls* is to dislocate any facile relationship between English reader and Irish joke. Thus (at perhaps excessive length) various famous bulls are found to have parallels in other cultures, including the English and French. The catalogue of non-Irish absurdities lays a foundation for the Edgeworths' second main contention, that the Irish bull is closely related to a propensity and a talent for elevated and imaginative expression. This is their challenge to the theory of comedy that holds that "laughter always arises from a sense of real or imaginary superiority" (*Bulls*, 39). Instead they envisage a laughter that is tempered with sympathy, even with admiration. In the later chapters of *Bulls*, the imaginative leaps made by the enthusiastic or agitated mind are justified by parallels, no longer with the lapses of English politicians and French academicians, but with the poetry of Milton, Gray, Ariosto, and Shakespeare (*Bulls*, 49–51). These writers had all been found wanting in decorum and intellectual consistency by neoclassical critics. The assertion that features of their admittedly sublime style were also to be found in the speech and idiom of the Irish peasant is important in the history of Irish literature since it makes at this early date the connection between the heroic and the peasant idiom that was later to be explored by Yeats, Synge, and Lady Gregory.

For the Edgeworths, what is important in a study of that essentially oral form, the joke, is the speaking voice of the people. The discussion in the latter part of their essay shifts from an analysis of the stale trivia of jestbooks to the vigorous and passionate expressions of a people who value and respond to the virtuosity of the spoken language. In recounting speeches of "pathetic remonstrating eloquence" on the cruelty of landlords, they include statements that might qualify as bulls: "he has just seized all I have, which, God knows, is little enough! and has driven my cow to pound, the only cow I have, and the only dependance I have for a drop of milk to drink; and the cow itself too standing there starving in the pound, for not a wisp of hay would he give to cow or Christian to save their lives" (*Bulls*, 81–82).

The narratives with which the Edgeworths illustrate this part of their work have, as in this passage, as much of the tragic, or at least the pathetic, as the comic in them. The speech of the poor widow lamenting her cow is a deliberately confusing example as it presently appears that the landlord is not a rich man and is also capable of dramatizing himself as a victim. Litigants, beggars, and petitioners are all able to express themselves in language that is artful and memorable, deeply rooted in the speaker's situation. Furthermore, the authenticity of the language is warranted by footnotes that assure us that "This was taken down a few minutes after it had been spoken" (*Bulls*, 83), a statement whose concern to assert historical authenticity can be frequently paralleled in authorial notes to Maria's fiction.

The spoken word is thus both deeply authentic and deeply ambiguous. It is our uncertainty about the identities and roles of the people we meet that forces our attention on their language, which is opaque, demanding our applause for its color and skill, its emotional virtuosity, rather than for its claim to truth or rationality. Unlike the written word, it can be subjected only with difficulty to tests of truth or falsehood. And the Irish speaker plays games with language and is opposed to the literal-minded Englishman who uses falsehood for gain. Thus, in the comic tale of an Irish adventurer in England that rounds off *Bulls*, Phelim O'Mooney, the hero, betrays his origins as much by his generosity of sentiment as by any verbal lapses or extravagance of wit; he meets an English adventuress, Miss Sharperson, more dishonest than himself in seeking for an advantageous marriage; and his experiences with the customs officers at his port of entry give the authors the opportunity of pointing out the political absurdity of British excise law, which continued to discriminate against Irish manufactures after the Act of Union.

Politically, *Bulls* is a protest against the relegation of the Irish to the role of childish buffoons and natural dependents, for whom the Union with England will mean a permanent tutelage. As a critical work on the nature of comedy, it locates the source of true comic delight in the fertility, energy, and resourcefulness of the folk idiom, while absurdity is exposed in the inequalities and corruptions of society rather than in the figure of the Irishman as clown. The prominence given to oral speech in the discussion, the way in which mere snippets of reported speech in the classic bulls are contrasted with examples of sustained, eloquent oral narrative or complaint, recall the importance throughout Maria Edgeworth's Irish writing of the voice of popular rhetoric, fueled by enthusiasm and passion. On the other hand, the wide reading she and her father display in their critique of standard English and European authors prepares us for the satiric approach of the novels about English society in which such cultural monuments play a large part, exploited to express doubts about stereotypes of human behavior and to construct ironic perspectives that cast new light on them.

The ease with which discussion of the absurd in *Bulls* slips into pathetic, melodramatic, or tragic examples suggests that for Maria Edgeworth as an anticlassical writer the tragic and comic will be frequently fused or disconcertingly alternated. This is indeed true of her fiction, especially when it places itself at a distance from the centers of power, dealing with Irish, or lower-class, or women's or children's experience. Her funniest novel, *Rackrent*, is a tale of destructive folly, obsession, and cruelty. Her most perceptive psychological study, *Belinda*, is about a woman, Lady Delacour, whose story can be viewed either tragically or comically—indeed Edgeworth hesitated between a tragic and a happy ending for the story, and readers have been divided by the same question. It is a novel in which, if women can handle language wittily and allusively as well as correctly, they have some hope of survival. In the

Irish setting of *Bulls* and *Rackrent* everything depends even more on point of view, and here the gender of the narrator is crucial.

We can listen to the voice of Thady Quirk in *Rackrent* telling the story of one Lady Rackrent's life in Ireland:

"There were no balls, no dinners, no doings, the country was all disappointed—Sir Kit's gentleman said, in a whisper to me, it was all my lady's own fault, because she was so obstinate about the cross—"What cross? (says I) Is it about her being a heretic?" [she is Jewish]—"Oh, no such matter, (says he) my master does not mind her heresies, but her diamond cross, it's worth I can't tell you how much, and she has thousands of English pounds concealed in diamonds about her, which she as good as promised to give up to my master before he married, but now she won't part with any of them and she must take the consequences. Her honeymoon, at least her Irish honeymoon, was scarcely well over, when his honour one morning said to me—"Thady, buy me a pig!"—and then the sausages were ordered, and here was the first open breaking out of my lady's troubles—my lady came down herself into the kitchen to speak to the cook about the sausages, and desired never to see them more at her table.—Now my master had ordered them, and my lady knew that—the cook my lady's part, because she never came down into the kitchen, and was young and innocent in house-keeping, which raised her pity . . . and from that day forward always sausages or bacon, or pig meat, in some shape or other, went up to table; upon which my lady shut herself up in her own room, and my master said she might stay there, with an oath; and to make sure of her, he turned the key in the door, and kept it ever after in his pocket—We none of us ever saw or heard her speak for seven years after that—he carried her dinner himself—then his honour had a great deal of company to dine with him, and balls in the house, and was as gay and gallant and as much himself as before he was married—and at dinner he always drank my lady Rackrent's good health, and so did the company, and he sent out always a servant, with his compliments to my Lady Rackrent, and the company was drinking her ladyship's health, and begged to know if there was anything at table he might send her; and the man came back, after the sham errand, with my lady Rackrent's compliments, and she was very much obliged to Sir Kit—she did not wish for any thing, but drank the company's health.—The country, to be sure, talked and wondered at my lady's being shut up, but nobody chose to interfere or ask any impertinent questions, for they knew my master was a man very apt to give a short answer himself, and likely to call a man out for it afterwards—he was a famous shot— had killed his man before he came of age and nobody dared scarce look at him whilst at Bath. (44–50)

Sir Kit is killed at last in a duel over a woman and "all the gentlemen within twenty miles . . . came in a body . . . to set [Lady Rackrent] at liberty, and to protest against her confinement, which they now for the first time understood was against her own consent" (59). The resolutely masculine point of view makes a farce out of the imprisoned woman's nightmare, which, as so often, is a story based on a true one of which Edgeworth had immediate knowledge: the notorious confinement, by her husband Colonel McGuire, of Lady Cathcart in County Fermanagh.

Lady Rackrent is like Lady Delacour and Rachel Hartley, the heroine of the subplot in *Belinda*. They are all women struggling for survival, trapped inside a male narrative convention. Thady's tone of calm acquiescence in his master's charade is part of the universal tolerance for masculine *play*, which can be as here, theatrical, or take the form of gambling, dueling, or sport. In *Belinda*, Lord Delacour loses his fortune at Newmarket before he marries; the hero of *Ennui* plays all the fashionable games in his search for distraction; in *Patronage*, the description of the horse race is in a tone of savage farce: "The gentlemen on the race-ground were all on tiptoe in their stirrups. The ladies in the stand, stretched their necks of snow, and nobody looked at them. — Two men were run over, and nobody took them up. —Two ladies fainted, and two gentlemen betted across them. This was no time for nice observances" (30). It is followed by a highly moral but also comic scene where two young men totally fail to communicate with each other because one of them can think only of sport: "'But I think it so wrong, so base . . . for money . . . for emolument . . . I cannot do it . . . I am not fit for the church—I know I shall disgrace it'—said Buckhurst, striking his forehead—'I cannot do it . . . I can not—it is against my conscience. . . . After all, I can't go to jail—I can't let myself be arrested—I can't starve—I can't be a beggar . . . if I got this living of nine hundred a year, how comfortable I should be. —Then I could marry, by Jove; and

I'd propose directly for Caroline Percy. . . . She certainly is a very pretty girl.'—'She certainly is,' repeated John.—'This devil of a fellow never cleans my gun'" (36–67). The voices drowned out by games and play need not be exclusively female. But they very often are; unlike Lady Delacour, Lady Rackrent and Rachel Hartley are not allowed to speak for themselves, to reject the genre they find themselves constrained by. The comedy comes precisely from the suppression of their protesting voices. *Rackrent* exists as an oral narrative, defined as such by, among other things, the contrast between Thady's idiom and the parade of literary and scholarly correctness in the author's notes. And the role of narrator is shown to be one of power and is liable to be abused as is every other kind of power surveyed in the book.

Lady Delacour, the central figure of *Belinda,* is another tragicomic narrator. She oscillates between witty conversation and pathetic monologue, in which she confides in her friend Belinda to whom she tells her life story. She believes herself to be dying of cancer and suffers from real guilt about her treatment of her children and of a man supposed to be her lover. The novel, in its plot as well as its dialogue, constantly reverts to the theme of the interchangeability, for women, of tragedy and comedy. Belinda and Lady Delacour dress for a masquerade as the comic and tragic muses but then exchange costumes. A woman who is foolish (folly being the traditional subject of comedy) will be punished as if she had been guilty, Lady Delacour remarks (1993, 26, 30). Lady Delacour's remorse for the past goes back to a duel between her husband and the man wrongly suspected of being her lover, Colonel Lawless, in which Lawless was killed. In tragicomic contrast, the symptoms in her breast that she wrongly supposes to be cancer are the result of another duel—of an injury received in a ridiculous encounter between two women in men's clothes—exacerbated by the effects of a medicine supplied by a quack doctor.

In the farcical subplot, a philosophically minded young man, Clarence Hervey, attempts to form a woman's character to make himself a perfect wife by bringing up a young girl in perfect seclusion. The girl "Virginia's" experience in this situation is not comic but acutely, painfully romantic, since she has fallen in love with another man, whom she has seen only in a picture. The reader, however, is forced to see it in a comic light because it is narrated unsympathetically, and its conclusion is manipulated to make Virginia's feelings appear in all their absurdity. The female duel, we learn from a letter of Maria Edgeworth's

(Butler, *Biography*, 243n), really took place; the story of Virginia too is based on the real experiences of Richard Lovell Edgeworth's friend, Thomas Day. Again, things that really happen are susceptible of both tragic and comic interpretations; the outlook of the narrator determines genre, but we are still made aware of the opposing possibilities.

In recognizing both tragic and comic stereotypes in Edgeworth's plotting (the death of Lawless; Lady Delacour's belief that she is being punished for leading him on; the transvestite duel; the quack doctor; and the school for wives), we must recognize too that they are being deliberately put in jarring juxtaposition with each other. We may also note how important is the gender of Edgeworth's narrator. The subplot is narrated in the third person but from the point of view of Clarence Hervey, the misguided educationalist. His intended wife has a name and surname, Rachel Hartley; he rechristens her Virginia St Pierre after the heroine of a romance, *Paul et Virginie*, and its author, Bernardin de St Pierre. This action symbolizes his total erasure of her actual character and experience from the narrative and symbolically guarantees all the characters' failure to listen to her story when she herself attempts to narrate it. As her outer life is entirely under Clarence's control, she takes refuge in telling her dreams, to which no attention is paid either.

Rachel's problem is her lack of education, deliberately brought about by the grandmother who hoped to shield her from knowledge of human wickedness and thus keep her pure and by Clarence, who protects her after the grandmother's death from life in the world, though he permits her to dream and read. She does not stand a chance of being able to speak for herself in a world of sophisticates who share a common literary culture—the comedy of *Belinda* is relentlessly bookish. The clashes between tragedy and comedy are signaled by quotations from Milton's *Il Penseroso* and *L'Allegro*, from Sheridan's *School for Scandal*, and from *Hamlet*. Fashions in feeling are marked by the quoting or naming of seminal works: such modish titles as Zimmerman's *On Solitude*, Buerger's romantic ballad *Lenore*, the novels of Anne Radcliffe, and, of course, *Paul et Virginie* are contrasted with the Augustan satire of Pope's *Rape of the Lock* (from which the heroine's name comes) and his verse epistle *On the Characters of Women* or with the mediaeval moralism of Chaucer's *Tale of Griselda*, which Edgeworth was to parody a few years later in *The Modern Griselda*. The quotations are displayed in polished, lively conversation; literature returns to oral currency, and the talent that enables a speaker to gain control of narration and determine genre is the key to being heard, not forced into silence.

A later Irish novel in which the speaking voices and the oral culture of the country are prominent, and in which the voice of the Irish woman gets a hearing, is *Ormond*, written as a last gift from Maria to her father, who in 1817, the year of its publication, was known to be dying. In this novel, the principal narrative voice is the moralizing, musing, often ironic voice of Maria Edgeworth's mature novels. But there are other narrating voices also, and it is through them that she creates space for her fine comic portrayals, especially of the Gaelic Irish. At the head of the representatives of traditional society is King Corny of the Black Islands, who delights in maintaining old customs, while his relative, the opportunistic Sir Ulick O'Shane, destroys himself by sacrificing his conscience to fashion and ambition.

The novel is full not only of absurd behavior by individuals but also of absurd social arrangements. Harry Ormond, the hero, at one point fights a duel in defense of Sir Ulick, who has brought him up but is later to attempt to defraud him. The occasion of the duel is Ormond's hearing recited a satiric poem that accurately describes Sir Ulick's propensity for "jobbery" or political corruption; Sir Ulick himself "would have laughed off the epigram with the best grace imaginable." Ormond is far less at fault than his patron, less so too than his opponent who has deliberately provoked him; the preliminaries for a tragic outcome are in place. But in the event, he is no loser by his misplaced loyalty and foolish adherence to the fashion for dueling. The voice here is the novelist's: "the man who deserved to have suffered, by the chance of this rational method of deciding right and wrong, escaped unhurt; Ormond received a wound in the arm. . . . as it was essential, not only to the character of a hero, but of a gentleman at that time in Ireland, to fight a duel, we may consider Ormond as fortunate in not having been in the wrong. He rose in favour with the ladies, and in credit with the gentlemen" (213–14). But while upper-class Anglo-Irish foolishness is shown to turn morality on its head, the strength of custom and sentiment is also illustrated at other social levels by tales of irrational behavior that—like the duel—borders on the tragic. The poor laborer Moriarty Carroll is shot by Ormond when drunk, and both men make this the basis of a lifelong friendship. Sir Ulick O'Shane vacillates comically between genuine affection for Ormond, whom he befriended as a penniless child, and absolute willingness to exploit him for selfish gain; he dies deserted and disgraced. King Corny betroths his daughter over a bowl of punch to the "eldest" son (but the sons are twins) of his friend Connal ten years before her birth. When one son, "White Connal," is killed in a farcically related accident (122–23), his brother, "Black Connal," an officer in the Irish Brigade in France, actually marries the girl and takes her to Paris where she is far from happy in her marriage. King Corny's death is absurd; he is killed by a gun he made himself, which explodes in his hands. He has a passion for ingenious manufactures (he had "with his own hands made a violin and a rat-trap . . . and had made a quarter of a yard of fine lace, and had painted a panorama"). The same propensity has serious consequences for his young friend Ormond, as he has also made his own will. This is badly worded, so that Ormond fails to receive a legacy, the price of an officer's commission in the army, which had seemed to assure his future when he had no other resources. Another death recounted with heartless good humor is that of Ormond's Anglo-Indian half-brother, which makes him a rich man. Such incidents, though their outcome may be ridiculous, cannot call up the "sense of real or imaginary superiority" of the traditional Irish joke, since the reader has already experienced the uneasiness generated by their macabre violence, blended with sympathy for their humanity.

Unlike those of *Rackrent*, *Ormond*'s comic effects do not come from the headlong narration of a succession of misadventures. Rather, misadventures occur as the by-product of passions and enthusiasms that are shown as the foundation of character—character not merely as an expression of personality but as constructed and accepted by popular feeling, which may be prejudiced but in the end is often shown to be just. The epigrammatist was in the right in satirizing Sir Ulick; the friendship between Moriarty Carroll and Ormond is based on a true appreciation in each of the other's qualities as shown in their reaction to the shooting. The comedy of King Corny includes his honorable consistency in absurdity, but most importantly the fact that those who live under him, over whom as landlord he really does possess almost absolute power, can see no absurdity in his behavior at all. His death is the occasion for the greatest possible mark of respect, the tribute Sir Condy Rackrent wanted so much and failed of: an enormous wake and funeral. The old housekeeper, Sheelah, describes the function of the wake in terms that are slightly apologetic; she knows that, to Ormond, the custom of keeping open house with whiskey and tobacco for all comers seems out of place at a time of mourning; just as Edgeworth knows it will seem paradoxical behavior to the English reader: "bear with us, dear, 'tis the custom of the country—and what else can we do but what the forefathers did—how else for us to show respect, only as it would be expected, and has always been? and great comfort to think we done our best, for *him that is gone*—and comfort to know that his wake will be talked of long hereafter, over the fires at night" (169; Edgeworth's emphasis). Ormond, guided by Sheelah, behaves "as expected" by making an offering of money at the Requiem Mass and responds to the strange dignity of the funeral procession: "King Corny's funeral was followed by an immense concourse of people, on horseback and on foot; men, women, and children; —when they passed by the doors of cabins, a set of the women raised the funeral cry—not a savage howl, as is the custom in some parts of Ireland, but chaunting a kind of funeral cry, not without harmony, simple and pathetic. Ormond was convinced, that in spite of all the festivity at the wake, which had so disgusted him, the poor people mourned sincerely for the friend they had lost" (171).

The mingled sympathy and disapproval of the author, her response and Ormond's to the strangeness of funeral and keening cry, are guided by Sheelah's words about the wake as a landmark in folk history. Folk narrative will also presumably relate the miserable funeral of Sir Ulick O'Shane, the corpse alone in a locked house "for fear of his creditors" and then attended to the grave by a few servants and poor neighbors and by Ormond, whom he has cheated. Again the comments of the peasants are closest to the truth about this complex character: "'and after all where is the great friends now? —the quality that used to be entertaining at the castle above? Where is all the favour promised him now? What is it come to? See, with all his wit, and the schemes upon schemes, broke and gone, and forsook and forgot, and buried without a funeral, or a tear, but from Master Harry.'

Ormond was surprised to hear, in the midst of many of their popular superstitions and prejudices, how justly they estimated Sir Ulick's abilities and character" (334). The voice of the people has the last word on Sir Ulick, the character who in the whole work comes closest to the world of the Irish Bull, his life a contradiction between natural kindness and acquired cunning, his marital affairs a jauntily carried-off history of cruelty and opportunism worthy of *Rackrent*, his house named absurdly "Castle Hermitage." At the novel's conclusion, Ormond has a choice between buying Sir Ulick's estate from his creditors and returning to the Black Islands and its people. His decision in favor of the Black

Islands shows which kind of folk hero he intends to become: the people there regard him as the legitimate successor to "King Corny" and have thus already incorporated him into their narratives.

The deep satisfaction of narrative is experienced by the people as capable of transforming disaster such as the death of King Corny or the unjust conviction of Moriarty Carroll for robbery (traceable to anti-Catholic prejudice) and his sentence of transportation to Botany Bay: "It would have done you good if you'd heard the cry in the court, when sentence was given for I was loved in the country. Poor Peggy [his wife] and Sheelah!" (316). The story of his escape from Kilmainham jail that follows is told with a different kind of relish and is succeeded by the episode, reminiscent of a ballad, that Ormond stage-manages, in which Moriarty is reunited with his faithful Peggy (331–32). Both of these were written by the dying Richard Lovell Edgeworth, the first being yet another authentic story told to him by its central figure.

The comedy of *Ormond* is then even more ambiguous than that of *Rackrent*. The hero accepts irrational behavior and behaves irrrationally himself on occasion. Maria Edgeworth has framed his character as, explicitly, a response to the hero of Fielding's *Tom Jones*, which Ormond reads at an impressionable age. His enthusiasm for Tom Jones almost leads him into justifying the seduction of the young Peggy, from which he is saved by his friendship with her lover, Moriarty Carroll. Later, his childhood affection for King Corny's daughter, Dora, is reborn among the corruptions of Parisian society under Louis XV; he is about to enter on an adulterous affair with her when he is stopped in his tracks by the reverence he bears for the memory of King Corny. In each case, the Irish absurdities of individual character, the Irish enthusiasms of Moriarty and Corny, are preferred to the stereotyped behavior of foreign societies. In fact, Ormond's final choice is foreshadowed in these responses: a return to live among people whose idiosyncrasies he has no expectation of reforming though he may hope to increase their happiness. We may add that his acceptance of their ways includes an acceptance of their religious beliefs as differing from his own, in line with the Edgeworths' lifelong opposition to Protestant proselytizing.

In the inheritance of the Irish past there are many elements that are at odds with the English present, but that Maria Edgeworth does not expect to be swept away by greater "civilization." The world as viewed from Edgeworthstown, or the Black Islands, is not the same as the one visible from the metropolis of her London publishers and English readers, and it will never speak with their accents or conform to their critical categories. The accounts of their own societies given by Sheelah or Lady Delacour, the account that Sir Kit Rackrent's lady would give if she could gain a hearing, must represent a divergence—a gentle plea for toleration, a critical differing, or a cry of fury—from the account of a male narrator.

WORKS CITED

Bakhtin, Mikhail. *The Dialogic Imagination*. Edited and translated by Michael Holquist and Caryl Emerson. Austin: University of Texas Press, 1983.

Burke, Edmund. *Reflections on the Revolution in France*. Harmondsworth: Penguin, 1969.

Butler, Marilyn. *Maria Edgeworth: A Literary Biography*. Oxford: Clarendon Press, 1972.

Edgeworth, Maria. *Belinda*. 1801. Reprint, London: J. Johnson, 1810.

———. *Belinda*. Reprint edited by E. Ní Chuilleanáin. London: J. M. Dent, 1993.

———. *Castle Rackrent*. 1800. Reprint, New York: Garland, 1978.

———. *Ormond*. 1833. Edited by W. J. McCormack. Gloucester: Alan Sutton, 1990.

———. *Patronage*. 1814. Reprint, London: Pandora, 1986.

———. *Tales and Novels*. 14 vols. London: Baldwin and Cradock, 1832.

Edgeworth, Maria, and Richard Lovell Edgeworth. *Essays on Practical Education*. 1798. Vol. 2. Reprint, London: J. Johnson, 1815.

———. *Essay on Irish Bulls*. 1802. In *The Book of Bulls,* edited by G. R. Neilson. Reprint, London: Simpkin, Marshall, Hamilton, Kent, 1898.

Owens, Cóilín. "Irish Bulls in *Castle Rackrent*." In *Family Chronicles: Maria Edgeworth's Castle Rackrent,* edited by Cóilín Owens, 70–78. Dublin: Wolfhound; Totowa, N.J.: Barnes and Noble, 1987.

Hyacinth and the Wise Man
Lady Gregory's Comic Enterprise

Mary Lowe-Evans

*I began to see how much William Butler Yeats and Lady Gregory dif-
fered on this all-important subject of audience. Yeats yearned for the
select few; Lady Gregory wanted them in the mass.*
GABRIEL FALLON, ACTOR, IN "FRAGMENTS OF MEMORY"

That the purpose of the Irish Literary Renaissance was to undergird
the country's cultural nationalism is by now an accepted fact of Irish
history. Just how that nationalism was to be defined, however, has been
hotly contended from the 1880s to the present. Heroic, spiritual, aesthetic, aggressive, independent, poetic, wise, innocent: the national character was to incorporate all of these sometimes contradictory qualities
and more. In combination, the myriad attributes of the emerging Irish
state would produce an island not only of saints and sages but of bards
and businessmen, soldiers and statesmen as well, each with attributes
esteemed in some corner of the nation. Early on, in the midst of all the
official scripting—the tracts, articles, speeches, and performances sup-
porting the cultural revival—there was little comic relief. The Irish character, it seems, was to be taken very seriously.[1]

A partial explanation for this grave national demeanor is that during the early years of the revival (roughly the 1880s through the early
1900s) debunking the image and sound of the stage Irishman was assigned a high priority in the plan for rehabilitating Ireland's image. In-

deed, the original statement of purpose for the Irish Literary Theatre includes the aspiration to "show that Ireland is not the home of buffoonery and of easy sentiment, as it has been represented, but the home of an ancient idealism" (quoted in Gregory, *Our Irish Theatre,* 9). This disclaimer was necessitated by a long tradition of stage Irishmen in the theater that culminated in the popular success of Irish playwright Dion Boucicault, believed by some critics, at least, to be an "exploiter of English prejudices toward Ireland [who] helped keep alive the traditional figure of the 'stage Irishman,' loud, drunken, violent, and sentimental" (Fallis, *Renaissance,* 6).[2]

But the perceived necessity for dignifying the Irish character brought about what amounts to a national psychic imbalance, a relentless seriousness of purpose unmitigated (at least officially) by intellectual playfulness. Even the blatant comic elements in the myths and folktales so widely disseminated in the early years of the revival were understated in favor of their heroic or mystical themes. Thus the "politically correct" had become sacred, and, as David Krause points out, "the sacred must . . . be mocked . . . because its original truths [had] become too hard and brittle" (*Profane,* 32). Accordingly, the humor implicit in the very project of national self-fashioning eventually could not be contained, and in the early 1900s comedy was legitimized by one of the official organs of reform, the Irish National Theatre Society, which had evolved out of the Irish Literary Theatre. As Ulick O'Connor imagines a meeting between Yeats, Lady Gregory, and Synge in the early days of the Abbey Theatre, the "patented" home of national drama, the three talked "in animated fashion about their plans. . . . The theatre could help to fuse the national image so that the people might find an identity" (*Celtic Dawn,* 367).

Apropos of the theater and Irish identity, Joseph Holloway, Dublin theater-goer, drama critic, and architect who transformed the old Mechanics Theatre into the original Abbey, records a letter of 4 February 1904 from Frank Fay, one of the two brothers who gave the Irish National Theatre its practical direction. Fay remarks "It is . . . curiously difficult to arouse Dubliners out of their lethargy to take a serious interest in the Arts. . . . The principal difficulty that I see ahead is to get strong modern plays and if possible plenty of comedy" (quoted in Holloway, *Abbey Theatre,* 34). Less than a month later, Fay wrote again: "What is your opinion as to the smallness of our audiences? Is it the sadness of the plays? . . . Next year I hope we shall have a historical play or two and perhaps more comedy, and Synge's next two plays will be devoid of corpses. . . . I have every sympathy with the desire for laughter, if it is kindly, but there is so much laughter around that is hard and cynical and cowardly, that I am not sorry we do pieces like *Riders to the Sea*" (36).

It had become clear to the founders then, that National Theatre audiences could neither find nor formulate themselves in esoteric verse dramas or poetic tragedies. As Lady Gregory succinctly put it in *Our Irish Theatre*, "The well-to-do people in our stalls [said], 'We have had enough of verse plays, give us comedy'" (78). In his 1929 history of Irish drama, Andrew E. Malone pointed out that "it was only when the idea of a National Theatre had definitely superseded that of [a national *literary* theater] that the necessity for popularization presented itself to the minds of the founders and directors. It was then that the *urgent necessity* for comedy began to be noted, and comedy began to be written" (*Irish Drama*, 221; my emphasis).

Although students of Irish literature outside of Ireland generally come to associate comedy of the renaissance period with male writers like J. M. Synge and Sean O'Casey, the person directly responsible for providing the comic balance needed to successfully "image" the Irish national character was Lady Gregory. Furthermore, although she would eventually create competent historical and tragic dramas, it was through her early comedies that she achieved an effect that Yeats could not, providing the necessary "lubricant" and "abrasive" to what we might call the machinery of Irish cultural nationalism.[3]

In assessing the nature, value, and effectiveness of Lady Gregory's comic contribution to cultural nationalism, I find it useful to view her as a foil to Yeats. Elizabeth Coxhead dates Lady Gregory's imaginative affiliation with Yeats at 1893, when his *The Celtic Twilight* was published. The opening chapters of Yeats's rather slight contribution to the plethora of works on Celticism flooding the literary market struck Augusta Gregory's fancy. Impressed by Yeats's invoking Paddy Flynn, the old Sligo storyteller of his boyhood, she saw in Paddy a counterpart to her own nurse, Mary Sheridan (Coxhead, *Portrait*, 41). But Mary had provided Lady Gregory a firmer grounding in the world outside the manor than Paddy had for Yeats. An Irish speaker, Mary had been a treasure trove of folktale and legend, a good Catholic, and a surrogate mother to Augusta. "At the time of the Fenian rising," Coxhead informs us, "Mary Sheridan had a discreetly veiled sympathy with the rebels, and the child [Augusta] found herself torn between the worlds above-stairs and below" (41). Thus, while Yeats's Paddy inspired recollections of Mary that would eventually find their way into Lady Gregory's plays, I would argue that those recollections sprang from a longer and deeper understanding of the complex problem of Irish identity than did Yeats's.

In the years between Mary Sheridan's tutelage and Augusta Gregory's association with the National Theatre of Ireland, Lady Gregory would travel the globe with her husband, the elderly Sir William Gregory, accruing life experiences that would render her apparently inconsequential comedies wise in the ways of the world as well as of Ireland. A woman in a man's world for most of her life, she was necessarily a keen observer and listener. Even the first of her comedies to be performed, *Twenty Five*—which represents the returned lover of a young woman, now married to an elderly man, who generously saves the couple's home—was likely inspired by her affair with poet Wilfrid Scawen Blunt.[4]

Lady Gregory began her playwriting career "by writing bits of dialogue, when wanted," for the already established dramatists, most notably Yeats (*Our Irish Theatre*, 80), and went on to fully collaborate with him on numerous plays. The history of that collaboration is a provocative discourse revealing an anxiety of influence and proprietorship (mostly on the part of critics) that ranges from misogynist to feminist.[5] While an exhaustive study of their professional collaboration is beyond the scope of this essay, I will approach the joint venture of Lady Gregory and W. B. Yeats in the National Theatre, and its ramifications for Irish cultural nationalism, primarily through an examination of one play from each author written during the period when the comic urge was erupting in official renaissance Ireland. Considered as two voices in a dialogue about the national vision Ireland was then developing, these counterpointed plays—where cultural beliefs and aesthetic ideologies collide—dramatize the making of the Irish character more accurately than would a comedy of Lady Gregory's alone.

The Abbey Theatre poster for Saturday, 9 March 1907, less than two months after the *Playboy* riots, boasted a program of four plays. Three of them, *The Rising of the Moon, The Gaol Gate,* and *Hyacinth Halvey,* were written by Lady Gregory. The fourth, *The Hour Glass,* is credited to William Butler Yeats, though Lady Gregory is purported to have "contributed largely" to its composition (Kelly, "Friendship," 213) and Lady Gregory's son Robert designed the costumes. Just two years earlier, at the opening of the Abbey Theatre on 27 December 1904, the bill had featured two Yeats plays, *Cathleen ni Houlihan,* and *On Baile's Strand* (both of which had been enhanced in one way or another by Lady Gregory's modifications or inspiration) and only one play by Lady Gregory, *Spreading the News.* Between December 1904 and March 1907, then, one might assume that something had increased the value of Lady Gregory's dramatic stock. Certainly the *Playboy* riots indicate that significant numbers of the Abbey audience were not willing to accept Synge's ironic image of the Irish hero (and hero makers) as their own likeness. They could handle seeing their "folks" satirized, even represented as murderers, as the popularity of *Spreading the News* attests. But they could sanction neither the cynicism that undercut the comic elements of Synge's play nor what Holloway called the "coarseness of the dialogue. . . . the outpouring of a morbid, unhealthy mind ever seeking on the dunghill of life for the nastiness that lies concealed there" (*Abbey Theatre,* 81). They wanted, specifically, Lady Gregory's brand of comedy, her more kindly version of the reluctant hero, to balance the highbrow depoliticization of Yeats's plays.

Although the 9 March 1907 performance was to be the premiere showing of *The Rising of the Moon,* the Yeats play would be first in order of performance. To be precise, the poster announces the "First Production of *The Rising of the Moon . . .* Preceded by *The Hour Glass . . . The Gaol Gate,* [and] *Hyacinth Halvey.*"[6] The arrangement of the program is consistent with Lady Gregory's early history with Yeats. Notoriously humble about her talents as a playwright, she invariably allowed Yeats's work to take precedence over hers even after it became clear that the Abbey Theatre's early success was due largely to the immense popularity of the comedies she insisted she was "forced to write . . . because [they were] wanted . . . to put on at the end of verse plays" (quoted in *Collected Plays,* v).

Quite consciously, then, she accepted the role of comic writer knowing that she was entering a dialogue about Irish identity. She would open the discourse of the National Theatre to carnival, forcing the polemic of identity formulation to become communal rather than autocratic. Even years after she had given up writing comedies, "whenever audiences were dropping off [at the Abbey] it became the thing to put on a Lady Gregory play to restore the box office receipts" (O'Connor, *Celtic Dawn,* 345). Her technique was to counter the unnatural with the natural, the esoteric with the popular, the universal with the particular, the ostensibly grandiose with the apparently trivial, thus evoking laughter at selected lies of the renaissance that centered on the heroic character of the Irish peasant.

In replicating on stage the rhetorical exchange about cultural nationalism, the Abbey plays provided the audience an opportunity to consider the extremes to which the cultural identity, its "character," was being distorted, thereby giving each viewer and the audience as a whole an opportunity to challenge, resist, or collude with the formation of that character. The antithetical tones and themes of Yeats's and Lady Gregory's plays created a synthesis of genre uniquely suited to the Abbey Theatre–going public of 1907, effectively yielding a means of mocking a self-image grown increasingly unsatisfactory through idealization or, in the case of Synge's playboy, ironic hardening.

Specifically, I will argue that the essentially conservative *The Hour Glass* gains vitality from the liberating force of *Hyacinth Halvey*. I have chosen *Hyacinth* to place in contention with *The Hour Glass* for the same reason that I suspect W. G. Fay and his brother Frank did, for it was they who orchestrated the voices of the playwrights. Taken together, the plays provide an ironic commentary on the latter day saints-heroes (Hyacinth) and sages (the Wise Man of *The Hour Glass*) of Ireland. Their placement on the same bill soon after the *Playboy* riots suggests a conciliatory move on the part of the Abbey Theatre directors. The remaining two plays, *The Gaol Gate* and *The Rising of the Moon*, both salved the suffering spirit of the Irish patriot in rather obvious ways— overturning the longstanding figure of the Irish informer—but *The Hour Glass* and *Hyacinth* replicate more subtle shades of the argument about Irish identity. The two plays were performed on the same bill at least one other time that I know of—for the twenty-first anniversary of the Abbey along with Synge's *The Shadow of the Glen*—and perhaps on many other occasions as well (Fallon, "Fragments," 33).

Despite Lady Gregory's reported involvement with the script of *The Hour Glass*, the work retains Yeats's well-defined stamp. Sustaining a tone of philosophical seriousness throughout, this little morality play pairs a humorless fool with an egocentric Wise Man, the personifications of intuition and reason respectively. The Wise Man, who is also a teacher (*the* Teacher), has effectively taught his pupils, family, and the community at large a particularly modern lesson—there is nothing to be known beyond this world, nothing that our senses cannot verify: "There's nothing but what men can see when they are awake. Nothing,

nothing" (200). The fool, being a fool, does not learn this lesson; however, the Wise Man does not take the fool's credulity seriously:

Fool: I have seen plenty of angels.
Wise Man: No, no, you have not.
Fool: They are plenty if you but look about you. They are like the
blades of grass.
Wise Man: They are plenty as the blades of grass—I heard that
phrase when I was but a child and was told folly. (200)

As the play progresses, we begin to understand that when the Wise
Man lost his childishness and failed to praise folly, he began to relinquish his soul. Confronted by an angel who challenges him to find even
one remaining true believer "before the sands have fallen" in the hour
glass or else be damned to hell for all eternity, the Wise Man is converted. Although he still must die, he is saved from damnation not so
much by the fool's faith as by his unreason. The play concludes with
the Fool's irrational verse: "I hear the wind a-blow, / I hear the grass a-
grow / And all that I know, I know. / But I will not speak, I will run
away" (211).

As is apparent from this brief summary, the play is fundamentally
conservative in spite of the experimentally spare, antirealistic setting
and dialogue that give it an avant-garde appearance. Although the Wise
Man's influence on his pupils seems to be considerable, we soon begin
to suspect that at least one of them has been putting him on—has
retained some doubt about the sufficiency of reason—while the Wise
Man's own egoism and fear of chaos prevent him from accepting a spiritual world. The Fourth Pupil's first line, "I will question him," establishes the catechetical nature of the play and this question/answer mode
is retained throughout. Later, when the Wise Man asks his wife, "Do
you believe in God?" she answers evasively, "O, a good wife believes in
what her husband tells her." Thus both in dramatic mode, the playing
out of a catechism, and in actual dialogue, the wife professes to support
her husband's projects, and the play reinforces a habit of mind quite
comfortable for the Irish public.

There is, however, a brief, unorthodox suggestion in the play that
belief in the supernatural creates heaven and that disbelief produces
hell:

Wise Man: I have a wife, children and pupils that I cannot leave:
Why must I die, my time is far away?

Angel: You have to die because no soul has passed the heavenly threshold since you have opened the school, but grass grows there, and rust upon the hinge; and they are lonely that must keep the watch.

Wise Man: And whither shall I go when I am dead?

Angel: You have denied there is a Purgatory, therefore that gate is closed; you have denied there is a Heaven, and so that gate is closed. (201-2)

Despite this provocative exchange, on the whole the play could have done little to challenge the ideals of its 1907 audience for it sustains a traditional religiosity masquerading as mysticism.

The conservatism of this play—which is representative of Yeats's oeuvre—is intriguing when considered in terms of the Irish National Theatre's role generally, and Yeats's specifically, as arbiter of cultural nationalism. In his 1918 assessment of *The Contemporary Drama of Ireland*, Ernest A. Boyd declared that Yeats had "come to be regarded as the embodiment of all that was, and is, represented by the Irish Literary Revival" (47). While I certainly would not presume to argue Yeats's right to that claim based on this one brief play, I find that *The Hour Glass* does incorporate the vision in embryo that Yeats elaborated throughout his life, one that he hoped would supersede contending images of the Irish character. What, then, is that vision as projected in the figure of the Wise Man?

In *The Hour Glass,* Yeats cautions against too facile a reliance on reason and science, too easy a dismissal of the supernatural. In doing so, he *conserves* an attitude already made dominant in Irish culture by religious and secular discourses seeking to control the Irish demand for material goods and psychological equity with other countries. Furthermore, in assigning responsibility to the Wise Man for the unbelief of the community (except the Fool), Yeats conserves another established, elitist tenet of Irish national identity: the notion that a natural aristocracy of the intelligentsia exists. The efficacy of the Wise Man's teaching implies respect for his power on the part of both the characters in the play and Yeats himself. But respect for the sage suggests a concomitant devaluing of the common people; a hierarchy is presumed.

Paradoxically, the fact that the Wise Man's salvation is effected by a masked *angelus ex machina* also aligns with a lifelong heart's desire of Yeats's: to displace ultimate responsibility for earthly well-being away from the priestly class (which of course includes not only sages but poets as well) and onto—not the community in its complexity and entirety—but a clockwork system of mystical forces. In sum, rather than inspiring a reformation of the Irish national character, *The Hour Glass* reproduces and reinforces an image of a hierarchical culture excessively reliant on its elite class, which in its turn seeks relief from the burden of vulgar, sublunar responsibility in metaphysical remedies. In addition, this conservative, escapist argument is conveyed with sanctimonious, catechetical, almost liturgical earnestness. In fairness to Yeats, I must mention that he was never quite happy with this play. But it seems significant that he never removed it from the repertoire of the Abbey Theatre, and, as I have noted earlier, it was still being performed, along with *Hyacinth Halvey*, in 1925 for a particularly festive occasion.

One might surmise from Joseph Holloway's reactions to the play throughout its history how few demands its actual content made on the audience in spite of the fact that its staging elicited enthusiastic responses:

> *Saturday, March 14* [1903]. The hall was thronged with an audience who listened enthralled to the clearly spoken and simple set representation of *The Hour Glass*—a simple legend beautifully and poetically expressed by our own particular mystic poet, the raven-locked W. B. Yeats. . . . It is wonderful the effect this little allegorical play had on the listeners, and the gentleman beside me inquired, "if a white flame really did appear at the end? For," he assured me, "I saw one . . ." This was cheating the imagination into belief with a vengeance, and was a great tribute alike to the power of the poet and the players. (*Abbey Theatre*, 21)

On the same bill with *The Hour Glass* that night was Lady Gregory's *Twenty Five*. Holloway found the "homely nature" of this play to be "in great contrast to *The Hour Glass*" (22). Although he declared the "vital incident" unconvincing—the game of cards where the wife's lover allows the husband to win the money that will save the couple's home—he pronounced this first of Lady Gregory's plays to be paired with one of Yeats's a "clever little work" whose "dialogue [was] very natural right through, and the characters cleverly suggested" (22). The significant point to be made here is that Holloway did note the intellectual content of Lady Gregory's work, even challenged its credibility, whereas *The Hour Glass*, based on a much more *incredible* premise, seems to have provided visual stimulation exclusively, the intellectual content having been *already* internalized. Viewing *The Hour Glass* twenty-two years later, Holloway remains consciously unaffected by the subject matter of the play: "The Abbey is playing a revival of Yeats's *The Hour Glass* with Gordon Craig scenery and new costumes this week. . . . W. B. Yeats and his wife were present at the Abbey on the first night of the revival of his play. His raven locks are now silvered, but he still looks distinguished and with his thoughts in the clouds" (246).

In 1906, three years after the first performances of *The Hour Glass* and *Twenty Five,* Lady Gregory completed *Hyacinth Halvey*. In the interim she had acquired considerable comic playwrighting skill, having revised *Twenty Five,* written and revised *The Poorhouse,* and completed the perennial favorite of Abbey audiences, *Spreading the News,* among others. Throughout the period during which she was writing *Hyacinth,* she was also working on a translation/adaptation of Molière's *The Doctor in Spite of Himself, The Rogueries of Scapin,* and *The Miser.* In addition to the recitative technique Lady Gregory employs in parts of *Hyacinth,* the name of her main character may have been suggested by Molière, for a Hyacinth appears in *Scapin.* In any case, the reluctant hero and mistaken identity are favorite subjects of Molière's, and both are crucial components of *Hyacinth.*

Very briefly, *Hyacinth* concerns the arrival in Cloon (Lady Gregory's fictional equivalent of the village of Gort) of the new, young Sub-Sanitary Inspector, Hyacinth Halvey from Carrow. He has attained this impressive office by producing "three pounds" of letters testifying to his excellent character. The testimonials turn out to be so effective that Hyacinth is provided a temperance button, invited to stay in a lodging "opposite the priest's house" where he will be on public display, and recruited to speak on the subject of "The Building of Character" at the local agricultural society. He is supported by a cast including Quirke, a butcher of questionable professional ethics; Fardy Farrell, the hapless telegraph boy; Sergeant Carden, guardian of the Anglo establishment; Mrs. Delane, the omniscient postmistress; and Miss Joyce, the priest's housekeeper.

In contrast to Yeats's virtually bare stage, the set for *Hyacinth* anchors the audience in mundane reality: "*Scene:* Outside the Post Office at the little town of Cloon. Mrs. Delane at Post Office Door. Mr. Quirke sitting on a chair at butcher's door. *A dead sheep hanging beside it,* and a thrush in a cage above. Fardy Farrell playing on a mouth organ. Train whistle is heard" (33; my emphasis). It would be hard to imagine a funnier or more potent symbol of the Irish character as represented in puffed-up official revival literature than the dead sheep hanging beside the butcher's chair. In contrast to Yeats's hour glass, the sheep is an earthy, familiar, but somehow outrageous sight. Signifying both the sacrificial lamb and the impotent hero, the sheep becomes the means to Hyacinth's fame. For, in stealing the sheep in order to ruin his own reputation, Hyacinth saves Mr. Quirke from arrest by removing the evidence of his selling spoiled meat to the military (but not to the residents of Cloon). Hyacinth soon finds the burden of the testimonials and his new, upstanding character irksome. The humor of the play derives from his unsuccessful attempts to destroy his own reputation and thus liberate himself from the confining image others have created for him. As in the *Playboy*, humor also springs from the townsfolk's insistence on having a hero whatever the truth of his character may be.

Hyacinth grew out of numerous impulses besides Lady Gregory's admiration for Molière and her growing appreciation of the need for comedy in the National Theatre. In her consciousness, a real-life incident became enmeshed with the cultural debate about the Irish character. She explains in the notes to the play: "I was pointed out one evening a well-brushed, well-dressed man in the stalls, and was told gossip about him, . . . which made me wonder if that appearance and behaviour as of extreme respectability might not now and again be felt a burden. After a while he translated himself in my mind into Hyacinth; and . . . he found himself in Cloon, where, *as in other parts of our country, "character" is built up or destroyed by a password or an emotion, rather than by experience and deliberation"* (*Seven Short Plays*, 205; my emphasis).

In both the play itself and this account of its origin, *Hyacinth's* antithetical premises with regard to *The Hour Glass* are clear. One might reasonably infer that the two pieces were chosen for the same program because of their polarities of theme as well as genre, for, while Yeats's play sustains a traditional image of the sage, Lady Gregory explodes the image of the respectable renaissance man. Her originating instinct for the play was a liberating one, inspired by a specific, well-defined incident in her life. Unlike *The Hour Glass*, which begins and ends with a conservative moral, *Hyacinth*, conceived from a moment's gossip, provides relief from the burden of respectability and an implicit lesson about the need to change certain rhetorical practices current in 1907 Ireland. Whereas *The Hour Glass* reproduces a sort of catechism of orthodox belief, *Hyacinth* reveals, in true Molièrean style, the intractability of misbelief:

Hyacinth: What are you going to do to me?

Mr. Quirke: Do, is it? (Grasps his hand.) Any earthly thing you would wish me to do. I will do it.

Hyacinth: I suppose you will tell—

Mr. Quirke: Tell! It's I that will tell when all is quiet. It is I will give you the good name through the town!

Hyacinth: I don't well understand. (42)

The cultural revival had rendered the burden of respectability, or "appropriate" patriotic behavior, onerous for many Irish citizens (one is reminded of Gabriel Conroy in Joyce's "The Dead"), and Lady Gregory was quick to realize that her original perception about the "well-dressed, well-brushed" young man had been conditioned by current discursive practices. Elaborating on the insight that character in Ireland is "built up or destroyed by a password or an emotion rather than by experience or deliberation," she reveals in *Hyacinth* the consequences of succumbing to character-building rhetorical pressures and releases her audience from those pressures by way of comic strategies.

In *The Hour Glass,* one might argue, the focus is on the "sage" component of the proverbial "isle of saints and sages," while *Hyacinth Halvey* features a secular "saint." Besides being the name of one of Molière's characters, "Hyacinth" recalls the thirteenth-century Polish saint. In the play, having stolen a look at some of the testimonials that have arrived in the mail, the postmistress decides that Hyacinth "must be a very saintly young man" (35). Later, after Hyacinth admits the testimonials are bogus, Fardy insists that it doesn't matter because the community already believes that "You are the next thing to an earthly saint" (40). Finally, when Hyacinth attempts to exonerate the beleaguered Fardy from a crime Hyacinth himself has committed, Mr. Quirke exclaims, "The preserver of the poor! Talk of your holy martyrs!" (55). It appears, then, that Hyacinth is permanently burdened with his saintly reputation.

The Hour Glass does not make clear where the Wise Man derives his earthly wisdom (presumably from another wise man/teacher like himself), though his conversion to a "higher" wisdom through a supernatural agent is played out on the stage. Conversely, Hyacinth's claim to sainthood is a decidedly communal affair, and we witness the formulation of that saintliness. One of Lady Gregory's comic strategies is to lay bare the otherwise unnoticed machinations of this communal enterprise. Recognizing the subversive nature of *Hyacinth Halvey,* David

Krause observes that: "Orthodox society and its repressive pieties are opposed and mocked by comic illusions. [Hyacinth] is defeated by the gullible people of Cloon who are determined to make him a saint. The play is therefore a comic desecration of saintliness; it mocks the psychological need to exalt excessive virtue in spite of the fallibility of ordinary human beings" (*Profane*, 125–26). But *Hyacinth* is more than a simple deconstruction of saintliness in the religious sense of the word. As both the play and the note on its origin show, it concerns itself with the burden of reputation, a burden weighing particularly heavy on Irish society just weeks after the *Playboy* riots. Furthermore, the play suggests that, while Hyacinth is "defeated by the gullible people of Cloon who are determined to make him a saint," as Krause observes, Hyacinth himself shares responsibility for his reputation since he originally colluded with the testimonial makers.

The list of tributes to Hyacinth's character and the sources of those tributes illustrate both the immediacy of Lady Gregory's message about character building and the wide-ranging culpability for Hyacinth's predicament:

> *Sergeant* (opening and reading one by one): "He possesses the fire of the Gael, the strength of the Norman, the vigour of the Dane, the stolidity of the Saxon"—
> *Hyacinth:* It was the chairman of the Poor Law Guardians wrote that.
> *Sergeant:* "A magnificent example to old and young"—
> *Hyacinth:* That was the Secretary of the De Wet Hurling Club.
> *Sergeant:* "A shining example of the value conferred by an eminently careful and high class education"—
> *Hyacinth:* That was the National Schoolmaster.
> *Sergeant:* "Devoted to the highest ideals of his Mother-land to such an extent as is compatible with a hitherto non-parliamentary career"—
> *Hyacinth:* That was the Member for Carrow.
> *Sergeant:* "A splendid exponent of the purity of the race"—
> *Hyacinth:* The Editor of the *Carrow Champion*. (36)

As this overdetermined list of character references shows, it is not the Church's method of canonizing its saints that Lady Gregory is satirizing but rather the overblown rhetoric of the cultural renaissance in its attempt to create modern secular Irish "saints." Unlike the spare poetic language of *The Hour Glass*, the language here is puffed-up yet very close to "the real thing." These testimonials, for all their emptiness, could easily have been lifted from actual letters of reference. And they represent a cross-section of clichés from nonsectarian official spokesmen for the cultural revival ranging from athletic societies to newspapers. Even the xenophobia inherent in some of the renaissance rhetoric is reproduced here: "A splendid exponent of the purity of the race." This concise statement of ethnocentrism is rendered ironic by the earlier comparison of Hyacinth to "the Gael," "the Norman," "the Dane," and "the Saxon." Notably, in the same year that *Hyacinth* appeared on the bill with *The Hour Glass,* James Joyce addressed the citizens of Pola about the history of "The Island of Saints and Sages," observing the contradiction in a polemic that claimed the purity of a race that had been infiltrated by a variety of invaders throughout its history.[7]

Whereas Yeats frequently employed supernatural agents in his plays to bring about their dramatic recognition scenes, Lady Gregory's comic strategy was to keep her satire just this side of the ridiculous or fantastic so that, however outlandish her plots may become, the events are within the realm of possibility. Mary Fitzgerald contends that Lady Gregory "yielded to truth and to history. . . . And to judge by her fidelity to her journals, her folklore collecting, and even the nature of her plays, Lady Gregory seems to have thought of herself as a recorder of her times" ("Perfection," 46). The foibles of Lady Gregory's Cloon citizens were familiar to her 1907 audience. And precisely because their failings were mundane and recognizable, they could be attended to and possibly overcome. It is in this sense of revealing the flaws and simultaneously implying their cure that Lady Gregory's comedy provides both an "abrasive" and a "lubricant" to the system of character formation in renaissance Ireland. In showing how Hyacinth is overwhelmed by the far-fetched, yet stock testimonials (which I take to be versions of the "password or . . . emotion" that she speaks of in the note on the play), she implies that Ireland, too, is at risk of being undone by its own rhetorical cleverness. At the same time, she implicitly requires a toning down of the language if the system is to work properly.

Recognizing the impossibility of living up to such a character as the testimonials have given him, Hyacinth responds to Fardy's insightful question:

Fardy (whistles): Maybe you're not, so, what those papers make you out to be?
Hyacinth: How would I be what they make me out to be? Was

there ever any person of that sort since the world was a world, unless it might be Saint Anthony of Padua looking down from the chapel wall? If it is like that I was, isn't it in Mount Melleray I would be, or with the Friars at Esker? Why would I be living in the world at all, or doing the world's work?

Fardy: . . . Who would think, now, there would be so many lies in a small place like Carrow?

Hyacinth: It was my mother's cousin did it. He said I was not reared for labourin—he gave me a new suit and bid me never to come back again. I daren't go back to face him—the neighbors knew my mother had a long family—bad luck to them the day they gave me these. (Tears letters and scatters them.) I'm done with testimonials. (40)

It is revealing that the testimonials are originally conceived as a way of getting rid of Hyacinth, a way of exiling the nonlaboring man from his home territory, and that decision too has been a communal one. Here Lady Gregory uncovers an important conflict in the fashioning of the new Irish character, a conflict that grew from the practical need to populate the island with working men rather than just saints and sages. Such subtle social notation is characteristic of Lady Gregory's plays generally and sets them off from Yeats's.

In spite of his vow to be "done with testimonials," Hyacinth is trapped both by what his relatives and neighbors have said of him and by the word of mouth they have released into the Cloon community. As she had done in *Spreading the News,* and as Synge had done in the *Playboy,* Lady Gregory foregrounds gossip in *Hyacinth Halvey,* exposing it as a fundamental source of power in the Irish community, greater even than the autocratic power of a Wise Man. It is this amorphous communication system among the people—personified in Mrs. Delane, the postmistress—that ultimately decides what to accept and what to reject with regard to character formation. Unlike Yeats's Wise Man, who is assigned responsibility for his community's unbelief, Hyacinth is only partially responsible even for his own reputation. The villagers from Carrow to Cloon, high and low, Catholic and Protestant, have made him what he is. And, unlike the Wise Man, Hyacinth is not saved from his predicament either by natural or supernatural forces. Having once tacitly agreed to allow the process of his character building to begin, Hyacinth must remain a hero in Cloon. Both anticipating and recalling Synge's Christy Mahon (since Lady Gregory wrote *Hyacinth* before *Playboy,* but it is here being performed in the wake of the riots), Hyacinth is lifted above a cheering crowd at the conclusion of the play and "chaired" through the streets as "an example and a blessing to the whole town" (56).

Joseph Holloway's *Impressions of a Dublin Playgoer* indicates that from the period of the *Playboy* riots in late January until late February 1907, a segment of the Abbey public had remained testy. In fact his own attitude toward Lady Gregory and Yeats, which had previously been quite fond and complimentary, had turned bitter: "One sack, one sample. Yeats, Synge, and Gregory are all degenerates of the worst type; the former pair indulge in sensuality in their later work, and the latter condones with them" (86). However, his entry for 9 March, the day when *Hyacinth, The Hour Glass, The Gaol Gate,* and *The Rising of the Moon* were performed together, suggests that "a fairly good" audience felt that the theater had regained its proper balance: "I found a fairly good audience present, though the weather was anything but inviting outside. . . . After an unusually long delay, *The Rising of the Moon* was presented, and from the start had the spectators interested. . . . It is a splendidly written little piece" (88). Holloway would naturally focus on *The Rising of the Moon,* the new play on the bill, rather than on *Hyacinth,* and he seems not to have arrived in time for *The Hour Glass.* Nonetheless, the audience couldn't have missed the affinities of *Hyacinth* with the beleaguered *Playboy* of just weeks earlier. Lady Gregory's hero, however, perhaps because he remains reluctant throughout the play, is acceptable to the audience. Holloway's initial reaction to *Hyacinth* suggests how the play was first received: "*Friday. February 23* [1906]. Lady Gregory's extremely amusing farce of country-town life, entitled *Hyacinth Halvey* . . . went like wildfire from first to last. If anything, it is funnier than *Spreading the News*" (70).

Interestingly, Hyacinth's fate left Lady Gregory so uneasy that in the 1910 play *The Full Moon* she devised his escape. In the note to that play, she explains: "It has sometimes preyed on my mind that Hyacinth Halvey had been left by me in Cloon for his lifetime, bearing the weight of a character that had been put on him by force" (quoted in Kopper, *Gregory,* 83). When she conceived the original play, however, it must have seemed expedient to represent a reluctant secular saint, trapped, like Ireland itself, in the rhetorical devices of his community.

Yeats would also revisit the characters of *The Hour Glass,* transforming the Wise Man and the Fool into shadow figures of Cúchulainn and Chonchubar, but his later plays would never attract the audiences that his earlier ones had done. The appeal of the earlier plays, however, depended largely on their pairing with Lady Gregory's comedies. The distance from real life that Yeats achieved in his poetic dramas, the strange events and enigmatic dialogue *demanded* a counterbalance. Furthermore, the pull backward toward an autocratic society that his plays exerted inspired the resistance of the communal will that Lady Gregory's comedies projected.

In an interview with a *Boston Herald* reporter in 1911 entitled "The Comedy Spirit of Ireland" (Mikhail, 43), Lady Gregory characterized her own work as "friendly satire." The reporter went on to note that "the too-serious is not part of her work, as she has explained 'All the young writers are so busy writing tragedy that I shall have to go on, as I am the only one old enough to laugh'."

NOTES

1. Representative views of the emerging Irish character can be found in such works as Daryl's *Ireland's Disease,* Gwynn's *Today and Tomorrow in Ireland,* Paul-Dubois's *Contemporary Ireland,* and Plunkett's *Ireland in the New Century,* and in *Ideals in Ireland,* edited by Lady Gregory.

2. Krause presents an opposing view of Boucicault in *The Profane Book of Irish Comedy:* "He took the vulgar buffoonery out of the stage Irishman and made him an attractive and articulate clown who dominated the stage" (175).

3. Martineau uses these terms to classify two of the social functions of comedy.

4. See Longford's piece on the Gregory-Blunt affair for a sympathetic yet fair assessment of this well-kept secret.

5. See Kelly's essay "'Friendship'" and the notes for information and numerous other sources on the Gregory-Yeats collaboration.

6. The poster is reproduced on the verso of page xv of *The Collected Plays.*

7. See Joyce's "The Island of Saints and Sages."

WORKS CITED

Boyd, Ernest A. *The Contemporary Drama of Ireland.* Dublin: Talbot Press, 1918.

Coxhead, Elizabeth. *Lady Gregory: A Literary Portrait.* New York: Harcourt, Brace & World, 1961.

Daryl, Phillippe. *Ireland's Disease.* London: Routledge, 1888.

Fallis, Richard. *The Irish Renaissance.* Syracuse, N.Y.: Syracuse University Press, 1977.

Fallon, Gabriel. "Fragments of Memory." In *Lady Gregory, Fifty Years After,* edited by Ann Saddlemyer and Colin Smythe, 30–34. Totowa, N.J.: Barnes and Noble, 1987.

Fitzgerald, Mary. "Four French Comedies: Lady Gregory's Translations of Molière." In Saddlemyer and Smythe, 277–90.

———. "'Perfection of the Life': Lady Gregory's Autobiographical Writings." In Saddlemyer and Smythe, 45–55.

Gregory, Lady Augusta. "Hyacinth Halvey." In *The Collected Plays,* 2 vols., edited by Ann Saddlemyer, 31–56. New York: Oxford University Press, 1970.

———, ed. *Ideals in Ireland.* London: The Sign of the Unicorn, 1901.

———. *Our Irish Theatre.* New York: Capricorn Books, 1965.

———. *Seven Short Plays.* Dublin: Maunsel, 1909.

Gwynn, Stephen. *Today and Tomorrow in Ireland: Essays on Irish Subjects.* Dublin: Hodges, Figgis, 1903.

Holloway, Joseph. *Joseph Holloway's Abbey Theatre: A Selection from his Journal "Impressions of a Dublin Playgoer".* Edited by Robert Hogan and Michael J. O'Neill. Carbondale, Ill.: Southern Illinois University Press, 1967.

Joyce, James. "The Island of Saints and Sages." In *The Critical Writings of James Joyce,* edited by Ellsworth Mason and Richard Ellmann. New York: Viking, 1959.

Kelly, John. "'Friendship is All the House I Have': Lady Gregory and W. B. Yeats." In Saddlemyer and Smythe, 179–257.

Kopper, Edward A. *Lady Isabella Persse Gregory.* Boston: Twayne, 1976.

Krause, David. *The Profane Book of Irish Comedy.* Ithaca, N.Y.: Cornell University Press, 1982.

Longford, Elizabeth. "Lady Gregory and Wilfrid Scawen Blunt." In Saddlemyer and Smythe, 85–97.

Malone, Andrew. *The Irish Drama.* New York: Benjamin Blom, 1965.

Martineau, William H. "A Model of the Social Function of Humor." In *The Psychology of Humor,* edited by Jeffrey H. Goldstein and Paul McGee. New York: Academic Press, 1972.

Mikhail, E. H., ed. *Lady Gregory: Interviews and Recollections.* Totowa, N.J.: Rowan and Littlefield, 1977.

O'Connor, Ulick. *Celtic Dawn: A Portrait of the Irish Literary Renaissance.* London: Black Swan, 1985.

Paul-Dubois, L. *Contemporary Ireland.* Dublin: Maunsel, 1908.

Plunkett, Horace. *Ireland in the New Century.* London: John Murray, 1904.

Saddlemyer, Ann, and Colin Smythe, eds. *Lady Gregory, Fifty Years After.* Totowa, N.J.: Barnes and Noble, 1987.

Yeats, William Butler. "The Hour Glass." In *The Collected Plays,* 196–211. New York: Macmillan, 1953.

"Humor with a Gender"
Somerville and Ross and *The Irish R.M.*

JAMES M. CAHALAN

Ever since the publication of the first story in 1898—"Great Uncle McCarthy" in London's *Badminton Magazine*—Somerville and Ross's *The Irish R.M.* (hereafter RM) stories have been among the most popular and successful works of comic fiction to have come out of Ireland. The three volumes of stories (subsequently collected in a single volume) deal with a cast of characters who develop in an ongoing fashion that makes these delectable short stories, when considered together, fairly similar in form to the Irish novel—episodic and filled with realistic Irish-English dialect and some rather fantastic occurrences. Here, however, I am interested less in the form of the RM stories than in how they were a product of the unique collaborative careers of the two women who wrote them, the cousins Edith Somerville and Violet Martin, and in how they interrelate with the cultural world of their time (and our own time) as reflected in their reception history. No fewer than seven biographies and critical books on Somerville and Ross have appeared during the past four decades, and a reestimation seems timely following the publication three years ago of their selected letters to each other. Gifford Lewis's recent biography and edition of the letters provide a valuable feminist perspective on their overall careers. Here I intend to focus more specifically on the RM stories.

The RM stories have enjoyed a persistent international popularity. They were first collected in three successive volumes of 1899, 1908, and 1915, and subsequently they were published all together in 1928, have always stayed in print, and are best known to the general public today through the British Channel 4/UTV/RTE television series that aired more than once beginning in the early 1980s. The latest inexpensive collected edition in paperback has been selling briskly in Dublin since the 1991 rebroadcast of the television series there. Ever since the turn of the century, the popularity of the RM stories has extended well beyond Dublin and London. In late 1901, during the Boer War, Edith wrote to Violet: "Mrs. Purdon told H that her son & his company came upon a dead Boer, & examined him for despatches & etc.—They found a copy of the R.M.—'He died of laughter-' . . . They took the copy, & it became the camp bible" (*Letters,* 258). The stories first appeared in *Badminton Magazine,* a kind of British *Field and Stream* of its day, and its publishers, Longmans and Green, immediately encouraged book publication of the stories and the subsequent sequels. Somerville and Ross were encouraged by the minor success of the earlier hunting stories of Robert Martin, Violet's brother. The closest fairly well-known earlier Irish analogue to RM was W. H. Maxwell's *Wild Sports of the West* (1832).

However, the RM stories have been repeatedly misunderstood, and Somerville and Ross had to endure considerable hostility, misogyny, and misdirected nationalism. Their protagonist, Major Sinclair Yeates— a well-educated, well-meaning chap with some Irish blood—is sent from England, in classic Irish fictional fashion, to remote southwestern rural Ireland as a resident magistrate (an archaic legal post whose closest American equivalent is the justice of the peace). There he—and subsequently his wife, Philippa—encounter many unforgettable Irish characters who really run the area, particularly Flurry Knox and his grandmother Mrs. Knox, and they participate in many racy Irish pastimes, most of which center on hunting. Many of these stories' early readers were incredulous that two women could write so effectively about traditionally male sites such as the courtroom and the hunt; typical was the reader cited by Somerville in *Irish Memories:* "First I read it at full speed, because I couldn't stop, and then I read it *very* slowly, chewing every word; and then I read it a third time, dwelling on the bits I like best; and then, and *not* till then, thank Heaven! I was told it was written by two women!" (288).

Added to such misogyny was the even more persistent Irish nationalism that misrepresented the RM stories as "stage-Irish" tales along the lines of Samuel Lover's novel *Handy Andy* (1842). This point of view completely misses the fact that in sharp contrast to Lover, who made fun of the peasant Andy's ignorance, Somerville and Ross adopted Yeates, an Anglo-Irishman, as their central comic victim as well as narrator. This was the Ascendancy laughing at itself more than at the peasantry—or more specifically, it was a case of two women making fun of an Anglo-Irish*man*, whose comedy is greatly leavened by the fact that he himself participates in it and narrates it: to some extent, he laughs at himself. (Their most foolish and most duped character is a visiting Englishman without any Irish blood at all, Leigh Kelway, especially in "Lisheen Races, Second-Hand.")

Yet partly because Somerville and Ross stayed out of the Literary Revival movement led by their protagonist's namesake, Yeats, and went their own way, nationalist critical commentators gave them at best backhanded praise. Ernest Boyd, in his canon-forming *Ireland's Literary Renaissance* (1916), briefly praised their great 1894 novel *The Real Charlotte* but lamented the supposed "subsequent squandering of the authors' great talent upon the trivialities of a superficial realism" (90). In *The Lonely Voice*, Frank O'Connor admitted that he enjoyed reading the RM stories but described them as "yarns, pure and simple" (4). Herbert Howarth omitted Somerville and Ross entirely from his 1958 study of their period; Vivian Mercier mentioned them only once in his pioneering but male-dominated study of *The Irish Comic Tradition* (1962); and, in *The Comic Irishman* (1984), Maureen Waters claimed that there was "a racist consciousness at work in Somerville and Ross, and they undoubtedly contributed to the stereotype of the Irish countryman as a tricky clown" (20).[1] I aim to show that, far from being racist victimizers, Somerville and Ross were victimized women who nonetheless managed to become successful, and that intermixed in the RM stories with a nostalgia for a dying way of life was a subversively gendered portrait of strong, vital women. In this sense, comedy could be—in the words of the title of a recent book by Nancy Walker about American women's humor—"a very serious thing."

Early criticism was dominated by misogyny and nationalism, but it also included such nuggets as the anonymous reviewer in the London *Daily Graphic* who noted, in Somerville and Ross's 1891 novel *Naboth's Vineyard*, "their keen sense of humour—qualities which many male critics deny to their literary sisters" (quoted in *Letters*, 178). And my own title is borrowed from a little-remembered, brief, but perceptive and trailblazing 1922 article in the *Atlantic Monthly* by Elizabeth Stanley Trotter: "Humor with a Gender." Trotter argued that men tend to laugh "at," while women tend to laugh "with," avoiding ridicule and often aligning themselves with the victims of jokes (as Somerville and Ross do by making Major Yeates their narrator). Suggesting that feminist humor, however, can be practiced by men as well as women, Trotter recounts an anecdote about Mark Twain having a joke at a Frenchman's expense (with the anecdote usually ending, in its common male retelling, with Twain's punch line). Then (in the part that interests Trotter), when the Frenchman complained about the insult, Twain offered to reverse positions and be the butt of the joke himself. The joke is the thing, not who wins and loses, not who is victim and who is victor. Best of all, Trotter quotes Somerville and Ross's "ideal of a woman of humor in the larger sense: 'Inherently romantic, but the least sentimental; the most conversational and the most reserved; silent about the things that affect us most deeply (which is perhaps the reason we are considered good company)—light-hearted, cheerful, and quite convinced that nothing will succeed!'" (787).

This perhaps rare combination of being at the same time both "cheerful" and "quite convinced that nothing will succeed" is understandable given the two cousins' personal—which is to say family—situations. Like their admired predecessor Maria Edgeworth, who (far from having a room of her own) had to write at the corner of the table in the family room, Somerville and Ross were compelled to eke out writing time whenever they could in the midst of bustling Big Houses for which they themselves became responsible after the deaths of parents. These authors had to develop what their narrator Yeates calls, in "The Friend of Her Youth," "that strange power of doing one thing and talking about another that I have often noticed in women" (RM, 463–64). Edith complained to her brother, "It is almost impossible to work quietly here: it is not the time so much as the want of mental tranquility plus the feeling that interruptions incessantly impend. It is impossible, I think, for anyone, who has not tried, to realise how exhausting interruptions are when one is engaged in imaginative creative work" (quoted in *Symposium*, 21).

Of course, Somerville and Ross's own interests were anything but entirely "quiet": both were avid hunters, though it was much more the chase than the kill that interested them. Somerville was the first woman in Ireland to become a Master of Fox Hounds, or MFH, in 1903. Yet even in this position she had to follow the repressive Victorian code of female decorum by riding sidesaddle, with her right leg swung across to the same side of the saddle as her left (as can be seen in photographs in Lewis's biography and edition of the letters). As a result, she developed serious "rheumatism" in her right leg that grew worse and worse as she got older. Violet Martin's 1898 riding accident—linked to the subsequent development of a brain tumor and her eventual death in 1915—has been mentioned by several biographers and critics as a postscript to Francie Fitzgerald's fatal riding accident in *The Real Charlotte*. Yet no one has ever stopped to wonder (at least in print) whether Martin would have been thrown from her horse if she had been permitted to ride securely in the normal, male position instead of the convoluted, precarious, and painful sidesaddle posture imposed on women at the time.

With Martin based until 1906 at Ross House near Galway, and Somerville anchored at the other end of the country at Drishane in County Cork, these two women had to struggle to find opportunities to collaborate as closely as they did. Nonetheless, they managed to achieve the most successful close coauthorship in Irish literature—arguably, in fact, the most successful among writers in English since the Middle Ages. Addison and Steele collaborated on the eighteenth-century *Tatler*, but they did not write everything together as did Somerville and Ross.

Carolyn Heilbrun's perceptive book *Writing a Woman's Life*—which rightly notes that the implications of women's friendship together, their collaboration, and their use of pseudonyms have been too little considered—would do well to include Somerville and Ross as more apt examples of such crucial collaboration than anyone in English or American literature. Similarly, Sandra Gilbert and Susan Gubar omit Somerville and Ross from their *Norton Anthology of Literature by Women* even though they would have provided a unique example of women's collaboration; that anthology, whose 148 writers are all individuals rather than coauthors, includes only four Irish ones. Ironically, the closest contemporary analogue may be the team of Gilbert and Gubar themselves; speaking together at the 1988 Summer Institute for Teachers of Literature to Undergraduates (sponsored by the National Council of Teachers of English), they described how they try to accept as many joint speaking engagements as they can since those provide them with relatively rare opportunities to get together (from Indiana and California) and write.

Collaborating without long-distance telephone calls and university budgets for air travel, Edith Somerville and Violet Martin spent the most productive twenty years of their careers, from 1886 to 1906, writing and traveling back and forth between Cork and Galway in order to get their work done. They talked out and wrote down everything to-gether, so closely that scholars have been unable to tell who wrote what or to identify separate segments of writing. Their collaboration was so close that after Martin's death in 1915, Somerville (who survived her by thirty-four years) insisted on publishing everything under their joint names; believed that she could maintain mystical communication with Martin; and took the idea for her most successful solo work of fiction, her 1925 novel, *The Big House of Inver,* from a suggestion in a 1912 letter from Martin (*Letters,* 294). Given the close nature of their col-laboration, their geographical isolation from each other, and the many distractions in their lives, they had to work very hard when they could work together at all.

The first RM stories were written between October 1898 and Sep-tember 1899, following Martin's accident when (as Somerville later re-called) "Martin hardly knew . . . what it was to be out of suffering" (quoted in J. Cronin, *Somerville and Ross,* 51). The bleakest RM story, "The Waters of Strife" (about a man who commits a murder and later commits suicide), was written just after Martin's accident. Each story "as we finished it, seemed to be the last possible effort of exhausted nature" (quoted in J. Cronin, 59). These stories were very carefully planned, as Guy Fehlmann has shown. Hilary Robinson records how Somerville and Ross made deliberate, extensive use of their own expe-riences and people they knew, keeping big notebooks they called *Stock Pot Irish Memories* and making notations when they incorporated ma-terials from the notebooks in the stories (51).

In order to succeed as two late Victorian women writers invading the male provinces of satire and hunting, Somerville and Ross needed each other. As Martin aptly put it to Somerville in 1889, thinking about the impediments facing women writers, "I am not man enough for a story by myself" (*Letters,* 153). They shared an inherited family code language of sorts, the vocabulary of the "Buddhs" (or descendants of Lord Chief Justice of Ireland Charles Kendal Bushe), which they col-lected in the form of a glossary (*Letters,* 297–302) and used in their letters for comic effects and sometimes for self-protective purposes. Their first novel, with the fitting title of *An Irish Cousin* (1889), was pub-lished under the pseudonyms "Giles Herring" and "Martin Ross," but thereafter Somerville insisted on signing all her books with her own habitually initialed name; as for Martin, all her friends (including Somerville, in her letters) addressed her as "Martin" rather than "Violet," and she was proud to carry the family Big House name of "Ross." Thus, at first, many readers assumed that Somerville and Ross were men, but their true status was generally known by the turn of the century.

The common and persistent view of Somerville and Ross as two wealthy Ascendancy "ladies" writing comic tales for a lark could not be further from the truth. With rents withheld during the Land War era, and given the general decline of the fortunes of Ascendancy families such as the Somervilles and the Martins, they wrote the RM stories in order to survive—to avoid the depression and total dependency on the family of unmarried women such as Martin's own pathetic sister Selina. As Martin wrote to Somerville in 1890, "I *must* make money—so must you" (*Letters* 164); Somerville replied, "I also am very poor, only for the *Art Journal*—as yet unpaid—I should be bankrupt" (*Letters*, 165). They always considered their somber, tragic novel *The Real Charlotte* to be their greatest work, but the RM stories sold much better, and when they saw they had a hit with those stories, they continued to write more of them.

J. B. Pinker—their agent and also agent to Henry James, Joseph Conrad, and D. H. Lawrence—was amazed at how well these stories sold. Martin's letters in particular are very hardheaded about sales and display a craftiness about making sure of the right reviews. In 1906 Martin complained to Somerville about a man who was working on a biography of her own brother Robert (author of some lesser-known hunting stories) and had asked her to contribute to it, to "'write all you like, and we can select what is wanted.' I at once said I was too busy to write stuff that might not be wanted and he seemed quite surprised—I don't think that he realises at all the position, or that I am a *professional writer*" (*Letters*, xxiii; my emphasis). Male critics such as Boyd (describing their work as "trivial") perpetuated this kind of sexist attitude.

It should be noted that Somerville and Ross felt quite removed from the Irish Literary Revival, despite the fact that Violet Martin was Lady Gregory's cousin, visited her at Coole Park, and was invited in 1905 to write a play for the Abbey Theatre. Martin wrote to Somerville that Lady Gregory told her, "A week at Coole would do it. We could give you all the hints necessary for stage effects etc—even write a scenario for you" (*Letters*, 274). It is clear that Martin was no more persuaded by this proposal than by the biographer's assurance that "we can select what is wanted." In response to Lady Gregory's invitation, Martin wrote Somerville, "I gave no further encouragement of any sort—and said we were full up" (*Letters*, 274). Martin had also met W. B. Yeats at Coole, and there remains the slight, teasing possibility that their Major Yeates might have been named partly as a private joke at the poet's expense. Years ago, Thomas Flanagan noted that "one can only hope that he was not given the name in malice" (19). In 1915, Lady Gregory wrote to Martin concerning RM that she "was reading the book slowly . . . because she was reading it aloud to W. B. Yeats. 'He at first mention of Major Yeates asked anxiously if it was spelt with a second "e," and hearing it was, gave himself up to uninterrupted enjoyment'" (quoted in Powell, *Cousins*, 166). A notoriously bad speller, Yeats did not meet Somerville until 1931, when he addressed an invitation to the inaugural meeting of the Irish Academy of Letters to "Miss Summerville." Edith "was so incensed," Violet Powell tells us, "that she threatened to address her reply to 'Major Yeates'" (119).

Criticism on the RM stories generally focuses on Major Yeates and Flurry Knox, though as I noted earlier, there has been a failure to fully appreciate the extent to which Yeates embodies the Anglo-Irish Ascendancy (an Ascendancy on the descent) having some fun at its own expense. Flurry Knox is a "half-sir," a Protestant who outfoxes Yeates and nearly everyone else and who is in fact as much a part of Somerville and Ross's own social stratum as Yeates. Flurry is Master of Fox Hounds (MFH), as was Somerville's brother Aylmer (on whom Flurry was based), and then Yeates becomes the MFH when Flurry leaves for the Boer War, just as Edith did when Aylmer left to fight in that war. However, here I want to attend to the stories' major women characters, who have been largely neglected, yet are very important. Somerville and Ross's depiction of Yeates—and even Flurry—as outmatched by the *women* who really control the Big House is parallel to their portrayal of the Ascendancy, in the person of Yeates, as rather hopelessly powerless in the face of the lower classes. Thus, in terms of gender as well as class, the RM stories are subtly and deliciously subversive.

The first story, "Great Uncle McCarthy," describes the arrival of Yeates (still a bachelor at this point) to Skebawn where he takes up residence in the windswept, rain-drenched house of Shreelane. Yeates may be the R.M., but his house is controlled by his inimitable cook, Mrs. Cadogan. We learn just how total her control is when it comes out that she has permitted a whole group of friends and relatives to continue to operate their fox-poaching operation in Yeates's attic, drinking his whiskey and producing noise and clatter that Yeates thinks is a ghost. Mrs. Cadogan's dialogue is marvelous; as Patrick Kavanagh recognized, Somerville and Ross "had a better ear for Irish dialogue than anybody except James Joyce" (quoted in A. Cronin, *Heritage*, 82), and, indeed, as Powell suggests, they influenced Joyce (*Cousins*, 102-3).

Much as in Joyce's "Cyclops" episode of *Ulysses*—where the narrative alternates between mock-heroic, pseudoclassical language and the folksy language of a bar-room wag—a good deal of the comedy of the RM stories has to do with registers of language shifting between Yeates's impeccably standard Oxford English and the racy dialogue of characters such as Mrs. Cadogan. RM's dialogue provides a veritable glossary of Irish-English usage: "Indeed it came into my mind on the way here," remarks Farmer Flynn to Yeates in "A Conspiracy of Silence," "to try could I coax you to come over and give us a day's hunting. We're destroyed with foxes" (RM, 304). As Lewis tells us, in this respect Somerville and Ross were influenced by Maria Edgeworth, who liked to write down Irish-English dialect "verbatim" and whose letters to her close friend Nancy Crampton, their great-grandmother, had been inherited by Martin (8–9). Somerville and Ross's realistic style could not be further from stereotypes about women's reputedly florid, romantic, "feminine" writing. A common stylistic feature in the RM stories is the deflating simile, as in the description in "The Friend of Her Youth" of "the small, rat-like head of Bill's kitchen-maid, Jimmy" (RM, 464).

Somerville and Ross's women tend to be strong and their men weak. In one of the very first references to Major Yeates's wife, Philippa, Yeates reports, "Philippa has since explained to me . . . a mere male fallacy" (RM, 21), and right through to the end of the stories, he notes, "I followed her, uttering the impotent growls of a husband" (RM, 476). When she first actually appears, in "Philippa's Fox-Hunt," she gives him a fierce piece of her mind for keeping her waiting at the train station, and she then proceeds to earn her spurs at the foxhunt. She gets on much more easily with Mrs. Cadogan and other female servants than Yeates does, and, unlike her husband, she makes an effort to learn Irish. As Maurice Collis noted in his 1968 biography, Philippa "is the stronger character of the two, a marriage relationship which Edith approved of" (126). Yeates is often ordered about while women cook, clean, and socialize, as in "A Royal Command," where he complains that his cigarettes, "in common with every other thing that I wanted, had been tidied into oblivion. From earliest dawn I had heard the thumping of feet, and the swish of petticoats, and the plying of brooms" (RM, 200–201). In the celebrated story "Poisson d'Avril," Yeates is under Philippa's orders to buy a salmon for an upcoming relative's visit and is gypped at the market by fish-hawker Eliza Coffey: "'How would the gentleman be a match for her!' shouted the woman on the floor. . . .'Sure a Turk itself wouldn't be a match for her! That one has a tongue that'd clip a hedge!'" (RM, 66).

The character closest to Edith Somerville herself is Bobby Bennett, who (Lewis tells us) "shares many characteristics with Edith herself" (*World*, 136); in "The Bosom of the McRorys," Somerville and Ross write of Bobby Bennett that "her dancing is a serious matter, with a Cromwellian quality to it, suggestive of jack boots and the march of great events" (RM, 533).

In these ways, Somerville and Ross show how the Big Houses were really run by women. At a time when the economic power of the Ascendancy was fading rapidly, the chief arena for Ascendancy activity was no longer the marketplace but rather the theater, the dinner party, and the hunt—a social world regulated very often by women. The character who most interests me, and the most dominant in all of the RM stories, is Flurry's grandmother, Mrs. Knox, the impressive materfamilias of the Big House of Aussolas. Even the usually fearless Flurry Knox is awed by her, and Flurry's wife is always referred to only as "Mrs. Flurry," never as "Mrs. Knox"—for only his grandmother can hold that title. And even Maurice Collis, who had trouble correctly understanding other gender issues in Somerville and Ross's lives, recognizes that Mrs. Knox is "much cleverer than any man. . . . What she stands for is Edith's feminine ideal, a matriarch. . . . Mrs. Cadogan is the same type in the world below stairs" (*Biography*, 154).

Mrs. Knox was closely based on Anna Selina Martin, Violet's mother—always called "Mama" in their letters, which recount anecdotes about her that are just as hilarious as anything in the stories. Somerville and Ross wrote much more about their mothers than about their typically aloof Victorian fathers. Martin remarked in 1910, "In her outdoor life, she was what, in those decorous days, was called a 'Tomboy,' and the physical courage of her youth remained her distinguishing characteristic through life" (*Letters*, 222). Lewis notes that Mrs. Martin "never had any idea of housekeeping. She used to have a special hiding place at Ross to avoid the servants when there was nothing to be cooked for dinner" (*Letters*, 69). "Mama" was the antithesis of Virginia Woolf's "Angel in the House," whose contemporary American analogue is the woman in the Lemon Pledge commercial of a few years ago—dusting the table until it shines while wearing high heels, a spotless dress, and a cheerful smile. In contrast, Martin's mother was an uninhibited woman interested not in housecleaning but in the hunt. Somerville and Ross admired Mrs. Martin (much more than Somerville's apparently overbearing and repressed mother). Unlike many of their other relatives, Mrs. Martin delighted in their work, even the unflattering novel *The Real Charlotte;* and perhaps partly as a result, their own "self-supporting literary lives . . . pre-figure," as Lewis notes, "the description given by Virginia Woolf in *A Room of One's Own* of the sort of life that intelligent women should work towards" (*World*, 10).

Mrs. Martin could also be an outrageous character in her own right, provoking in her daughter a remarkably loud laugh that her collaborator, Somerville, often described as penetrating and nonstop. As for RM itself, recalled Somerville in 1944, "One reviewer described it as a book no self-respecting person could read in a railway-carriage with any regard to decorum" (*Experiences*, vii)." There is a riotous series of 1888 letters (*Letters*, 79–80, 87) from Martin to Somerville recounting an ongoing feud between Mrs. Martin and the local R.M. and his wife over the occupancy of a church pew that had traditionally been the Martins'; Mrs. Martin wins the day by smiling pleasantly at her foes, moving to another pew, and allowing the R.M. and his wife to encounter a resultant virtual boycott by the rest of the congregation before they agree to restore the pew to its rightful occupants. Around the same time, when visiting tenants began dancing in the hallway of Ross House, "Mama who was attired in a flowing pink dressing-gown and a black hat trimmed with lilac," recorded her daughter, "became suddenly emulous, and with her spade under arm joined in the jig. . . . Mama is indeed a wonderful woman" (*Letters*, 81). Throwing feminine stereotypes and conventions to the winds, "Mama" was completely unselfconscious and eccentric about her clothing. In 1892 her daughter described at length how at one point "Mama" was wearing, on top of everything else, a red kettle holder that she had been unable to find around the house, and at another point a woman came up to her in the street and alerted her to the fact that "her sponge *and* her sponge bag were hanging from her waist at the back" (*Letters*, 181).

The unforgettable fictional Mrs. Knox is a close copy of the unforgettable Mrs. Martin. Figuring impressively in several of the earlier

RM stories, Mrs. Knox takes over completely in the third volume of 1915. This suggests that following Mrs. Martin's death in 1906 (after which her daughter moved to Drishane, the Somerville estate, until her own death in 1915), Somerville and Ross were determined to memorialize her properly. Mrs. Knox is introduced in the first volume in "Trinket's Colt," where we learn that she danced with Yeates's grandfather and she discovers (and appreciates) Flurry's ruse of hiding her colt in a bush. "The Aussolas Martin Cat" and "The Finger of Mrs. Knox," the first two stories of the final volume, are my own favorites—in contrast to the preferences of some critics who see this volume as a weaker one, perhaps because the central men, Yeates and Flurry, are less substantial in it. Mrs. Knox was already eighty-four when first encountered in an earlier volume and thus is presumably several years older in the final volume. Here Mrs. Knox is seen "swathed in hundreds of shawls, in the act of hurling . . . tongs and some unseen object" (RM, 434), and she is described by Lady Knox as "a rag bag held together by diamond brooches'" (RM, 437).

Mrs. Knox governs all at Aussolas; as Yeates notes: "She pervaded all spheres" (RM, 436), "her personality was the only thing that counted" (RM, 437), and "I hope it may be given to me to live until my mood also is as a dark tower full of armed men" (RM, 425). Her admiring grandson Flurry, who is quite an operator himself, adds: "There's no pie but my grandmother has a finger in it" (RM, 436). Mrs. Knox's voice is so commanding, Yeates feels, that it "would have made me clean forty pig-sties had she desired me to do so" (RM, 63).

In "The Finger of Mrs. Knox," a tenant comes to her complaining about his neighbor Goggin, who has seized his livestock because he owes him five pounds. Mrs. Knox's ominous statement (in this period following the Wyndham Land Act of 1903, which legislated a peasant proprietorship) and the tenant's reply are both memorable: "'I have no tenants,' replied Mrs. Knox tartly; 'the Government is your landlord now, and I wish you joy of each other!' 'Then I wish to God it was yourself we had in it again!' lamented Stephen Casey; 'it was better for us when the gentry was managing their own business'" (RM, 440). Despite her remonstrations, the next morning Mrs. Knox has Yeates take her to Killoge Wood to lay Goggin low. The story ends when, believe it or not, she convinces Goggin to lend the five pounds to himself, in effect, and leave the offended tenant alone.

This is no romantic heroine, though. Somerville and Ross describe her impressively but unflinchingly; Yeates observes how Mrs. Knox "blinked her eyes like an old rat. . . . I felt as if I were being regarded through a telescope, from the standpoint of a distant century" (RM, 507). She even speaks Latin (RM, 539). Mrs. Knox is the old, dying Ascendancy at its best in the view of Somerville and Ross: a powerful woman who lords it over her house and lands—and they do seem to be *hers*, despite Victorian convention—and takes joy in life.

These are funny stories with a serious point behind them. As Langston Hughes wrote in *The Book of Negro Humor*, "Humor is laughing at what you haven't got when you ought to have it. Of course, you laugh by proxy. . . . Humor is your own unconscious therapy" (quoted in Walker, *Women's Humor*, 101). Laughing "by proxy" seems a particularly appropriate notion when applied to Somerville and Ross, who were active in the women's suffrage movement. Somerville was president of the Munster Women's Franchise League in the period around World War I. As early as 1889, Martin angrily wrote to Somerville, "I certainly think it is absurd that the people Mama employs should have a vote, and that she herself should not have one. After all most women who have to stand alone and manage their houses or places themselves are competent" (*Letters*, 141).

As Nancy Walker notes, the long tradition in African-American humor of "laughing at the man" takes on a new relevance when applied to women's humor (*Women's Humor*, 109). In another of the relatively few recent considerations of women and comedy, Regina Barreca writes: "Comedy is a way women writers can reflect the absurdity of the dominant ideology while undermining the very basis for its discourse. They can point to the emperor's new clothes" (*Last Laugh*, 19)—or the R.M.'s, permit me to add. Of course, Somerville and Ross *forgive* the R.M.; they even allow him to narrate these stories, following the pattern of identification and role-reversal with the comic victim, as outlined in that now obscure but insightful essay by Trotter, "Humor With A Gender." If Major Yeates is made a fool of, we are nonetheless permitted to emerge from the RM stories liking him. As Maria Edgeworth wrote to Somerville and Ross's great-grandmother, Mrs. Bushe, in 1832, "It is good to laugh as long as we can . . . and whenever we can" (quoted in Lewis, *World*, 220).

NOTE

1. As innovative as it purports to be in its groupings of Irish writing, the recent *Field Day Anthology of Irish Writing,* edited by Seamus Deane, is quite traditional in filing Somerville and Ross among realist practitioners of "Prose Fiction 1880–1945." This section, edited by Augustine Martin, includes only a selection from *The Real Charlotte* (2:1046–59) and a brief author's note referring to their "strange literary partnership" (2:1217). The inclusion of four chapters from a long novel rather than any complete story seems an odd decision; apparently none of the RM stories was deemed serious enough for the *Field Day Anthology.*

WORKS CITED

Barreca, Regina, ed. *Last Laughs: Perspectives on Women and Comedy.* New York: Gordon and Breach, 1988.

Boyd, Ernest. *Ireland's Literary Renaissance.* 1916. Reprint, New York: Barnes and Noble, 1968.

Collis, Maurice. *Somerville and Ross: A Biography.* London: Faber and Faber, 1968.

Cronin, Anthony. *Heritage Now: Irish Literature in the English Language.* Dingle, County Kerry: Brandon, 1982.

Cronin, John. *Somerville and Ross.* Lewisburg, Pa.: Bucknell University Press, 1972.

Deane, Seamus, ed. 3 vols. *Field Day Anthology of Irish Writing.* Derry: Field Day Publications, 1991.

Gilbert, Sandra, and Susan Gubar, eds. *The Norton Anthology of Literature by Women: The Tradition in English.* New York: Norton, 1985.

Fehlmann, Guy. "The Composition of Somerville and Ross's *Irish R.M.*" In *The Irish Short Story,* edited by Patrick Rafroidi and Terence Brown, 103–11. Atlantic Highlands, N.J.: Humanities Press, 1979.

Flanagan, Thomas. "The Big House of Ross-Drishane." *Kenyon Review* 28 (1966): 65.

Heilbrun, Carolyn. *Writing a Woman's Life.* New York: Norton, 1988.

Howarth, Herbert. *The Irish Writers, 1880–1940: Literature under Parnell's Star.* London: Rockliff, 1958.

Lewis, Gifford. *Somerville and Ross: The World of the Irish R.M.* New York: Viking, 1985.

Mercier, Vivian. *The Irish Comic Tradition.* New York: Oxford University Press, 1962.

O'Connor, Frank. *The Lonely Voice: A Study of the Short Story.* Cleveland: World, 1962.

Powell, Violet. *The Irish Cousins: The Books and Background of Somerville and Ross.* London: Heinemann, 1970.

Robinson, Hilary. *Somerville and Ross: A Critical Appreciation.* New York: St. Martin's, 1980.

Somerville, E. OE. [Edith Somerville]. *Experiences of an Irish R.M.* 1944. London: J. M. Dent, 1957.

————. *Irish Memories.* London: Longmans, Green, 1917.

Somerville, E. OE. [Edith Somerville], and Martin Ross [Violet Martin]. *The Irish R.M.* 1928. London: Sphere/Abacus, 1989.

————. *The Selected Letters of Somerville and Ross.* Edited by Gifford Lewis. London: Faber and Faber, 1989.

Somerville and Ross: A Symposium. Belfast: Institute of Irish Studies, 1969.

Trotter, Elizabeth Stanley. "Humor With A Gender." *Atlantic Monthly* 130 (1922): 784–87.

Walker, Nancy. *A Very Serious Thing: Women's Humor and American Culture.* Minneapolis: University of Minnesota Press, 1988.

Waters, Maureen. *The Comic Irishman.* Albany: State University of New York Press, 1984.

The Crumbling Fortress
Molly Keane's Comedies of Anglo-Irish Manners

RACHAEL JANE LYNCH

Molly Keane's acerbic portrayals of life in the rotting world of what has been nicknamed the Descendancy have become in her most recent novels so bitter and shot through with violence that one hesitates, almost, to refer to her work as comic. However, horrifying at times as her vision of impotence and decay can be, she is unquestionably funny. Keane's humor adheres, I will argue, in many respects to a tradition identifiably Irish. Although Irish women's humor is not discussed in Vivian Mercier's seminal *The Irish Comic Tradition*, Keane's viciously funny novels clearly illustrate the Dionysian comic impulse that Mercier sees as central to Irish literature and describes as "the mockery of Irish laughter," from which "no aspect of life is too sacred to escape" (248). Keane's irreverent comedy also serves as a perfect illustration to Regina Barreca's theory that women's often hostile humor "brings down the house" literally as well as metaphorically, that one of its purposes is to resist, even dismantle, hegemonic and male-dominated power structures through laughter. Women's humor, Barreca argues, is subversive, "often a thinly veiled indictment of the society that trivializes a woman's life." It offers "some sort of challenge to the system. . . . Feminist humor is serious, and it is about changing the world" (*Snow White*, 182–85).

The constructive power of women's humor is that it exposes and withers the roots of patriarchal power by refusing to take it seriously. That several of Keane's "patriarchs" are in fact women renders them no less patriarchal in their values and their tyranny and illustrates another of the great strengths of women's humor—unlike classic male humor in which an Other (often female) is objectified and rendered ridiculous, women's humor, as well as being protective of self and mocking of others in function, dares to engage in self-examination. Indeed, the power of Keane's satire derives in part from the fact that the world she displays and ridicules in her fiction—Anglo-Irish society in its death throes—is her own. Struggling for what little power remains within this crumbling realm, the last of the Anglo-Irish bring down their own house with very little outside help. Watching the process of self-destruction, we are torn between laughter and horror. The power retained by this increasingly powerless group is that of inflicting pain within the community; the fading survivors of a former ruling class are the last to take themselves seriously, and we watch with delight and with pleasure. Laughter wins, because the world of Keane's fiction does not deserve to survive; we sense that Keane herself is bringing down her house, killing and burying a decaying microcosm with an overwhelming sense of relief.

Keane achieves detachment from her dying heritage through her creation of an ironizing distance, defusing the helplessness that she feels as she witnesses the rot by means of a humor we are coming to recognize as gendered. Just as the narrator of Edna O'Brien's "A Scandalous Woman" renders the vicious and powerful local priest comfortingly ridiculous by noticing his prominent Adam's apple, Keane defuses the menacing by noting the absurd. Such unpleasant scenes as Nicandra's miscarriage in *Queen Lear* (hereafter *Lear*) while her husband is on the phone to his mistress can perhaps never be neutralized, but Keane enables us to laugh even as we recoil, and, perhaps for the author herself and her Anglo-Irish readers, to laugh *because* they recoil. Without the ironic distance provided by Keane's humor, her Anglo-Irish readers could not observe themselves so truthfully.

Keane's ten earliest published novels[1] are easier than her later works to categorize as funny, or at least as more funny than ominous; frothier than their descendants, they are in many respects comedies of manners. Yet beneath the froth, Keane displays a grim awareness that comedy can be, especially for women, serious business. As Barreca comments, "Often women's humor deals with those subjects traditionally reserved for tragedy: life and death, love and hate, connection and abandonment" (*Snow White*, 33). The focus, in Keane, is on the women:

their roles; their ambitions and aspirations (or lack thereof); their blindness and illusions, occasionally pierced through with the dim light of embryonic self-awareness; their weaknesses; their needs; their difficulties with self-esteem; and their strengths. Her early novels, many of them hunting romances, were highly popular when first published. In her introduction to *Devoted Ladies*, Polly Devlin recounts that a "devoted" following reveled in what she calls their "horsy habitat" (v). Yet they fell out of favor, and of print, only to be rediscovered after Keane herself reappeared triumphantly on the scene in 1981 with *Good Behaviour* (hereafter GB). That many of the early books have recently been reprinted by the Virago Press, accompanied by serious introductions by admirers like Polly Devlin and Russell Harty, one can attribute to both a climate that is welcoming of women's writing and an awareness on the part of the publishers and a sophisticated reading public appreciative of Keane's later novels that her early books are also funny and serious in important ways.

Taking *Loving Without Tears* (hereafter *Loving*) as representative of these earlier novels, we can see the many ways in which the comic elements and serious issues notable in her later work occur, albeit initially in a bubblier form, from the time Keane started to write. I choose to discuss this novel in particular because as a family comedy rather than a hunting romance it is particularly close in its concerns to the three late novels.

With certain important exceptions, *Loving* reads like a trial run for Keane's later fiction. We note the manipulative Keane Mummy, who is to recur in GB and *Time After Time* (hereafter *Time*), and the ancestral mansion filled with manipulated offspring common to all three later novels. Owlbeg, the mansion in *Loving*, has not yet fallen into disrepair; the War has just come to an end, and Angel and her children can still afford to live an approximation of the Good Life. Yet in Owlbeg, the "silly castle" "perched hysterically on the edge of a cliff" (16, 6), we see foreshadowed the later crumbling fortresses. As Devlin warns in her introduction to *Devoted Ladies*, "M. J. Farrell's [that is, Keane's] houses are never safe places, never sanctuaries, though they may appear so. . . . the accumulation of ancient passions turns them into emotional archaeological sites, where an outsider stepping unwarily can set off shattering reverberations" (xi). The sun that floods this house cannot disguise the tensions or block the entry of the outsider, Sally, who (like Leda in *Time*, but without her malevolence) is responsible for a series of "shattering reverberations."

Presiding over the household is the widowed Angel, mother of twenty-one-year-old Julian who is returning from the war, and of beautiful, gawky Slaney, at eighteen struggling into adulthood. Also "caught and tamed" (41) on the estate are Oliver, Angel's lover and land agent; Birdie, the nanny; and Tiddley, the disparagingly named and disparaged orphan cousin. Angel is a self-obsessed, jealous, and possessive woman, closely identified with her house and determined to manipulate her way to a permanent position of power within her family. The plot is driven by her wildly erroneous assumption that her children are still incapable of an existence not arranged and supervised by her and by her allied concern with finding for them appropriate mates. She plans on assembling the "'right young girls' for Julian to play with" (8), and she leads Slaney "by a ribbon towards the supreme sacrifice and glory of the right marriage" (15).

All does not proceed as Angel plans, however; Slaney falls in love with Chris, a young man who for no apparent reason does not meet with Angel's approval, and Julian returns to Owlbeg in the company of Sally, his American fiancée. The lovers' tales unfold in a breathless series of comic and often improbable plot twists reminiscent of a comedy of manners like *The Country Wife*, resulting in the simultaneous unions and escape from Owlbeg of Julian and Tiddley, Slaney and Chris, Sally and Oliver, Birdie and Walter. All ends more or less well, but lurking in the shadows are tragedies barely averted and ill will scarcely contained.

Angel's viciousness, in particular, frequently threatens to break the comic frame. She understands as well as any man how to hurt and that the appearance of good behavior can and does hide the real business of tyranny. In an attempt to control her children's choices, for example, she lies repeatedly, warning Slaney that Chris will be repelled by her "eager" display of genuine affection and telling Chris that Slaney's love for him stems simply from pity for his war experiences (178). Angel is amusing only because she is eventually defanged; her children detect and dismantle her tissue of lies, and Sally matches her aggressive humor, line for line. In response to Angel's nasty "What is your skin like?" as her eyes "bored" Sally's make-up, the American coolly responds, "if I had your skin and you had my bottom, what a knock-out we two would be" (149). Sally defuses aggression by appreciating humor as power; as Barreca says, in such a situation, ideally "you take control, take a risk, and try to bring the house down" (*Snow White*, 61).

Sally's bringing down of the house is ultimately, if barely, contained within the comic framework. Angel acknowledges her hatred of the intruder, reaching for the vestiges of her controlling authority and insisting that her children need her still. She nearly loses everything: a "feather on a flood," she is almost drowned by the incoming tide that "sucked and swirled at the rocks" (239) beneath *her* house, as her children defy her outright and then leave her. In a pair of scenes too grim for humor, Slaney declares, "I shall marry to please myself, not my mother. It's all turned into her" (246), and Julian repels Angel's ugly attack on Tiddley, reaffirming his choice and leaving his mother chilled with "the terror of defeat" (250–51).

In order to survive, Angel's children have no choice but to leave on the now fortuitously turning tide. The tide, possibly signifying societal changes threatening the Ascendancy, functions both literally and metaphorically, simultaneously liberating for the escaping children, as they use the moment of its turning to launch a boat to carry them away from Angel's control, and threatening to their mother. Chris says firmly, "Tide's turning. Come on, Slaney. We're off to make the midnight express—Dublin tonight—London tomorrow" (254). All the escapees recognize the urgency of the moment; it is "now or never" (254). The dangers of the strongly running tide are not underestimated by anybody, but the occupants of the boat recognize that it is better to move with the turning tide of change rather than to resist and risk annihilation from its sucking, swirling force.

The closure of the novel is firmly lighthearted, magically forgiving. Angel, her lesson to some degree apparently learned, is comforted by the thought of her incipient grandchildren and aware that she had better behave herself; and her children "felt not so much relief at their escape, as a feeling that they were out of the fun—they would have to come back to her" (256). A quick review of the final chapters will remind us, however, that the process of separation was anything but fun and that the illusion of fun is only possible because the tide turned just in time.

Keane's satire in her three most recent novels grows increasingly merciless. Through GB, *Time,* and *Lear,* there unravels a thread of comedy so black (and arguably blacker in each succeeding novel) that Sir William Collins, who had published most of her earlier books, expressed himself unable to accept the manuscript of GB "on the grounds that it was too black a comedy." Keane refused his suggestion to make the characters "more pleasant" and put the manuscript aside (*The Rising Tide,* v–vi).

Collins's horror prompts several interesting questions. Just what about GB did he find so dark, so threatening to the very notion of what he obviously considered satisfyingly humorous? And was what he found so unpleasant precisely what the readers of this highly successful book liked? Do we see in the response to this black comedy the results of a shift in the acceptably funny, a shift forced by women's increased (and in Keane's specific case, the Ascendancy's decreased) economic control and the resultant "legitimization" of women's perspectives?

Our questions answer themselves as soon as we appreciate that in GB and its successors we witness the self-delusion, misery, and even self-engineered destruction of a series of "good girls" and the triumph of Bad Behaviour. Keane's mature fiction is divided from her earlier work by virtue of the overwhelming and unavoidable presence in the later novels of the abyss. Most of the main characters are old, and all are in some way blind or maimed, lacking in some way. Instead of watching a character from outside bring down a house, forcing self-awareness and a happy ending in a comedy of manners in which the narrator's poignard is carefully blunted, as we do in *Loving*, we wince as we observe the women in the later fiction bearing responsibility for and then failing to extricate themselves from their misery. Now their creator does not rescue them from their follies. Keane's later comedy is serious business indeed; loving without tears becomes impossible.

Perhaps Collins was appalled by GB and unable to see it even as darkly funny because it recounts in explicit detail the story of a woman's entrapment and abuse at the hands of the values of her social milieu and, in particular, of her mother, followed by her triumph and admittedly disgusting revenge. This powerful come-back novel dissects the world of Keane's youth to expose the vulnerability of children of privilege, using the power of gendered humor to focus particularly on the plight of young women. GB faces the loneliness and frailty of a young Anglo-Irish woman. It details the sufferings that can be imposed, by oneself and others, as a result of a rigid adherence to the "good girl" strictures of the societal superego in a world where women's potential as active contributors to the society is assumed not to exist. Keane herself has commented about the world of her youth: "It would have never been considered that I should get a *job*. Girls stayed at home. Many of them grew very sour over that; others adored their fathers and did everything for them" (quoted in Quinn, *Portrait*, 70). Her portrayal of the difficulties of surviving womanhood as well as of the virtual impossibility of emerging intact from beneath the rubble of the collapsing Ascendancy sears in its intensity. In GB, Keane does not merely bring down the house; she uses humor as a means of escape from the ruins and allows her narrator to choose her new dwelling place.

Iris Aroon St. Charles, the huge, ungainly narrator of her own unpleasant life and ultimate act of revenge, is not a lovable heroine. Yet she not only survives but actually triumphs, perhaps more than any other character in Keane's later work, and to achieve her triumph she turns the tables on her manipulative "patriarchal" mother, the goddess of "Good Behaviour," seizing control of her own and her mother's lives. In so doing she revenges herself on the representative of a world that clipped her wings, laughed at her size, denied her a raison d'être, and reduced her to an object of pity. As Alice Adams has pointed out, Aroon, totally at the mercy of her family, is not given a fighting chance to find a husband: "Aroon is denied a coming out and a London season on the marriage market, effectively cancelling her prospects for finding a mate her mother would find worthy" ("Coming Apart," 27). Fat, deemed so unlikely a prospect for marriage that economies are made at the expense of the only permissible future (other than with her family) open to her, prone to drink beyond the point of self-control to escape from her own feelings, Aroon is judged by her mother to be a social disaster and sentenced to an ignominious, insult-laced adulthood of dependency in a world of increasing poverty, chilliness, and literal decay as the family "big house" crumbles around them.

Aroon's story unfolds against a backdrop of paralysis and decline, literal and metaphorical. Adams links the social decay of the Ascendancy in the novel with "the slow spread of disfigurement and death. The cook dies of cancer; the governess commits suicide. Neither is replaced. Papa loses his leg in the war. . . . Hubert [Aroon's homosexual brother] dies after smashing up his car. Papa suffers a stroke that reduces him to mumbling invalidhood until another attack kills him. At last Mummie dies, done in by her 'dicky heart' and Aroon's malice, until only Aroon is left to carry on" (27).

It would perhaps be more accurate to report that Mummie is murdered, symbolically at least. The novel is structured so that we observe the destruction of what is left of Mummie at the start, and then, in a flashback that lasts for the rest of the book, ending with Aroon's accession to power and setting the scene for what we witness in chapter 1, we are made acquainted with the story behind the controlling, controlled, self-justifying woman who begins with a description of her mother's death.

The details of Mummie's death are important; the black humor of the occasion depends on our connecting the manner of her dying with that of her abusive living, and our resultant appreciation that her daughter's revenge is perfect. In the opening pages of the novel, Mummie is Aroon's prisoner in Gull's Cry, where Aroon has moved her from Temple Alice, the decaying mansion where Aroon was herself a prisoner. The generous leaning windows of Gull's Cry, in an identification of the narrator with *her* house, remind Aroon of "bosoms on an old ship's figurehead," and Aroon records her relief that "bosoms are all right to have now" (5). Such relief stands in marked contrast to her misery throughout her fat teen years as she strapped down her unwieldy Bad Girl breasts "with a sort of binder" in a despairing effort to make them less remarkable (5). Aroon has decorated the rooms in her new house herself. The walls of the drawing room feature photographs of Papa "riding winners" (as Aroon herself now is) and of various meals in the making—"the model of a seven-pound sea trout and several rather misty snapshots of bags of grouse" (4).

Against this caloric background, Mummie exudes misery. Her dislike of food always bordered on the anorectic and is contrasted sharply throughout the novel with her daughter's rebellious eating. In the scene leading to Mummie's death, Aroon force-feeds her a meal that she knows Mummie will not be able to keep down, however well it is disguised as chicken. As the servant Rose warns when she sees the deliberate act of aggression that Aroon has planned, "Rabbit sickens her. . . . She couldn't get it down. . . . You couldn't deceive her, Miss Aroon" (3).

Aroon, however, is bent on betrayal and bears down on unwilling Mummie with destructive firmness and "a delicious chicken mousse" (5). In response to her daughter's treacherous attentions, Mummie "gave a trembling, tearing cry, vomited dreadfully, and fell back into the nest of pretty pillows," dead (6). Aroon denies her appalled response, her desire to "cry out." "I controlled myself," she reports, and, struggling to remain calm in the face of "this abyss," she orders Rose to "Just take that tray down and keep the mousse hot for my luncheon" (7). Feeling "quite strong" again, she stands "tall as a tree" in resistance to the imprecations hurled at her by the servant, accusations that she has brutally abused her power, killing her mother and turning elderly relatives out of Gull's Cry so that she could get her hands on the house (9). Aroon, swelling with a consciousness of her own power, plans to be "generous" with Rose, the old enemy who, in her devotion and closeness to Aroon's father, had made Aroon herself feel "in second place" (145). This first, "narrative present" chapter ends with Aroon basking in, "apart from my shock and horror about Mummie, a feeling of satisfaction" and with her claim that "I do know how to behave. . . . All my life I have done everything for the best reasons and the most unselfish motives. I have lived for the people dearest to me" (9).

Aroon then spends the rest of the book exploring her past, from her earliest remembered youth right up until the narrative present, and it does not take the reader long to appreciate that if the controlling, force-feeding daughter is monstrous, her monstrosity has been learned at home. The dominant Aroon behaves toward her mother exactly as her mother has always behaved toward her, cloaking her malevolent intentions in exactly the same excuses, rationalizing her behavior in exactly the same ways. Aroon turns upon Mummie that matriarch's own most powerful controlling force, that of Good Behaviour. Following Mummie's rules, she represses the emotions that threaten her supremacy and destroys her mother just as Mummie almost destroyed her. Under these rules, aggression, domination, and control are disguised as attention and nurturing (just as rabbit is disguised as chicken); hunger, whether physical or emotional, is seen as inappropriate Bad Behaviour; and powerful positive emotions such as love and grief are repressed in the name of restraint.

A few details from Aroon's early life show beyond doubt that finally she does unto Mummie exactly what Mummie always has done, and would clearly have continued to do, unto her, had not a last-minute reversal of fortunes occurred. The young Aroon spends her life chafing at her mother's controlling ways, finding what little happiness she knows basking in her father's rare attentions, and enjoying the companionship of her homosexual brother Hubert and his lover Richard. Even here the relationship is less than honest and satisfying for Aroon; she is deceived, and deceives herself, as to her importance in this triangular friendship. Good-looking Hubert uses her company to shield himself from the attentions of other girls, and Richard pretends sexual interest in her to foil Aroon's father, who is becoming suspicious of the relationship between the two young men.

Aroon does derive pleasure from her friendship with Hubert and Richard. However, her inclusion in the group is shown to be increasingly tenuous and sustained by illusions on her part; she is clearly not wanted, for example, when she knocks on Richard's door looking for gin to ease her period pain. Richard answers her knock "not quite at once" (95), pours her some gin and asks her to leave, yet she is slow to take the hint. Her connection with the lovers is further marred by the self-deprecating humor she is forced to accept as the price of her admission. Never seen by the male lovers as an object of desire, she acts the clown to capture Richard's attention. We see Aroon's complete lack of self-esteem in her reaction to Hubert's advice to be her "natural self" in front of his friend; she literally swallows her pride and fear in an attempt to be an acceptable "happy joke," gobbling "sensational quantities of food" in order to keep their attention (86–87). This and other shared "jokes," such as Richard's demeaning nickname for her, "Our Pig-Wig," indicate in a painful manner the pitifully limited basis of Aroon's sense of inclusion and the hurts she suffers in return for acceptance and small pleasures.

The self-destructive societal prescription for repressive self-control so internalized by Aroon poisons every emotion throughout the novel and dampens even the most explosive and wrenching of occasions. After Hubert dies in an accident, "normal" life in Temple Alice is grimly pursued. "There was to be no sentimentality. It was the worst kind of bad manners to mourn and grovel in grief" (115). Anger was as forbidden as grief; when Aroon is humiliated and insulted at a party where she is obviously unwanted and made to feel her position keenly, she struggles with her hurt and anger, unable to express it: "I wish I knew how to be rude" (201). In the grip of Good Behaviour, she has lost all sense of autonomy.

The High Priestess of Good Behaviour is of course impeccable Mummie. Aroon does not battle for supremacy over her mother until she can do so on more than equal terms, but the antagonism between mother and daughter is always in evidence. It remains more or less submerged, however, until Aroon's father's death drives her so wild with grief and despair that she crosses the line. By bringing hidden tensions into the open, Papa's death also sets the scene for the violent climax with which the book opens.

After Papa's final seizure, as after Hubert's death, "Mummie was rigorously set on perfect behaviour" (216), yet she repeatedly and very unfairly blames Aroon, in the nicest possible way, of course, for her father's death. After the disastrous party during which she hears the news about Richard, the car's engine freezes and Aroon is brought home by the solicitor. Mummie tortures her daughter, who is genuinely grief-stricken: "Rather a pity about the car. But you mustn't blame yourself. . . . If only the car had been here last night" (216–18). Aroon is "stunned" by the unfairness of the assumption but is powerless to stop her mother; she can only beg the doctor to clear her of guilt.

Aroon's grief for her father is real; she adored and admired him, and despite the relative indifference shown at times to her in return, father and daughter do actually share a relationship. Before Aroon leaves for the ill-fated party, she shares a moment of intimacy with her father, during which he renders her rapturous by expressing a desire to see her "dressed up" (193). Inevitably her self-display is ruined by the dismissive presence of Mummie, who deflates her father's admiration by pronouncing her daughter "Stupendous," with all its hurtful implications of the oversized and overgaudy (194). Aroon has another powerful reason to grieve for her father, however; he functioned as a barrier between her and her mother and was necessary for her emotional survival. The grieving daughter, "shovelling down" (217) enormous meals in a desperate attempt to feed her emptiness, analyzes the situation accurately and rightly fears the worst: she imagines her future as "the unmarried daughter who doesn't play bridge, letting the dogs out for evermore. Mummie and Rose would be in power over me, over Temple Alice, until I was old. . . . They may starve me too—the idea filled me with panic. Mummie doesn't eat and Rose won't cook for me alone. They will enjoy starving me. It will be called economy" (219–20).

Driven to desperation by this grim and all-too-probable vision of the future, Aroon misses the funeral, drinking until she is unable to walk, and then falling, spraining her ankle. Lying alone and hungover on the library sofa and forced to acknowledge, despite her most determined illusions, that Richard might not come back to her from Kenya, Aroon weeps for "Papa, out there in the cold," and "future days for me with Mummie in power and Rose to abet her power" (235). Overwhelmed with visions of mean, undersized "future luncheons and dinners," Aroon feels "like a rat in a trap, and too big for my trap" (326–27).

It is at this point that Aroon's paternal and authorial creators—not, it should be noted, Aroon herself—intercede, altering the balance of power completely and irrevocably in her favor. After a particularly demeaning attack on Aroon by her mother, and during loud uncontrolled sobbing from Aroon herself, Papa's will releases her from her servitude. "Everything of which he dies possessed, with the exception of those small legacies . . . is left to his daughter, Iris Aroon" (243). The novel ends with a dry-eyed Aroon, "empowered by Papa's love" (248), conveniently represented by his money and property, imperiously ordering Tio Pepe sherry and a delicious evening meal and promising kindness for Mummie and Rose. Symbolically standing "above" her "shrivelled" mother, she promises, in a voice "humid with kindness" but nonetheless extremely firm, that she will look after her "always" (245–46).

The feminist reader puts down GB with mixed feelings, acknowledging both the positive and negative implication of the outcome of the novel. Clearly, after the scenes that end Aroon's flashback, we reread the first chapter with sympathy, even with a smile of guilty pleasure. In a macabre way, Mummie's fate *is* funny; she unquestionably dies of a dose of her own medicine, and only Papa's will puts an end to her machinations.[2] Mummie's death, we realize, is brilliantly conceived and perfectly fitting; in this bosomy little house the tables have been carefully turned, but according to all the rules of Good Behaviour learnt by Aroon from her mother. Like her mother, Aroon refuses to "grovel in grief" (115), to lose her calm or her ordinary voice, to deviate from the norm in any way, even though such calm clearly costs her an effort. The details of the revenge have been so carefully pursued that even the choice of rabbit is significant; not only does Mummie hate it, but she also used it as a weapon in her campaign against Aroon's needy appetite. Under the disguise of making economies, she puts Aroon in her place, suggesting that her daughter "and the dogs could sometimes manage with rabbit," a dish even the maids refuse (178).

Aroon betrays Mummie, as Mummie betrayed her, without ever betraying her upbringing. No longer forced to participate in jokes against herself, Aroon is given the last laugh, and lasts. While she does not bring down her old house, she does move her mother, on her own terms, to "her" generously fronted new one. Such triumphant revenge does not come without an unpleasant aftertaste, however. First, much as we may rejoice in her seizing of power and control, this power is derived from her father's legacy; she is funded by the patriarchy in the most literal sense, and her last laugh is a present from Daddy. Keane is perhaps emphasizing that money and property indeed result in power, but that inherited money can provide only inherited power. If Ascendancy women wish to control their own lives, perhaps they need to direct these lives themselves rather than living out a reaction to those of their forebears (as, despite her power, Aroon does).

Second, Aroon, although much wronged, is unreliable enough as a narrator that we are left with the impression that she has learned remarkably little from her experiences. When she wreaks her revenge by behaving like her mother, for example, she appears to draw solace from her adherence to the laws of Good Behaviour rather than to acknowledge her transgression. It is as if she were offered an escape only to run right back into the inviting twin traps of illusion and self-denial as soon as the opportunity presents itself. Aroon may be a woman revenged, but she is not freed into self-knowledge. We are distressed not so much, perhaps, by what Adams rightly identifies as "the spite and selfishness that drive her" as by her "personal biases and blind spots. . . . Aroon is a whole-hearted devotee of the code" ("Coming Apart," 28). As Adams puts it, Aroon's "determination to cling to the code of behavior that has made a fool of her has serious implications" (33). Aroon's sanctimoniousness affords us a last laugh, but our pleasure is marred by our awareness that she herself does not share our insight.

Keane's second mature novel, *Time*, continues to explore the issues raised in GB. From its earliest pages, we recognize a familiar world. Again we are presented with a crumbling "big house," Durraghglass, its occupants elderly and all in some way maimed or defective. Three sisters, all childless and all but one unmarried, live with their brother. Jasper, the aging scion, blind in one eye and socially inept, is a selfish man who expresses himself through his cooking and gardening. Shy and yet manipulative, and veering between homosexuality and asexuality, Jasper Swift tries to rule a roost peopled with three sisters and their dogs, all with a lifetime claim to live on the family estate. It is in the stories of the four siblings and their Bad Girl nemesis, Leda the German Jewish cousin, that the issues probed in GB receive continued attention here.

When the novel opens, April-Gaye, eldest of the sisters, is the still-beautiful, moneyed, and stone-deaf widow of Colonel Grange-Gorman, a man "from the right family" who was, we gather, determinedly kinky in bed (49–50). Her "married mystique," as well as her money, "floated her on a superior cloud above her single sisters and bachelor brother" (23). May-Blossom, the second sister, has a withered hand and is possessed with a passion and a genius for restoring old china, particularly rabbits. Last comes "Baby" June-Rose, dyslexic and "a little slow" (46), so much so that she has remained illiterate. An inspired if extravagant farmer, it is June who works the overgrown land and raises her beloved pigs and hens. She had been an excellent horsewoman in her youth and spends much of the narrative present teaching a local boy, Christy Lucey, all she knows. Presiding over the whole brood in their youth was another Keane Mummie, this time an over-protective nurturer, who, in her attempts to cover up and compensate for her darlings' disabilities and deformities, destructively determined that they would never have to fight their own battles.

The comedy in *Time* is frequently black, even macabre, but it is more hopeful, too, as it is played out in the lives of the Swift sisters and the manipulative cousin who forces change in all their lives. The plot is driven by the return late in the lives of all the characters of Leda, a childhood favorite thrown out of the house for her affair with the family patriarch (as a result of which he apparently committed suicide) and since forgotten, presumed dead in the concentration camps during the war. (It turns out that the family need not have worried: Leda, an archmanipulator, collaborated early and, according to her daughter, ensured for herself "a very comfortable war" [183].) She returns to Durraghglass after her daughter has placed her in a convent functioning as an old age home, in which she is bored. She has an old score to settle with Mummie Swift, now dead from cancer, who engineered her original exclusion from Paradise, and she is further fueled by the ridiculous hope that Jasper might marry her and make her chatelaine of Durraghglass.

The savage comedy of the book derives primarily from what, for Nicole Hollander's Sylvia, is the bedrock on which women's humor rests: an exploration of "the disparity between the ideal and the real" (Barreca, *Snow White*, 145). This comic approach is also well suited for an examination of Ascendancy blindness and evasion. The returning Leda is literally blind, as she clearly has been for quite some time, and she completely fails to recognize the nature and scope of the changes that have taken place in her or in Durraghglass since the days of her youth. The precipitous descent of the fortunes of the Ascendancy does not enter her reckoning, and neither does the fact that she, her victims, and their chilly, crumbling house, have aged beyond repair. We laugh nastily at somebody who deserves and invites such laughter; Leda has returned to Durraghglass vengeful and power-hungry, and, unlike Aroon, she gives us little reason to take her part. Leda's blindness, her complete, unseeing, and uncomprehending resistance to inevitable change, both her own and that of her environment, are symbolic, perhaps, of the resistance of the Ascendancy to which she half-belongs. The narrator describes her at one point, with a symbolic touch, as "sure and contented in her ascendancy" (165), despite the fact that her over-reaching machinations are about to place everything she desires firmly outside her reach. As Keane has said, "People simply didn't visualize any change coming. They believed life would go on like that for all time" (quoted in Cahalan, *Irish Novel*, 208).

Herself a gold standard of decay, Leda simply refuses to acknowledge that she is no longer young and lovely, and she is hilariously, terrifyingly unaware that she is ungainly and overweight and has lost her powers to charm. The book returns time after time to sad yet very funny scenes in which the "toad-like" (140) Leda's lack of beauty, as seen through the eyes of her beholders, is all too apparent. For example, in a comic scene bordering on the slapstick, Leda seeks out Jasper in his bedroom, attempting to seduce him as he lies with his lovingly prepared cup of Complan, absorbed "absolutely and entirely with the propagation of azaleas" (165). Faced with the advancing and determinedly seductive Leda, Jasper "determined on an immediate evacuation of his bed" (166) and eventually succeeds in thwarting her.

The effects of Leda's presence at Durraghglass are not entirely malign, however, despite her best efforts. When she first arrives, stirring up old rivalries and internal strifes and eager to seek out, as she did when she was a child, her cousins' weaknesses, she initially stimulates a pleasant "mirage" from the past: "Since she could not see Durraghglass in its cold decay, or her cousins in their proper ages, timeless grace was given to them in her assumption that they all looked as though all the years between them were empty myths" (103).

However, like a mirage, Leda is not what she seems. Always a manipulative seeker of victims, she wishes to divide and conquer her cousins. What Leda desires above all is power; just as when the cousins were all children she liked to fondle May's "terrible little mole hand" (177) and kiss the empty socket of Jasper's eye, she now seeks "a power over each against each, and to steal even the secrets they didn't know they kept" (145). Content at first to play the sisters against one another as she works on her pursuit of the unwilling Jasper, her resentment explodes with destructive force after Jasper's rejection of her advances. At this point in the novel, Leda is once more symbolically allied to the aging, deluded, and increasingly impotent Ascendancy hegemony that is, at this point, as withered as May's hand; Leda descends to breakfast, and from power.

In the climactic scenes that follow and close the book, Leda's descent is irreversible and not completed without great suffering for almost all concerned. During breakfast, Leda uses her supposed "power over each" cousin to wound and humiliate them as individuals and as a group. She is so unsuccessful in her venture, however, that despite our revulsion at her filthy tongue and worse intentions, we are permitted a series of chuckles. Enraged and disarmed by Jasper's "light indifference" and "polite dismissal" (174), Leda looses her tongue, first dismissing June as a "mental defective" in thrall to her stable boy. Moving on to April, Leda insults her deafness and kinky married life, then focuses on May's hand, artistic abilities, and (recently revealed under promise of secrecy) "dangerous thrills"—May has, for years, been shoplifting her "little fancies" (177). Jasper she saves until last, but he preempts and disables her, reducing her completely by his refusal to rise to her bait. A taunter can have no power without the cooperation of the tauntee. Feeling that "it would be fairer to the girls to leave it undenied," Jasper "agreeably" acknowledges his homosexual tendencies and adds casually that they are all, surely, "a bit old for these gambols" (178).

It is at this point that the tables are magnificently turned. "Leda turned her head away as though in refusal to see or imagine change. 'We're not *old*,' she said in a different voice, forbidding the subject" (178). After Leda's incursion into private territory, however, the cousins retaliate by trampling upon her forbidden ground, and they are "pitiless" in their response. Despite a brief rallying on Leda's part, as she tries to claim that her daughter is the cousins' half-sister, the final defeat comes when the daughter herself arrives, further to expose her mother's lies and to return her to the convent; Leda spends her last hours at Durraghglass "old, pale, powerless" (180).

Despite the unpleasantness of the scene just described, *Time* is the most guardedly optimistic of Keane's three later chronicles of crumbling fortresses. First, the sharp definition of the final exposure is highly gratifying. In GB, Mummie the destroyer is herself destroyed, but under a cashmere blanket of good manners and unacknowledged resentment. Aroon's victory is tainted by her own unself-reflexive manipulations. With the partial exception of Jasper, Leda's victims in *Time*, on the other hand, either face, painfully but honestly, their defects or are spared from facing them at all.

Keane is at her gentlest in her handling of the future of Baby June, reinforcing the truth of Barreca's assertion that women's comedy takes no pleasure in humiliating the powerless and disadvantaged: "Women's humor picks on the powerful rather than the pitiful" (*Snow White,* 150). June, after Christy's desertion and a riding accident, survives to hire and train a new stable boy, this time a tinker. This new bond contains its own share of optimism, suggesting as it does a breaking down of the mistrust that so divides Irish social classes.

April, married off by a manipulative mother who concealed the full extent of her deafness from her husband until after the marriage, also receives gentle treatment. It is given to April, herself responsible neither for her disability nor for the fortune she inherited at her husband's death, to extract unwittingly and appropriately the full measure of the family's revenge upon Leda. While Leda was still in the ascendant, she had planned "how, after she had won Jasper, she might best contrive to eliminate her sisters. She thought her nuns might suit April very well— they would be patient as angels with her deafness, sympathetic with diets and disciplines and understanding and worldly over the nips of vodka" (159). As Leda predicts, the nuns turn out to suit April very well indeed; what Leda does not envisage is that it is April who will continue to control her situation. April never learns of Leda's breakfast insults; unable to hear, she is spared by Jasper, who destroys Leda's vindictive scribbles and inscribes a compliment instead. Completely unaware, therefore, that Leda bears any malice toward her, April decides to accompany her to the comfort and cosseting of the convent. Once there, the moneyed April arranges everything to her satisfaction, choosing "every possible convenience" (247) for herself and gaining complete mastery of Leda's life.

In the richly funny closing pages, containing none of the unpleasantness of the ending of GB, Leda gets what she deserves, a tailor-made existential hell. April treats her with kindness (unlike Leda, she is not motivated by malice) but as her plaything and possession, as a child would a doll, and her ascendancy over her blind captive is complete. Unable to read Leda's writing and in possession of the best bedroom in the flat for two, April pays for everything, plans for them both the healthy meals and extended keep-fit sessions that Leda so loathes, and gloats, just a little, over the totality of her control. "'You'll never find your way out, darling Leda,' she said, 'without me'" (249). We leave April enjoying her warm, clean surroundings, a new fortress so unlike Durraghglass, and Leda acknowledging, "There was to be no escape" (249).

Jasper, intermittently self-reflexive and not without courage, provides us with both hope and characteristic evasion as he contemplates his own future and that of Durraghglass. He emerges from the family crisis stronger and more generous than before; as we have seen from his intervention on April's behalf and his acknowledgment of his homosexuality, he breaks through his wall of detachment and acts, in crisis, from pure altruism. He is further generous in his acceptance of June's new stable boy. What he is less willing to accept is that he can make a difference to the future, that he can, through conscious and deliberate action, do something to prevent "worse things to come" (244). With a resistance to change that makes the reader scream with frustration, Jasper ultimately refuses to learn and to gain strength from the near disestablishment of Durraghglass forced by Leda. Jasper has long dreamed of selling the now untamed land attached to Durraghglass, and until the end of the book we accept the good faith expressed in his reasons against so doing: the sale of the land would deprive June of her life's work. When, however, the opportunity arises for Jasper to come to a mutually advantageous agreement with the monastery adjoining his property, one that would literally encourage new growth without dispossessing Jasper and his sisters, he panics, and we realize with a pang that it is Jasper himself who is standing in the way of progress and cooperation: "The prospects [of partial sale to the monks in return for labor in Jasper's beloved gardens] were so vast as to be nearly unacceptable. Jasper . . . trusted that, given more time, he would grow accustomed to the idea" (244). Bolstered by the comforting belief that "There was no hurry," Jasper manages to delude himself that life at Durraghglass "could now return to its accustomed importances, their establishment unshaken by Leda's appallingly embarrassing behaviour" (244). Jasper fails to take seriously the looming threat of disestablishment so harshly presented by Leda or the possibility that he, through his actions, could alter the future, and we are left with the uncomfortable awareness that time in Jasper's crumbling fortress is running out.

The most optimistic note is struck by the indication at the end of the novel that May, potentially the strongest sibling, does profit from her brush with destructive forces (from which, unlike April and June, she is in no way shielded, either by her own limits in perception or by the intervention of another) and will have some chance to test her potential and control her fate outside the fortress. In an interesting final twist bearing out Barreca's contention that "bad" behavior in oppressed women can indicate strength and the ability to survive, May's uncontrollable shoplifting finally leads to the empowerment that she has presumably always sought through her illicit actions. That a woman with a withered hand engages in an activity requiring light fingers certainly suggests that the activity itself works to restore self-esteem; she gains "potency" (227) from her actions. May, with her petty pilfering, is a "secret bad girl" (*Snow White*, 51) and emerges as a strong, adaptable, survivor. In the final pages of the book, it is May who is in the ascendant. After Leda's attack upon the deformity that she has always bravely tried to overcome, May sits "entirely disestablished and betrayed" (177).[3]

Rachael Jane Lynch

When arranging with Ulick the antique dealer the details of the packing of April's delicate possessions, she succumbs to the temptations posed by "a rabbit, flowered gown to his feet, seated on a chaise perçe, his nightcap lying in the dust beside him. Here was the mate and pair to her own. . . . No question, the two must be united" (226). May is driven here not simply by a petty criminal impulse but by the artist's desire for completion, and it is also notable that although she can be compared to Leda in that she takes a great, potentially self-destructive risk in pursuit of her own happiness, she does not seek destructive power over others, nor does she place anybody but herself at risk. Her worst crime is that she steals something that is Ulick's.

Ulick, it turns out, has just installed two-way mirrors, and May is caught. Despite a degree of dislike on both sides, it does not take Ulick long to realize that he has caught not simply another shoplifter, but somebody who shares his own artistic passions. The potentially disastrous situation ends with Ulick's offering May a full-time job. Of course May is a novice in the "outside" world of employment and wages, and Ulick offers her considerably less than her worth, but she does bargain for a car and gasoline. She walks away through her new workshop as if "through cloudcapped towers and glorious palaces" and has found her own, gratifying fortress (232). May and Ulick both feel as "matched" as the pair of rabbits, and we leave her exultant, planning small but significant expressions of her new power: "she would return to Durraghglass with the week's shopping, paid for by herself—only the account shown to Jasper, shown to him with a careless: that's OK I've paid. Don't worry. It would be a way of keeping him in his place. His proper place" (235). Alone of Keane's women, May steps outside the fortress, symbolically deciding to destroy, rather than attempting to clean and repair, Mummie's clothes upon which Leda is discovered to have defecated. May secures for herself a measure of independence, a sense of control other than that over the preservation of the soiled and decaying past, a future in a "place" of her own.

May's triumph, her redefinition of her "place" and of Jasper's, tests what Judy Little refers to as the "norm" (*Comedy*, 11). Although Little does not discuss Keane, her analysis of the nature and extent of such norm-testing in women's fiction, particularly that of Woolf and Spark, is particularly applicable to *Time*. Little carefully draws an important distinction between what she identifies as comedies of manners or "classic comedy," like that of Molière, in which "a constant, a trusted norm" is upheld through the satirizing of, for example, "a social eccentricity that becomes extreme or vicious" (15) and comedy in which the norms themselves are held up to examination. Keane's May belongs to a comic world "mocking conventions, values, and stabilities against which a comic writer traditionally would judge some odd deviation" (*Comedy*, 8). May's undeniably "odd," deviant behavior, initially criminal and then social, is linked to her survival; Jasper, as he clings to his normative belief in the stability of his environment, is at the end of the novel a figure more ridiculous than authoritative.

The shakiest and most decayed of all Keane's houses appears in her most recent book, *Lear*. As the title suggests, the novel concerns itself, as do its predecessors, with the intersection of family, power, property, and gullibility. Simultaneously a tragedy and a comedy, it is resplendent with all the insights that gendered humor can provide. It is hard for the reader to empathize with the feeble and masochistic Nicandra; she is as caught up as the other characters in a belief in Ascendancy superiority, and when this belief is joined with a desperate dependency, perhaps as a result of her mother's early disappearance from her life and the substantial financial support she receives from her loving Aunt Tossie, she absorbs her husband's abuse in a way that is as pathetic as it is horrific, but that is not without its humorous edge. For Nicandra, the appropriately named Andrew Bland is the embodiment of the genetic ideal, and because they both "recognize the invaluable importance of belonging to the Anglo-Irish 'Family'" (88), Nicandra remains willfully blind to his laughable failings as a husband and friend. If she had looked beyond their shared gene pool, perhaps we might not have laughed at her, but her learned self-positioning as a member of a master race earns our snickers, tempering our sympathy for her as a woman who places undue faith in her powers as nurturer, only to be abandoned for her socially unacceptable, suntanned, duplicitous, "hard-to-get" best friend.

The device of the contrasting Good Girl and Bad Girl is a classic component of humor about and appealing to women. Clearly Nicandra, despite having been named after an "outstanding winner" of a horse (3), is a parody of the Good Girl stereotype rather than a "winner" herself. Her Bad Girl counterpart in a Good/Bad pairing is her best friend Lalage, a "practical and calculating" (92) connected thinker and a winner every time. The aptly named Lalage Lawless is the daughter of "a rich and respected solicitor—not quite the right breeding, socially speaking, in County Westcommon, but Lalage's charm and silly looks guaranteed her welcome in many houses to which her mother had never been invited" (56).

From their earliest scenes together in the book, the Good Girl/Bad Girl dynamic joining and separating Nicandra and Lalage is in evidence. Nicandra climbs into Lalage's dirty bath water as the girls prepare for a Hunt Ball because "refusal might seem ungrateful or unkind" (56), while Lalage titillates and slightly shocks Nicandra by producing the very latest in feminine hygiene: her bottle of Odor-O-No deodorant (67). Perhaps we see the psychic gulf separating the two young women at its widest when they discuss the critical comments of Lalage's cousin Deirdre. In response to Deirdre's statement that she is like a "ripe plum," Lalage contemplates her revenge: "'I hate her,' Lalage spoke seriously, 'I'd like to stick a knife in her, and when I got it in—you know what I'd do?' 'Pull it out.' Nicandra saw no other solution to this ugly and childish idea. 'No, when I got it in, I'd twist it.' Lalage's eyes widened, their pupils melting in the pleasure of her thoughts" (68).

Nicandra, on the other hand, cannot consciously think vengeful thoughts, no matter how unhappy, neglected, or betrayed she is. What is terrifying in Nicandra, and what separates her from Keane's other Good Girl, Aroon, is that unlike Aroon, whose final actions, however she rationalizes them, are the Bad Girl's revenge, Nicandra has so internalized the Good Girl imperative that she appears genuinely incapable of life-saving, independent, Bad Girl thought. The plight of the vulnerable Nicandra is made infinitely worse by her inability to achieve emotional distance from her situation or to laugh at herself or anybody else. She is emotionally crippled rather than strengthened by the lesson dangled before her by her mother; perhaps unable to break free without leaving, Nicandra's mother, in marked contrast to the other Keane Mummies, departs "with a little skipping step towards the door" for the 4:30 train, never to return (39). Nicandra is understandably devastated by the resulting "frightening loss of love" (202) but never moves beyond it, never wonders what might have driven her mother away in what Aunt Tossie refers to as "that shaming elopement" (202). From an early age, therefore, Nicandra wilts under and is finally destroyed by a desperate need for security and love and an externally and internally imposed mission to be a Good Girl.

Nicandra lives her life in the service of others, in trying at all costs (and the costs are all too high) to avoid confrontation and crisis and doing her utmost to "excite, please, soothe" (45). She takes to marriage with a "slavish contentment" (112) and so bores Andrew with her compliance and "total generosity" (128) that Andrew flies into Lalage's Bad Girl embrace as much for amusement and challenge as for pleasure.

Even when she is able to confirm her suspicions that Andrew and Lalage are having an affair, even after a painful miscarriage to which Andrew responds with frank relief, Nicandra's reactions stem not from fury but vulnerability, grief, distress, despair. Emotionally *in extremis* after her miscarriage, she is briefly filled with joy by her (unfounded) belief that Andrew has prepared her a dinner tray, and when she learns that the cook was responsible for the food and its arrangement, she blames the servant for her presence rather than Andrew for his complete emotional absence. When Andrew finally asks Nicandra for a divorce, planning to use Lalage's brother to obtain in England the document forbidden under Irish law, she still submits patiently to his knife, rather than twisting her own: "Of course. You can have anything. You know I'd give you anything" (165).

The book ends in a shocking climax with Nicandra's death, yet even her final moments are tinged with a kind of desperate humor. After Andrew's betrayal and departure, with the divorce still pending, she has returned to the decaying old house in which she grew up, an Ascendancy seat in such disarray, permeated with damp, dust, and filth, with "a sweet horrible smell of bats in the lavatory" (111), that even the stalwart Aunt Tossie has abandoned it in favor of a caravan outside its doors. After trying hard to move her aunt back inside the rotting mansion, in a hopeless attempt to bind with family ties the crumbling edifice of Anglo-Irish traditions, Nicandra receives a phone call from her husband in which he announces his intention of returning to her. Still dependent upon others for her happiness, Nicandra crumbles in a matter of seconds, and, in a flurry of nurturing "surrender," her mind "spinning fatally towards cooking and cosseting," she falls through the equally crumbled "floors of Paradise" and dies on the flagstones in the basement below, "coffined and certain in her happiness" (231–32). As an elegant metaphor engendered by the insights that only gendered humor can provide, Nicandra's happy plunge through the rotten boards is darkly, satisfyingly funny. We may not laugh outright, at least on a first reading, but how can we not be amused, if we are honest? In her portrayal of Nicandra's last minutes, Keane does not bring down the house; it is toppling of its own accord. She does, however, use black comedy to warn us that if we are not watchful, bringing down our houses ourselves or not knowing when to leave, we ourselves could be brought down so far that we could fall right through.

Keane's black comedies place her firmly in the tradition of women's comic writing. We have seen how *Time* fits Little's model for women's comedy; *Lear* also functions as a comedy of the norm as defined by Little. As Barreca warns, women's comedy is "dangerous" because "it refuses to accept the givens and because it refuses to stop at the point where comedy loses its integrative function" (*Untamed*, 30). Unlike carnival, a temporary defuser, "certain forms of comedy can invert the world not briefly but permanently. . . . comedy can effectively channel anger and rebellion by first making them appear to be acceptable and temporary phenomena, no doubt to be purged by laughter, and then by harnessing the released energies, rather than dispersing them" (32–33). Barreca's words can effectively be applied both to the matricidal Aroon and the triumphant May, who in going out to work and evading, even laughing at, Jasper's authority, truly does refuse to "accept the givens," transcending and redefining the norm. As Barreca says, "This kind of comedy terrifies those who hold order dear. It should" (*Untamed*, 33).

Keane's comic world is further destabilized through her superb use of a strategy Barreca opposes to traditional joke-telling (where the supposedly literal is reduced to comfortingly figurative status) and calls "metaphor-into-narrative" (*Untamed*, 163). Barreca argues that the comic effect depending on "reliteralizing," on "the error of believing language to be used figuratively when it is used literally," is integral to women's "apocalyptic" humor (*Untamed*, 162–63). The vivid, often violent literalism of the swirling tide in *Loving*, Aroon's immense hunger, Leda's blindness, the maimed children of the Ascendancy in *Time*, and Nicandra's unsuspecting and fatal fall through the floor of her rotten ancestral home, demonstrate Keane's effective mastery of this device.

The Irish comic strain asserts itself vigorously in Keane and must not be overlooked. Among the comic motifs David Krause identifies as part of the "comic catharsis" provided by the Irish comic tradition are "denied expectation," "the principle of disintegration," and "the desecration of Ireland's household gods" (*Profane*, 11). While Krause believes that the "barbarous sympathies" he describes "strike a universal impulse, a common cause . . . to mock conformity and authority" (12) and are, as we have seen, also vital components of women's humor, he emphasizes the centrality of such ridicule of the sacred to Irish comic drama. He observes that the "barbarous affinities" of "the mythic Oisin or Usheen, the last great playboy of the pagan world," still "hover like a giddy spirit of defiance over the tradition of Irish comedy," emerging like an inherited trait in a long line of characters created by authors both Anglo-Irish and Catholic, including Goldsmith's Tony Lumpkin, Synge's Christy Mahon, Behan's Borstal Boy, and Beckett's Gogo and Didi (10, 22–23). Krause continues: "These comic characters must be failures or outcasts before they can be mythically liberated, for low comedy is the last and perhaps the only refuge of the defeated. They are defeated or dispossessed from the start; they enter defeated; and it is precisely their ability to live cheerfully and resourcefully with defeat that distinguishes them from tragic characters, who are broken and destroyed by defeat. . . . comic hubris affirms individual freedom through merry indulgence in outrageous deeds" (23).

These revealing comments on the Irish comic tradition can be extended to include many of the inhabitants of Keane's novels, where the characters sustained by their "barbarous affinities" are, in the strikingly similar tradition of women's comedy, predominantly female. Surely the similarities between the traditions are not coincidental; both women and the Irish understand what it is to "enter defeated," and in Keane's later comedies the once dominant Anglo-Irish are nearing extinction. Krause's observations, like Little's and Barreca's examination of women's apocalyptic humor, are particularly pertinent when applied to Aroon and May. Both "enter defeated" and, rejecting renunciation, survive; both defy the household gods; and both gain what Krause calls a "psychic triumph" (25). In Aroon destroying her tormentor and planning delicious meals, and in May, delighting in her one-handed dexterity and putting Jasper "in his place," we recognize "the Satanic sympathies of Prometheus' and Dedalus' *non serviam*" (*Profane*, 37). Yet the "desecrating laughter" Krause notes in Joyce, O'Casey, and so many other Irishmen (26) is also that of women, the irreverent and irrepressible chuckling for which Judith Wilt named an essay on women's humor: "The Laughter of Maidens, the Cackle of Matriarchs." Keane dances in the crossroads where two comic traditions meet.

Notes

1. *Young Entry* (1928), *Taking Chances* (1929), *Mad Puppetstown* (1931), *Conversation Piece* (1932), *Devoted Ladies* (1934), *Full House* (1935), *The Rising Tide* (1937), *Two Days in Aragon* (1941), *Loving without Tears* (1951), and *Treasure Hunt* (1952) were published under the name M. J. Farrell. Polly Devlin quotes Keane as saying that she needed a nom de plume because "For a woman to read a book, let alone write one was viewed with alarm. I would have been banned from every respectable house in County Carlow" (*Rising Tide*, v).

2. As Ann Owens Weekes has noted, "the final irony" of *Good Behaviour* "is the murder of the mother through the powers first depicted as the source of her own superiority." Weekes also stresses the importance of the transfer of "means" from Mummie to Aroon, seeing in the novel Keane's suggestion "that erotic fulfillment is merely the spice of women's fiction—economic independence and the murder of the fictional collaborators mark the real foundation of women's texts" (*Irish Women Writers*, 172–73).

3. The word *disestablished* is interesting in context. Many Church historians argue that the Church of Ireland was liberated in 1869 by disestablishment, after which it rebuilt itself entirely. In this subsequent reconstruction, undertaken from within with no support from the establishment, it displayed courage and ingenuity and prospered in a smaller way. From an establishment point of view, Leda performs a dual role in the novel: first she is herself a half-member of the Ascendancy, aiming for continued ascendancy, wishing to reign over the "establishment" of Durraghglass and refusing to accept change; and, second, she is herself an outside, "disestablishing," force, wreaking havoc upon the establishment.

Works Cited

Adams, Alice. "Coming Apart at the Seams: *Good Behaviour* as an AntiComedy of Manners." *Journal of Irish Literature* 20 (September 1991): 27–35.

Barreca, Regina. *They Used to Call Me Snow White, But I Drifted: Women's Strategic Use of Humor.* London; New York: Penguin, 1991.

———. *Untamed and Unabashed: Essays on Women and Humor in British Literature.* Detroit: Wayne State University Press, 1994.

Cahalan, James M. *The Irish Novel: A Critical History.* Boston: Twayne, 1988.

Keane, Molly [M. J. Farrell, pseud.]. *Conversation Piece.* 1932. Interview by Polly Devlin. Reprint, London: Virago, 1991.

———. *Devoted Ladies.* 1934. Introduction by Polly Devlin. Reprint, London: Virago, 1984.

———. *Good Behaviour.* New York: Alfred Knopf, 1981.

———. *Loving and Giving.* 1988. Reprinted as *Queen Lear.* London: Penguin, 1990.

———. *Loving without Tears.* 1951. Introduction by Russell Harty. Reprint, London: Virago, 1991.

———. *The Rising Tide.* 1937. Introduction by Polly Devlin. Reprint, London: Virago, 1984.

———. *Time After Time.* 1983. New York: Alfred Knopf, 1984.

Krause, David. *The Profane Book of Irish Comedy.* Ithaca: Cornell University Press, 1982.

Little, Judy. *Comedy and the Woman Writer: Woolf, Spark, and Feminism.* Lincoln: University of Nebraska Press, 1983.

Mercier, Vivian. *The Irish Comic Tradition.* Oxford: Clarendon Press, 1962.

O'Brien, Edna. "A Scandalous Woman." In *A Fanatic Heart: Selected Stories of Edna O'Brien*, 239–65. New York: New American Library, 1984.

Quinn, John, ed. *A Portrait of the Artist as a Young Girl*. London: Methuen, 1986.

Weekes, Ann Owens. *Irish Women Writers: An Uncharted Tradition*. Lexington: University of Kentucky Press, 1990.

Wilt, Judith. "The Laughter of Maidens, the Cackle of Matriarchs: Notes on the Collision Between Comedy and Feminism." In *Women and Literature*, edited by Janet Todd. New York: Holmes & Meier, 1980.

Iris Murdoch's Moral Comedy

The novel is a comic form.
Language is a comic form, and makes jokes in its sleep.

MURDOCH, *The Black Prince*

Iris Murdoch was born in Dublin in 1919, to parents Irish on both sides. She received through her parents an awareness of her Irish antecedents, and she has said, looking back on her upbringing in London, "I've only recently realized that I'm a kind of exile" (quoted in Haffenden, *Novelists*, 200–201). Her fiction frequently includes Irish characters, often, like herself, Anglo-Irish, and possessing a kind of outsider quality, as in the case of Jake Donoghue in *Under the Net* (1954). An aspect of the Easter Rising of 1916 and the collision between English and Irish views of Ireland are central in *The Red and the Green* (1965). Recent Irish history is discussed in *The Sea, The Sea* (1978), focused through an Ulsterman's revulsion against terrorist violence in Northern Ireland. In *The Philosopher's Pupil* (1983), the Northern Irish troubles create for Emmanuel Scarlett-Taylor a crisis of identity: he rejects his Irishness but still recognizes that he is not an Englishman. In *The Unicorn* (1963), an accumulation of references to past burnings of houses, fairy stories, and accents either English or incomprehensible, makes clear that this Gothic fiction is generated in an Irish setting, out of interaction between Irish and English characters.

In this essay I examine aspects of Iris Murdoch's comedy, focusing first on two novels that have distinct Irish connections: *Under the Net*, in which she adapts materials borrowed from Samuel Beckett's *Murphy*, and *The Red and the Green*, in which she deals with Dublin in 1916. Turning to a novel with no apparent Irish dimension, *The Black Prince* (1973), I suggest that there is a gendered aspect in her comic treatment of love. Murdoch's assimilation to English culture has meant that her relationship with other Irish comic writers is a complicated one. Her affinity with Beckett is especially important at the beginning of her career, but in many respects her work deviates from what David Krause has outlined as salient characteristics of Irish comic writing. Krause suggests about Irish comedians that theirs is "a world without truth or justice . . . that encourages . . . anarchic games and disguises of comic survival" (*Profane*, 31), whereas Murdoch's comedy is largely corrective. For her, truth and justice do exist, and Krause's suggestion that knockabout comedy gives the comic artist the capacity to endure repressive order is alien to Murdoch, who does not contest political or religious order and sees the moral order as liberating and enriching (371–72).

Similarly, Murdoch resists easy classification as a woman writer. Her writing subject position is largely formed from a masculine perspective, and Murdoch herself has commented interestingly on her preference for writing through male narrators: "I think I identify more with my male characters than my female characters. . . . a male represents ordinary human beings . . . whereas a woman is always a woman" (quoted in Johnson, *Murdoch*, xii). Her careful adoption of a male position as representative, which implies refusal of identification with women's marginal status, is unsurprising in an academic philosopher of Murdoch's generation. It indicates that she is not a writer to whom we can apply Regina Barreca's arguments that women's humor is subversive, and that it works to challenge male-dominated power structures (*Snow White*, 182–85). Similarly Judy Little's ideas about women's comedy, based on the idea that those who perceive themselves as outsiders will create comedy that mocks hierarchies and norms in a radical way (*Comedy*, 6), are scarcely applicable to Murdoch, who, despite seeing herself as an Anglo-Irish exile in England, shows no awareness that being a woman has caused her to suffer exclusion.

In the opening chapter of *Under the Net*, Jake Donoghue's friend Madge asks him to leave her apartment. She emphasizes the request by removing from the bookshelves his copies of Samuel Beckett's *Murphy* and Raymond Queneau's *Pierrot Mon Ami*. Thus the author indicates her debt to two important influences, confirmed in her 1962 interview with John Fletcher: "I imitated these two great models with all my heart" ("Beckett," 8). It may be significant that, as Vivian Mercier has pointed out, Queneau was crucially influenced by the work of James Joyce, and in particular by *Ulysses* (25, 45–46). Queneau is the dedicatee of *Under the Net*, and the comic melancholy of Murdoch's novel and episodes such as the theft of the film star dog, Mr Mars, which echoes Pierrot's journey with a vanload of trained animals, are attributable, as Frank Baldanza suggests, to her reading of the French and Irish-inspired novelist (*Murdoch*, 31).

The influence of Beckett, which establishes a connection with a tradition of Irish writing, is seen in several aspects of *Under the Net*. Murdoch has said that she was "enslaved" by *Murphy*, and she reworks material from it in her own novel (Fletcher, "Beckett," 8). Beckett's Neary, under whom Murphy had studied in Cork, has a relationship with a "man-of-all-work" named Cooper, and this provides a basis for the strange relationship that exists between Murdoch's Jake and Finn, the distant relative whom he allows to be mistaken for his servant. Cooper is an invaluable servant as long as he can be kept off the bottle; has a curious hunted walk; never sits down; and never takes off his hat. Murdoch transmutes Cooper, with his "morbid craving for alcoholic depressant" (41), into the richer figure of Finn, who normally waits for Jake leaning up against the side of the door with his eyes closed and "has an almost psychic capacity for finding drink at all hours" (122).

Beckett's study of a relationship between two Irish characters is turned by Murdoch into a vehicle for examination of different racial and cultural identities, combined with a comic scrutiny of the artist as outsider. She plays on the stereotyping of Irish characteristics, showing Jake secure in his own complacent perception of Anglo-Irish superiority to the more authentically Irish Finn. Finn appears to accept a role that, to complement the philosophical Jake, combines practical activity and resourcefulness with limited thinking. But Jake assumes wrongly that Finn does not possess an inner life, and his self-absorption is comically exposed at the end of the novel when, having failed to take seriously Finn's voicing of his desire to go back to Ireland, he is greatly surprised and upset by the news that Finn has actually done so. Murdoch develops Jake into an outsider figure whose Anglo-Irish identity prevents him from truly belonging in either country. He is aware of not being English but also recognizes that his connection with Ireland is a distant one and that he is separated from the genuinely Irish Finn by not sharing his Catholic and Gaelic background. Finn's return to Ireland, Donna Gerstenberger notes, puts an end to their relationship because it has depended on their shared sense of displacement, and in Dublin Finn has moved back into his own world where Jake cannot fully belong (*Murdoch*, 75).

While Beckett's preoccupation is principally with the philosophical, Murdoch's interest in moral issues is seen in her adaptation of Murphy's game of chess with Mr. Endon at the ironically named Magdalen Mental Mercyseat to produce Jake's important conversation with Hugo Belfounder in the hospital. The outcome of the game for Murphy is a perception of nothing, appropriate to the ultimately philosophical concerns of Beckett's novel. Murdoch replaces this with a recognition scene in which Jake acquires a moral understanding of his misapprehensions. The recurrent pattern of *Under the Net* is derived from Jake's inability to see other people clearly, and the comedy is based largely on the processes by which he is compelled to correct mistaken assumptions.

Murdoch adapts for her own purposes in *Under the Net* an episode from *Murphy* in which Neary, driven to distraction by frustrated love, and displaying something of the comic desecration of "whatever is too sacred in Ireland" that David Krause sees as one of the characteristic varieties of Irish comedy (*Profane*, 9–12), seizes by the thighs the statue in the General Post Office of the dying hero Cúchulainn, and dashes his head against its buttocks. Murdoch turns this, stripped of its Irish national significance, into the scene in which Jake and his friends visit the General Post Office in London to make use of its late-night facilities and are turned out for singing. This episode in Murdoch's novel turns on the comic contrast between the extreme rationality with which the men pursue a series of political questions and their anarchic drunken progress through London. Although Murdoch removes the Irish significance that lies in Beckett's profane treatment of dying hero and holy ground, her polarizing of order and chaos has an affinity with characteristic features of Beckett's comedy in *Murphy*. Just as Beckett plays off an obsessive concern with method against uncontrollable disruption, as when he juxtaposes Murphy's careful strategies for obtaining 1.83 cups of tea for the price of a single cup and his contemplation of the possible permutations of a meal of five different biscuits with his discomfiture when the biscuits are eaten by Miss Dew's dachshund, so Murdoch derives comedy from an elaborate interplay of ingenuity and method with accident and chaos. While Murdoch's use of comic interaction between rationality and chaos shows an affinity with Beckett's work, the significance in her writing is somewhat different. She is fascinated by the way in which human efforts and aspirations are at the mercy of accident, but she sees such accidents as coming into conflict with a framework of moral values alien to the absurdity and subversiveness of *Murphy*.

The Red and the Green, Murdoch's only historical novel, is set in the events of the week leading up to the Easter Rising in Dublin in 1916. Several central characters are poised between Irish and English identities, either because they are Anglo-Irish, like Andrew Chase-White and his mother Hilda, or because, like Christopher Bellman and his daughter Frances, they are technically English but have become identified with Irish affairs and interests. Much of the comedy in this novel is derived from satiric exposure of English ignorance and prejudice. Ironic juxtapositions make the point forcefully, as when a condescending remark about Irish volunteers drilling is followed by a revelation of the poor state of British equipment and the recent mysterious loss of a British rifle. Murdoch satirizes prejudiced attitudes by skillful use of cliché, as in the misguided Anglocentric views expressed by Hilda about Roger Casement: "He does it for love of gold. . . . It's the traitor mentality" (40). Frances Bellman, objecting, is accused of "parroting" the views of her nationalist uncle, although it is perfectly clear that it is Hilda whose opinions are no more than parroted commonplaces. A significant sequence of political argument is brought to a climax when Hilda reveals how ill-qualified she is to make any judgment on Irish affairs or history by enquiring, "What exactly did Wolfe Tone do?" (Theobald Wolfe Tone, a leader of the United Irishmen, was captured in the unsuccessful rising of 1798, and committed suicide while awaiting execution.)

In *The Red and the Green*, Murdoch manipulates voices to create a critique of English intolerance and complacency but at the same time to produce an awareness of the complex forces in the events of Easter week. The impulses that bring about the Rising are treated with both respect and criticism, and Donna Gerstenberger notes that the Epilogue to the novel asks the same question as Yeats's "Easter 1916": "Was it needless death after all?" (*Murdoch*, 15–16). The two conflicting positions are brought into sharp focus through the confrontation between Andrew, commissioned in the British army, for whom the Rising is insane, and his cousin Pat Dumay, for whom it is necessary. Christopher Bellman's analysis, while disposing of Hilda's facile simplifications, expresses awareness of areas of weakness in the nationalist position. He exposes Irish sentimentality, countering his daughter's quotation from Yeats's *Cathleen Ni Houlihan* with the retort that in Dublin a reading of the telephone directory could have people shedding tears. But Christopher's negative view of the Rising's prospects is belied by the vividness with which he speaks of the volunteers he saw, and it is ultimately proved mistaken by the events of the narrative and by his own death in an apparent attempt to join the defenders in the Post Office.

Through the textual treatment of Frances Bellman, Andrew's intended bride, Murdoch brings together issues of nationality and gender. Although she is, as Gerstenberger points out, an outstanding horsewoman, possibly to be associated with the *Sidhe* of Irish mythology (*Murdoch*, 54), Andrew regards Frances condescendingly as representing, along with his mother, a little feminine world, as opposed to the important things of the world, which are masculine. Related perceptions link weakness with the feminine, as when Hilda says of Millicent Kinnard that she "really might have been somebody if she'd been born a man" (31), while Christopher attributes Irish sentimentality to the habit of personifying Ireland as a tragic female. But these negatives are comprehensively overturned: Frances and Millie both emerge as strong and competent figures, and the female figure of Ireland finally precipitates action, not sentiment. Murdoch allocates to Frances the observation that "being a woman is like being Irish. . . . Everyone says you're important and nice, but you take second place all the same" (31), and the text as a whole addresses the implications of Frances's remark by demonstrating that the strengths both of Ireland and of women have been too easily dismissed.

Murdoch's comedy frequently turns on men's inadequate handling of relationships, and it is difficult not to see a gender-related significance in the consistency with which her texts display a selfish or self-deluded male figure incapable of seeing things clearly and of paying proper attention to other people. Something of this is present in Jake Donoghue; and Andrew Chase-White's insight into himself and his relationship with Frances is similarly defective. His emotional inadequacy is interwoven with the political dimension as one of the major narrative strands in the novel. He does not recognize that his "love" for Frances is a matter of familiarity rather than passion. His unrealistic expectation that marriage will resolve all his personal difficulties is juxtaposed with a revelation of sexual repression made clear by the difference between his sexless approach to Frances and his easy response to the sexual attractiveness of his aunt, Millicent Kinnard. Murdoch indicates Andrew's emotional incompetence through the naive idealism that makes him see Frances in chivalric terms as presenting to him a trial of his own worth.

Angela Hague has drawn attention to a close relationship in comedy between the comic character's manipulation of people and events and the creative activity of the artist, suggesting that in Murdoch's work the hero who is a writer may play the role of buffoon, calling into question the value of artistic activity. Hague recalls Murphy's mind in chapter 6 of *Murphy*, divided into three zones—light, half light, and dark—and she suggests that the first of these zones, in which the imagination can rearrange the elements of physical experience, is an excellent paradigm for the fantasy consciousness of many comic characters (*Vision*, 37–39). As Beckett has it: "Here the kick that the physical Murphy received, the mental Murphy gave" (65). In Murdoch's work, the folly of confusing art and life is typically seen in the lives of male characters, and it is tempting to see as significant the absence from her work of women artists similarly confusing fantasy and reality. The life of Bradley Pearson, the artist-protagonist in *The Black Prince*, is marked by this confusion. The comedy issuing from his inability to understand and control his sexual passion is at some level related to his view of himself as an artist. Fantasy and reality become inextricably woven together in his mental and emotional life in a way which Murdoch, in her philosophical and critical writing, identifies as morally dangerous ("Dryness" 16–20).

In *The Black Prince*, Murdoch also develops a complex and witty exploration of the relation between writers and the texts they create, which embraces the female as well as the male by including metafictional reference to Murdoch's own writing practice. Based on *Hamlet*, this exploration bears a resemblance to Stephen Dedalus's *jeu d'esprit* in *Ulysses* on connections between this play and Shakespeare's life. Bradley Pearson passes on to Julian a simplified version of Ernest Jones's reading of the play, arguing that Hamlet is created out of the dramatist's own crisis of identity. Pearson's words, "The unconscious delights in identifying people with each other. It has only a few characters to play with" (195), are applicable not only to *Hamlet* but also to the text within which Pearson himself has his existence. It may confirm the suggestion teasingly trailed before the reader in a heavy-handed analysis proposed by Francis Marloe, that the attraction Pearson feels in turn for Baffin's wife and his daughter is a displacement of a homosexual attraction to Baffin himself.

Further, his elaboration on the relation of writer to text points to the way in which the two contrasting novelist characters, the high-minded, relatively unproductive Pearson and his rival, the successful, populist Arnold Baffin, appear to correspond to different aspects of Murdoch herself as a writer. As Peter Conradi points out, Julian's suggestion that Baffin's fiction is characterized by "Jesus and Mary and Buddha and Shiva and the Fisher King all chasing round and round dressed up as people in Chelsea" (137) parodies the more sensational aspects of Murdoch's own fiction (*Saint*, 197–98). Apollo figures in a foreword and postscript as the editor of Murdoch's text, and the myth of the flaying of Marsyas by Apollo is applied to the relation between suffering and art. Hamlet is "the god's flayed victim dancing the dance of creation" (199), and Hamlet's voice is also the voice of Shakespeare himself. A. S. Byatt identifies here the figure of Apollo as the puppetmaster, "setting the artists, including Shakespeare, dancing in their excruciatingly funny agonies" ("Postwar," 35). Even the pain is brought within the comic vision.

Iris Murdoch's writing positions are characteristically situated on borders. The Anglo-Irish experience of having affinities with both Ireland and England while remaining conscious of belonging in neither nation provides her with material that can be treated in a direct political manner as in *The Red and the Green* or that can, as in *Under the Net*, allow exploration of wider implications of the position of outsider. Occupying this displaced position, she transmutes characters and incidents from Beckett into something that is less Irish, and corrective rather than absurd, but that retains Beckett's comic juxtaposition of order with wild disruption. In her situation as a novelist who is a woman but who prefers not to be categorized as a "woman writer," she does not write to challenge existing order and subvert hierarchies. Yet there is in much of her moral comedy an intriguing insistence on applying her wit to male characters who cannot free themselves from self-absorption and fantasy. As an Irish-born woman writing from a traditional English academic environment, she possesses an element of double vision that adds complexity to her comic writing.

Works Cited

Baldanza, Frank. *Iris Murdoch.* Twayne's English Authors Series, 169. New York: Twayne, 1974.

Barreca, Regina. *They Used to Call Me Snow White, But I Drifted: Women's Strategic Use of Humor.* New York: Penguin, 1991.

Beckett, Samuel. *Murphy.* London: Picador, 1973.

Byatt, A. S. "People in Paper Houses: Attitudes to 'Realism' and 'Experiment' in English Postwar Fiction." In *The Contemporary English Novel,* edited by Malcolm Bradbury and David Palmer. Stratford-upon-Avon Studies, 18. London: Edward Arnold, 1979.

Conradi, Peter J. *Iris Murdoch: The Saint and the Artist.* 2d ed. Basingstoke: Macmillan, 1989.

Fletcher, John. "Reading Beckett with Iris Murdoch's Eyes." *AUMLA* 55 (1981): 7–14.

Gerstenberger, Donna. *Iris Murdoch.* Irish Writers Series. Lewisburg, Pa.: Bucknell University Press, 1975.

Haffenden, John. *Novelists in Interview.* London: Methuen, 1985.

Hague, Angela. *Iris Murdoch's Comic Vision.* Selinsgrove, Pa.: Susquehanna University Press, 1984.

Johnson, Deborah. *Iris Murdoch.* Key Women Writers. Brighton: Harvester Press, 1987.

Krause, David. *The Profane Book of Irish Comedy.* Ithaca, N.Y.: Cornell University Press, 1982.

Little, Judy. *Comedy and the Woman Writer.* Lincoln: University of Nebraska Press, 1983.

Mercier, Vivian. *The New Novel: From Queneau to Pinget.* New York: Farrar, Straus and Giroux, 1971.

Murdoch, Iris. "Against Dryness." *Encounter* 16 (January 1961): 16–20.

———. *The Black Prince.* London: Penguin, 1975.

———. *The Philosopher's Pupil.* London: Chatto and Windus, 1982.

———. *The Red and the Green.* London: Penguin, 1972.

———. *The Sea, The Sea.* London: Chatto and Windus, 1978.

———. *Under the Net.* London: Penguin, 1960.

———. *The Unicorn.* London: Chatto and Windus, 1963.

(S)he Was Too Scrupulous Always

Edna O'Brien and the Comic Tradition

Michael Patrick Gillespie

Although a desolate, unforgiving atmosphere informs the narrative discourse in much of Edna O'Brien's writings, seeing her fiction as dour and pessimistic imposes a narrow, even reductive, view of her craft.[1] One can, in fact, gain a great deal of interpretive insight into O'Brien's work by remaining attentive to the way that she incorporates into her narratives common features of Irish humor. Indeed, by using the guidelines articulated in Vivian Mercier's classic study *The Irish Comic Tradition*, one quickly finds that humor—albeit at times quite singular—stands as an integral part in O'Brien's fiction.

Mercier's approach presents the modest proposal that Irish humor draws particular strength from a legacy of sardonic, polemic critiques of society through a commentary that clarifies the complex forces that produce necessarily paradoxical views of Irish culture. His book clearly demonstrates—by tracing the formative influence of a heritage of acerbic chronicles of national foibles and failings that stretches from Jonathan Swift to Brendan Behan—that a significant selection of this humor comes out of a polemic Anglo-Irish[2] comic tradition antithetical to the amusement produced by ostensibly neutral anecdotal discourse. Such social commentary juxtaposes—through extravagantly distorted descriptions and exuberantly idiosyncratic characterizations—the grotesque and the banal to enforce searing, though generally oblique, critiques of Irish life and mores. Despite the clarity and insight of Vivian Mercier's study, however, a full delineation of Ireland's comic tradition remains elusive, in part because the historical conditions shaping the Irish consciousness have produced a brand of humor that often mixes amusement with the restraining cynicism of a sophisticated satirical consciousness. That paradoxically can create a false sense of verisimilitude because, as Mercier notes, "really subtle irony can be mistaken for the literal truth" (2).

More than any other feature, however, a biting if often dissipated anger frequently interposes itself and obscures the comic spirit of many pieces. Frank O'Connor has offered a particularly mordant view of the way that diffused indignation shapes and misshapes Irish humor: "None of us could ever fashion a story or a play into a stiletto to run into the vitals of some pompous ass. Oliver Gogarty, like Brian O'Nolan of our own time, could make phrases that delighted everybody, but the phrases never concentrated themselves into the shape of a dagger; they were more like fireworks that spluttered and jumped all over the place, as much a danger to his friends as to his enemies. Irish anger is unfocused; malice for its own sweet sake, as in the days of the bards" (quoted in Mercier, 182).[3]

O'Connor sees the Irish comic tradition as still fighting the influence of centuries of English cultural imperialism—represented in performances by Paddy, the stage Irishman, and characterized in newspaper caricatures of simian versions of Irish men and women—and responding to its slanders with the lacerating indignation of the consciousness aptly noted by W. B. Yeats in "Remorse for Intemperate Speech": "Out of Ireland have we come; / Great hatred, little room, / Maimed us at the start."

Edna O'Brien's writings manifest no less anger than any other Irish author. Nonetheless, she brings a distinctive perspective to a previously male-dominated genre.[4] Without the same cultural resources that men enjoy, O'Brien operates at an additional disadvantage, and consequently one cannot group her manipulation of comic techniques too quickly or too easily within the tradition noted above. Indeed, the organizing premise of this essay (and of the entire volume) rests upon an assumption of the singularity of the experiences and perspectives of Irish women writers like O'Brien.

Primarily, a both/and incorporating impulse rather than an either/or exclusivity stands as the feature distinguishing O'Brien's humor from that of most Irish male writers. Like Swift, she possesses a keen, satiric voice, but her commentary on Irish society generally—though not always—stops short of the enmity one finds in *Gulliver's Travels* and "A

Modest Proposal." Her invocation of the fantastic and her respectful treatment of superstition recalls *At Swim Two Birds*, but, unlike Flann O'Brien, she integrates rather than displaces the quotidian with the fabulous. Even her anger retains a sense of proportion and asserts the value of plurality. If her characters take the roles of green fools, they do not voice the all-encompassing anger found in Patrick Kavanagh's works. Instead, they critique Irish society without alienating themselves from it.

Thus, while keenly aware of the achievements and influence of her literary antecedents, O'Brien's comic inclinations draw back from their gender-based methods. Without completely rejecting their system of Cartesian cause and effect linearity, her writing shows a marked partiality for liberating ambiguities. In this disposition she aligns herself—more overtly than many of her male counterparts—with Ireland's foremost (and perhaps most imaginatively androgynous) writer of prose fiction, James Joyce.

At first glance, Joyce and O'Brien may seem to operate under very different aesthetic and artistic dispensations, but important creative convergences illuminate the works of both. While no twentieth-century Irish author could avoid the influence of Joyce's canon, male responses to Joyce's writings have varied greatly. Near contemporaries like Samuel Beckett frankly admired his work. Subsequent writers like Frank O'Connor overtly criticized him. Seamus Heaney evoked his ghost in *Station Island* in a complicated form of exorcism. All, however, while acknowledging his shaping impact, endeavored to establish their independence.

One sees in O'Brien's canon this anxiety of influence working with both greater and lesser force than in her male counterparts, and she uses such ambivalence to good effect time and again in her novels and short stories. Writing as a minority within a minority—a female Irish writer seeking to establish a reputation among English-speaking readers—O'Brien's rich literary allusiveness sharply acknowledges the competitive presence of her artistic predecessors. At the same time, while pursuing many of the same topics and employing many of the same methods as male writers, in both proportion and exposition her deployment differs. In James Joyce, she finds the guidance of a mentor and not the challenge of a competitor. Joyce's comic inclinations show the rich diversity of a powerful creative imagination, with each manifestation highlighting a particular artistic perspective and specific aesthetic goals. O'Brien's narratives, highlighting multiplicity and ambiguity,

Michael Patrick Gillespie

resonate with the same understanding of the Irish comic tradition marking Joyce's process of creation.

Such comparisons, of course, require careful qualification. One can find in O'Brien's work echoes of Joyce's entire canon, but generally parallels with *Dubliners* assert the strongest artistic and aesthetic links to Joyce's social awareness and his comic sense. O'Brien's commitment to conventional realism leads her to imitate the tart, desperate comedy of *Dubliners* rather than the broad, slapstick humor of *Ulysses* or the fantastical raillery of *Finnegan's Wake.*[5] The implications of such a choice—both for O'Brien and for Joyce—emerge from passages appearing in two letters that Joyce wrote in 1906 to Grant Richards, the eventual publisher of *Dubliners:* "My intention [in writing *Dubliners*] was to write a chapter of the moral history of my country, and I chose Dublin for the scene because that city seemed to me the centre of paralysis" (2:134); "It is not my fault that the odour of ashpits and old weeds and offal hangs round my stories. I seriously believe that you will retard the course of civilisation in Ireland by preventing the Irish people from having one good look at themselves in my nicely polished looking-glass" (1: 63–64).[6] These sentiments affirm an intention to inculcate a serious social critique within even the most sardonic discourses of the collection. In following these aims, however, Joyce avoided the heavy-handed didacticism of an author like Bernard Shaw by liberally employing an idiosyncratic brand of humor throughout the discourse. O'Brien's writing shows this same inclination to balance censure with raillery.[7]

In fact the short stories examined here neatly fit the aesthetic and polemic paradigm of *Dubliners* outlined above. Since the Irish comic tradition assumes that irony increases our sensitivity to the Irish consciousness, such critiques rest upon abilities to manipulate and to foreground the complexities and ambiguities of a national character. Consequently, attention to conventions established in Joyce's stories allows one to measure the impact of similar techniques in O'Brien's writing.

Specifically, one can explore how Joyce's writings set up expectations influencing both the composition and the interpretation of O'Brien's works. While such impressions cannot, of course, impose programmatic readings upon her stories, they do increase our tolerance for ambiguity and multiplicity in O'Brien's writing. As a result, because we have read Joyce, we have the capacity for finding greater aesthetic satisfaction in O'Brien; and because O'Brien has read Joyce, she has cultivated the artistic ability to appeal to that capacity. The rural stories by O'Brien considered in this essay—"The Connor Girls," "Irish Revel," "A Scandalous Woman," and "The Small-Town Lovers"—facilitate this perception by easy associations with the *Dubliners* collection: as in most of Joyce's stories, O'Brien's narrators stand at the periphery of Irish society—children or young women on the brink of becoming adults. All of the stories establish a common ethos through recurring settings and characters. And they all sustain imaginative ambiguity by deferring closure and inviting multiple interpretations.

"The Connor Girls" clearly illustrates the links between O'Brien and Joyce as it represents a village's changing relations with the two women of the title—Miss Amy and Miss Lucy Connor—the adult daughters of a local Protestant landowner. Over the course of the story, the unnamed young girl who acts as narrator contrasts, with a growing perceptiveness, the social aloofness of these two women with a genuine need, felt especially by Miss Amy, for male companionship. (The villagers, with a satirical sense of the situation, have long since nicknamed a frequent male visitor to the Big House the "Stallion.") After several disappointing love affairs and a prolonged absence, Miss Amy returns to her family home. The narrator, now a grown woman with a husband—"a man who was not of our religion" (14)[8]—and a son, also comes back to the village for a visit. In the story's closing scene she meets the much-changed Connor girls. A measure of charm and graciousness have replaced their thoughtless aloofness, and the narrator finds herself quite taken by their demeanor. Her husband's rudeness, however, forestalls an invitation to tea, a prize that the entire family had at one time sought. Apprised of this, the husband can only respond, "don't think we missed much," but the narrator's interior monologue gives a far subtler view, tinged with the caustic humor of self-reflexivity: "At that moment I realized that by choosing his world I had said goodbye to my own and to those in it. By such choices we gradually become exiles, until at last we are quite alone" (16).

Despite its rural, Protestant setting, one can gain interpretive insights by comparing "The Connor Girls" with Joyce's "The Sisters": both works deal with eccentric families set apart from the community. Both have their isolation scrutinized and implicitly judged by a young child who stands simultaneously as an outsider kept apart from their lives and as someone inadvertently exposed to the rhythm of their daily affairs. And both stories show a fascination with the way loneliness and alienation develop within Irish society, be it urban or rural. At the same time, O'Brien softens the picture, making the world of the Connor girls considerably less harsh than that inhabited by Father Flynn and his sisters. In fact, she presents the story with humorous touches—evident in the villagers' grudging awe of the Connor girls and in the superciliousness of the narrator's husband—that mute the tragic overtones so insistent in Joyce's tale.

Further, "The Connor Girls" shows an emphatic shift in perspective from that of "The Sisters," highlighting O'Brien's achievement in revivifying a topic so common in Irish literature. Father Flynn's sisters—Nannie and Eliza—occupy positions in the discourse so peripheral as to raise questions about the ironic nature of the story's title. Miss Amy and Miss Lucy, on the other hand, stand at the center of the narrative and thus of the social commentary made by the story. In tracing the course of Miss Amy's blighted loves, O'Brien conveys cynical and sentimental views of the lives of Irish women without privileging either, and readers see the pathos and the bathos of this rural society without feeling pushed toward reverence or condescension.

"The Sisters" takes a very different approach, with the title characters highlighting the reader's exposition of the complex personality of their dead brother. For example, at the end of Joyce's story, Eliza explains, as definitively as she can, her brother's degenerative condition: "Wide-awake and laughing-like to himself. . . . So then, of course, when they saw that, that made them think that there was something gone wrong with him." (18). These observations, made by an uneducated woman who nonetheless deeply loved her brother, offer the reader a sense of a parochial society's judgment of the behavior of one of its highly sensitive, though deeply troubled, members. A certain defensive regard for communal norms gives a brittleness to Eliza's response to Father Flynn's aberrance, yet one would be mistaken to ignore the deep concern also imbedded in her remarks. Indeed, Eliza's fragmented comprehension captures the tragic features of the story, and we are obligated to fit Father Flynn's actions into our own interpretation.

In the final lines of "The Connor Girls," quoted above, the story's unnamed narrator provides a more ambivalent impression. Her husband's condescension (unknowingly mimicking the earlier behavior of Miss Amy and Miss Lucy) has invited readers to make amused comparisons with those foolish young women. Now, however, terms like "exiles" and "alone" give the conclusion a poignancy similar to that evoked by the final lines of "The Sisters." At the same time, a discordant contrast arises between this trivial encounter and the narrator's articulation of such a profound sense of loss. It underscores the hyperbole punctuating all of her impressions and suggests a self-dramatization of the inevitable distancing that comes from growing up and older.

In this context, judging Joyce's story as more profound than O'Brien's has little significance. Instead, the unwillingness of both writers to gloss their characters' lives with glib moral pronouncements comes through as pivotal. In "The Sisters," the seriousness of the occasion, the priest's wake, overlays with dignity and complexity the embarrassment felt by Father Flynn's sisters over his behavior before he died. In "The Connor Girls," the youthful foolishness of Miss Amy and Miss Lucy—replicated at the end of the story by the intolerant fatuousness of the narrator's husband—enforces a tolerant but knowing view of human behavior that makes the final lines of the story less chilling and not so ominous. The ambivalence that both refuse to relinquish reflects a profound respect for their central characters and all who inhabit the worlds that they have evoked.

O'Brien's "Irish Revel" tells of Mary, a young country woman who has gone to a party in the local village on a cold November evening with the groundless notion of meeting again an English painter who had briefly stayed in the village two years previously. From the opening lines, the story contrasts Mary's romanticism with hints of her exploitation: "The invitation had come only that morning from Mrs. Rodgers of the Commercial Hotel. The postman brought word that Mrs. Rodgers wanted her down that evening, without fail" (177). At the Commercial Hotel, Mary not only finds no trace of the English painter but, to her shock, also realizes that Mrs. Rodgers expects a great deal of help preparing for the party: "Now, first thing we have to do is to get the parlor upstairs straightened out" (181).

The narrative continues with alternating descriptions of the preparations for the party and Mary's recollections of John Roland, the painter, unself-consciously ironic because of their ingenuous tone. Shortly after leaving the village, for example, Roland had sent "a black-and-white drawing of her": "[Her family] hung it on a nail in the kitchen for a while, and then one day it fell down and someone (probably her mother) used it to sweep dust onto; ever since it was used for that purpose. Mary had wanted to keep it, to put it away in a trunk, but she was ashamed to. They were hard people, and it was only when someone died that they could give in to sentiments or crying" (185). As the night goes on, Mary reaches an increasingly clear sense of the occasion—"She . . . thought to herself what a rough and ready party it was" (190)—so that the drunken belligerence and aggressive sexuality at the end of the evening seem to her merely anticlimactic. The story concludes as Mary approaches her family's home: "Walking again, she wondered if and what she would tell her mother and her brothers about it, and if all parties were as bad. She was at the top of the hill now, and could see her own house, like a little white box at the end of the world, waiting to receive her" (198).

"Irish Revel" shows the same general concern with ritual, celebration, sexual frustration, and social alienation that one finds in "The Dead," but two other pieces in *Dubliners* illuminate equally significant if less obvious issues examined in O'Brien's story: versions of youthful expectations and awkwardness comparable to those in "Araby" and in "After the Race." Like the central characters of those stories, Mary finds herself caught up by fanciful illusions that she would disdain in others but that, in the context in which they occur, exert a powerful influence over her. O'Brien also picks up a theme that appears in "Clay," Joyce's tale of a party that takes place on Hallow's Eve. There, Maria, though older than her namesake in "Irish Revel," seems driven by a similar mixture of independence and naiveté. In each of these accounts, an individual struggles to sustain a carefully cultivated and generally naive view of the world while uneasily and ultimately unsuccessfully holding at bay its quotidian realities.

Whether these fantasies induce vulnerability or imperviousness remains open to interpretation, for in each story the reader occupies the privileged vantage point. Our distance allows discernment of the illusions conditioning the way the central characters perceive events in the worlds they inhabit, but the narratives of Joyce and O'Brien's stories deflect pessimistic responses and circumvent a single predictable reading. Humor forestalls the inevitability of a bleak assessment of events and inculcates into the discourses the potential for a range of equally valid alternate responses.

Such multiplicity may not seem immediately evident. The final lines of "Araby," for example, appear to give little doubt as to the unavoidable pain that sentimental idealism produces: "Gazing up into the darkness I saw myself as a creature driven and derided by vanity; and my eyes burned with anguish and anger" (35). Similarly, Jimmy Doyle's final thoughts in "After the Race" seem an unambiguous acknowledgment of the cost of naiveté: "He knew that he would regret in the morning but at present he was glad of the rest, glad of the dark stupor that would cover up his folly. He leaned his elbows on the table and rested his head between his hands, counting the beats of his temples" (48). Nonetheless, while the consequences of the actions described in these stories remain clear, their impact upon the protagonists does not evince the same certitude.

The sardonic tone and muted self-deprecation of the final lines of "Araby" in fact reflect the mature thoughts of an experienced adult looking back from a much more secure emotional position upon a childhood incident. This retrospection affirms an immediate poignancy while diminishing its significance over the long term. Likewise, Jimmy's ambivalent mixture of incipient guilt and pleasure conveys images of a young man both shamed and protected: able to make mistakes, to take cognizance of their consequences, and yet to escape any permanent effect.

Similarly, Mary's thoughts at the end of "Irish Revel" project both new realizations and continuing security. The loutish behavior of the men and women at the party, though initially shocking, has taken away their power to hurt or menace Mary in any but the most trivial ways. The narrative's gentle parody of Mary's temperament has humanized her, but, like Joyce before her, O'Brien effectively uses humor to forestall the simple-minded conjunction of naiveté with weakness or stupidity. Instead, she can gently lampoon Mary's sentimentality while broadly ridiculing the fatuousness of the putatively more sophisticated villagers.

"A Scandalous Woman," set in an unidentified portion of rural Ireland, ostensibly follows a conventional plot line, recounting the friendship between two young girls, Eily Hogan and the story's unnamed narrator. Eily becomes infatuated with a young bank clerk, and the narrator helps her devise ways to "walk out" with him unbeknownst to Eily's family. Eventually—perhaps inevitably—Eily becomes pregnant, the couple is forced to marry, and Eily and her husband leave the village. Later, the narrator hears rumors of Eily's declining mental health, and when, after four years, Eily returns to the village for the Christmas holidays, she seems preoccupied and distant. In a clever false ending, the narrator and her mother subsequently see a madwoman on a city street who might be Eily. The close of the story overturns such a possibility, however, when the narrator, now married, visits a shop owned by Eily and her husband. There Eily appears as the cunning merchant, now having little in common with the narrator: "To revive a dead friendship is almost always a risk, and we both knew it but tried to be polite" (264).

Like Joyce's "Eveline," O'Brien's story plays out themes of claustrophobia and rebellion in the tight-knit society of an Irish household. As with "Eveline," attention oscillates between the sentimental romanticism of a young girl's daydreams and the starker reality of the consequences of pursuing those dreams. The striking difference, however, between Joyce's treatment of these issues and O'Brien's lies in the skeptical perspective that the latter invites her readers to assume.

For Joyce and for his readers, Eveline's condition remains grave and even tragic. Her indecision about leaving home takes form through an interior monologue that emphasizes how seriously she considers her proposed elopement and, at the same time, confronts readers with her profoundly naive view of the world: "Now she was going to go away like the others, to leave her home. . . . Perhaps she would never see again those familiar objects from which she had never dreamed of being divided. . . . She had consented to go away, to leave her home. Was that wise? . . . What would they say of her in the Stores when they found out that she had run away with a fellow?" (37). Perceptions of Eily, on the other hand, evolve quite differently through the mediating vision of the narrator, which unconsciously depicts the nature of the narrator as much as the nature of Eily.

From the start of the story, the narrator advances her claim to having a privileged perspective of Eily: "Hers was the face of a madonna. She had brown hair, a great crop of it, fair skin, and eyes that were as big and as soft and as transparent as ripe gooseberries. She was always a little out of breath and gasped when one approached, then embraced and said, "Darling." That was when we met in secret. In front of her parents and others she was somewhat stubborn and withdrawn, and there was a story that when young she always lived under the table to escape her father's thrashings" (239). The final sentence says a great deal more than the narrator intended about the girls' relationship. It conveys a sense of the duality of Eily's nature, but it also insinuates the idea that much of what the narrator learns about Eily comes from hearsay. (One can also see in these lines dual Joycean resonances: the image of the child under the table evokes both the riveting scene of the second page of *A Portrait of the Artist as a Young Man* and the increasing brutality of Eveline's father.)

In fact, despite the putative closeness of the two girls, the narrator seems to know little of what Eily actually thinks. That distance and the distorting medium of second-hand information lead the highly imaginative narrator to presume the worst: "Eily began to grow odd, began talking to herself, and then her lovely hair began to fall out in clumps. I would hear her mother tell my mother these things. The news came in snatches, first from a family who had gone up there to rent grazing, and then from a private nurse who had to give Eily pills and potions. Eily's own letters were disconnected and she asked about dead people or people she'd hardly known" (262). Though apparently straightforward, the above description relies more on the observations of others than on any personal insight, and the last sentence leaves ambiguous whether the letters to which the narrator refers come to her or to Eily's family. (Also, the hearsay motif links this gesture with Old Cotter's vaguely articulated insinuations about Father Flynn in "The Sisters.") In any case, in the closing pages of the story, we find evidence of what sort of life may have waited for Joyce's Eveline had she gotten on the boat to Buenos Aires with Frank. Significantly, however, Eily refuses to sustain the part.

Joyce's story ends with Eveline paralyzed with fear, apparently (though not certainly) unable to sever her ties to Dublin society and to board the soon to be departing ship with Frank: "[Frank] rushed beyond the barrier and called to her to follow. He was shouted at to go on but he still called to her. She set her white face to him, passive, like a helpless animal. Her eyes gave him no sign of love or farewell or recognition" (41). Terror holds Eveline in a form of catatonic mania. Analogously, the narrator of "A Scandalous Woman"—as if recalling Eveline's story and applying it to her friend—mistakenly imagines Eily trapped by fear and derangement in an environment that she lacks the courage to escape. These assumptions produce the false ending alluded to above: "I was pregnant, and walking up a street in a city with my own mother, under not very happy circumstances, when we saw this wild creature coming toward us, talking and debating to herself" (262). Although her mother says "I think that was Eily" (263), the discourse never resolves the matter, and, reading that conjecture as certitude, it overlooks the highly subjective narrative perspective that conditions the story.[9] In fact, the eminently sane, if somewhat dowdy, Eily that the narrator visits in the final scene gives the lie to the image of the crazed figure driven mad by her society. More to the point, it gently mocks the unvoiced insularity of the narrator and her mother on several levels: they reflexively assume that any woman who had allowed herself to become pregnant before marriage must inevitably come to a bad end, and they shrink from analyzing the full impact of the less melodramatic, more prosaic lives led by Eily and themselves.

While the discourse never dispels the ambiguity surrounding Eily's mental condition, her relatively secure existence at the end of the story balances the potentially comic against the potentially tragic. The possibility for tragedy does not disappear altogether, however, for the story's ending foregrounds the narrator's undisciplined imaginative powers and the disparity that they create between her perceptions and the events that she perceives. Thus, by the final lines, one sees an overt depiction of the misery, anger, and confusion represented implicitly at the close of "Eveline": "[Eily] kissed me and put a little holy water on my forehead, delving it in deeply, as if I were dough. They waved to us, and my son could not return those waves, encumbered as he was with the various presents that both the children and Eily had showered on him. It was beginning to spot with rain, and what with that and the holy water and the red rowan tree bright and instinct with life, I thought that ours indeed was a land of shame, a land of murder, and a land of strange, throttled, sacrificial women" (265).

However one interprets the final sentence of the paragraph, its meaning clearly does not derive logically from those immediately preceding it. In fact, it seems more likely that the narrator's bitter condemnation of Ireland's treatment of women comes out of her own experience and attitudes than from an assessment of Eily's condition. That, of course, does not in itself diminish its accuracy, but it shifts interpretive emphasis. In a deft insinuation of the role of literary antecedents that the narrator evokes—at least for readers familiar with Joyce—the experiences of Eveline offer a way of comprehending both Eily and herself, giving an added dimension to our sense of the precise identity of "A Scandalous Woman."

"The Small-Town Lovers," like other O'Brien short stories, stands ostensibly as a straightforward account of pedestrian events in rural Ireland, and again, as in the other stories, one gets a much sharper sense of the interpretive potential of "The Small-Town Lovers" by setting it against the creative expectations established by stories like "The Dead." "The Small-Town Lovers," narrated by another of O'Brien's unnamed young girls, traces events surrounding the marriage of the title characters—Hilda and Jack Donnelly. The opening paragraphs make a great deal of their demonstrative affection and public concern for one another. As the story progresses, however, one gets a sense of the isolation and loneliness characterizing their lives. When Hilda dies under mysterious circumstances, Jack's unconcern at the funeral suggests how little he actually cared for his wife. In the final pages the narrator recounts Jack's decline into drunken seclusion, and she closes with a description of his ineffectual efforts at seduction. In her final thoughts, the narrator sums up her lasting impression of Jack and unconsciously offers an overview of the couple's life together: "I still believe he killed her, just as I believe it was clear what he wanted from me that dewy morning, but not being certain of these things, I told no one; yet as the years go by, the certainty of them plagues me. Indeed, it has become a ghost, and the trouble with ghosts is that no one but oneself knows how zealously they stalk the everyday air" (353).

More directly than any of the three stories already considered, "The Small-Town Lovers" confronts concepts of love, both as characters manifest it and as they feel it. Thus, the stark difference between the behavior of Jack and Hilda when walking through town and when in their home gives an aura of hypocrisy to everything they do. At the same time, their lack of introspection raises interesting questions about their level of self-awareness. Finally, the shocking degeneration of Jack after the death of Hilda suggests a dependence upon her for a civilizing, humanizing influence of which even he did not seem aware.

The narrator's distance from the principal characters and her often inaccurate assessment of the events that she observes signal an irony informing the story that invites pluralistic readings of the events: a number of comic interludes playing upon the foibles of country folk punctuate the narrative and, to a degree, stereotype rural life. At the same time, a series of poignant interchanges—like the growing friendship of Hilda for the narrator's mother, and the children's visit to the Donnelly house for tea—forestall reductive conclusions about forces motivating characters.

Joyce's version of enduring love, depicted in "The Dead," also takes up the issue of how one holds in equilibrium physical desire and emotional commitment. In "The Dead"—in contrast to "The Small-Town Lovers"—it is the urbanity of Gabriel Conroy that works against him. He finds that his love for his wife Gretta cannot match the feeling once expressed by the young Michael Furey, and the final paragraph underscores the significance of this epiphany as it gradually reveals the full effect of Michael Furey's fatal gesture upon Gabriel's consciousness:

Yes, the newspapers were right: snow was general all over Ireland. It was falling on every part of the dark central plain, on the treeless hills, falling softly upon the Bog of Allen and, farther westward, softly falling into the dark mutinous Shannon waves. It was falling, too, upon every part of the lonely churchyard on the hill where Michael Furey lay buried. It lay thickly drifted on the crooked crosses and headstones, on the spears of the little gate, on the barren thorns. [Gabriel's] soul swooned slowly as he heard the snow falling faintly through the universe and faintly falling, like the descent of their last end, upon all the living and the dead. (223–24)

One comes away from Joyce's story with no prescription for interpretation but rather with an assurance of the poignancy of its closing lines. Just as "The Dead" moves from the cynicism of previous stories in *Dubliners*, "The Small-Town Lovers" takes a tone strikingly different from other O'Brien stories considered here. For once, ambiguity does not potentially mitigate pain. Instead, a bitter, rural coda to "The Dead" rebuts Gretta's romantic visions by emphasizing the odious behavior of Jack Donnelly when last seen by the narrator and by revealing the starkness informing the lives of Hilda and Jack.

As I note in my introductory remarks, the Irish comic tradition that I find so apparent and so appealing in all of the stories considered in this essay grows directly out of conventions laid down by social commentary from Swift's satires through Brendan Behan's diatribes. The biting tones and harsh assessments inherent in such views clearly remove them from lighter forms of humor, but they nonetheless reflect the particularly Irish literary inclination to integrate comedy (especially when tinged with elements of ridicule) into the most tragic of topics.

The O'Brien stories to which I have referred gain additional effectiveness from the links that the reader makes with Joyce. Unlike many contemporaneous male Irish writers, O'Brien does not view Joyce's literary legacy as a threat to her own creative efforts. While easy generalizations about male competitiveness—like Alan Alda's theory of "testosterone poisoning"—seem too reductive (and, admittedly, for a male critic, too embarrassing) to serve as an adequate explanation, no clear alternative emerges. At the beginning of this essay, I set O'Brien within the tradition of writers (implicitly male) from Swift to Behan. It may be more instructive, however, to place her in an analogous but separate context. In the narrowly defined, claustrophobic, and still predominantly male artistic society of modern Ireland (very much like the one that Joyce himself rejected when he left his country in 1904), O'Brien has the advantage of being so far outside the structure that she can acknowledge Joyce's achievements without the need for the pugnacious posturing characteristic of so many Irish male writers.

Instead, O'Brien draws inspiration from the model of Joyce's fiction, and she plays upon our expectations created by memories of his to infuse more humor into her own work by subtle contrasts with Joyce's. To say that she draws upon the Irish comic tradition to feminize Joycean themes would in and of itself trivialize the works of both writers. On the other hand, to use that idea as a point of departure for a more detailed examination of both writers acknowledges the interpretive multiplicity inherent in their respective stories.

NOTES

1. See, for example, Darcy O'Brien's "Edna O'Brien," and Peggy O'Brien's "The Silly and the Serious."

2. My emphasis is on the linguistic, not the political, sense of the term *Anglo-Irish*. Lyons, however, sees both senses as inseparable.

3. Frank O'Connor, "Is This A Dagger?" *Nation* 186 (1958): 170. Quoted in Mercier, *The Irish Comic Tradition*, 182.

4. For a commentary on this aspect of O'Brien's fiction, see Hargreaves's "Women's Consciousness."

5. One can, of course, find analogues between O'Brien's writings and Joyce's later works. Her short story "Over," for example, evokes the same sense of a powerful, complex female voice as does Molly Bloom's monologue at the close of *Ulysses*. Admittedly, O'Brien's narrator speaks in a more articulate and sophisticated voice (and thus, paradoxically, stands as a less demanding creation), but both figures, through an unbalanced mixture of cynicism and optimism, enforce for readers their multifarious sense of the conditions that delineate their lives.

6. See Edna O'Brien's analogous remark in *Night*: "Mirrors are not for seeing by, mirrors are for wondering at, and wondering into" (3).

7. Contextually as well as formally, O'Brien's work follows Joyce's creative trajectory. Although his idea never went beyond an initial proposal, Joyce once planned to write a series of stories set in the country and entitled *Provincials* as counterparts to the urban chronicles of *Dubliners* in a volume that surely would have resonated with O'Brien's writings of rural Ireland. Joyce's reference to such a project appears in a 12 July 1905 letter to his brother Stanislaus. Joyce, *Letters* 2:92.

8. For the sake of simplicity, citations from all of the stories under consideration here will be taken from *A Fanatic Heart*.

9. For contrasting views of Eily's mental condition, see Haule's "Tough Luck."

Works Cited

Hargreaves, Tamsin. "Women's Consciousness and Identity in Four Irish Women Novelists." In *Cultural Contexts and Literary Idioms in Contemporary Irish Literature,* edited by Michael Kenneally, 290–305. Totowa, N.J.: Barnes and Noble, 1988.

Haule, James M. "Tough Luck: The Unfortunate Birth of Edna O'Brien." *Colby Library Quarterly* 28 (1987): 216–24.

Joyce, James. *Dubliners: Text, Criticism and Notes.* Edited by Robert Scholes and A. Walton Litz. New York: Penguin Books, 1969.

———. *The Letters of James Joyce.* 2 vols. Edited by Richard Ellman and Stuart Gilbert. New York: Viking Press, 1957–66.

Lyons, F. S. L. *Culture and Anarchy in Ireland: 1890–1939.* Oxford: Clarendon Press, 1979.

Mercier, Vivian. *The Irish Comic Tradition.* Oxford: Clarendon Press, 1962.

O'Brien, Darcy. "Edna O'Brien: A Kind of Irish Childhood." In *Twentieth-Century Women Novelists,* edited by Thomas Staley, 179–90. Totowa, N.J.: Barnes and Noble, 1982.

O'Brien, Edna. *A Fanatic Heart: Selected Stories of Edna O'Brien.* New York: Farrar, Straus, Giroux, 1984.

———. *Night.* New York: Farrar, Straus, Giroux, 1987.

O'Brien, Peggy. "The Silly and the Serious: An Assessment of Edna O'Brien." *Massachusetts Review* 28 (Autumn 1987): 474–88.

8

History, Gender, and the Postcolonial Condition

Julia O'Faolain's Comic Rewriting of *Finnegans Wake*

Theresa O'Connor

The figure of the detective may be seen as an inevitable product not only of the nineteenth century's concern with criminal deviance, but also, more simply, of its pervasive historicism, its privileging of narrative explanation, accounting for what we are through the reconstruction of how we got that way.

PETER BROOKS, *Reading for the Plot*

Just as Jean Rhys sets out to rewrite *Jane Eyre* in *Wide Sargasso Sea*, Julia O'Faolain sets out to rewrite *Finnegans Wake* (hereafter FW) in *No Country for Young Men*. Rooted in a signifying structure of intertextual revision, O'Faolain's work is a comic double for Joyce's (hi)story of history. Both works are, on one level, inquiries into the sexual logics behind history; in both works the postcolonial nation is portrayed as a split consciousness, a dreamer suffering from traumatic amnesia. In both works, the quest to find the (w)hole truth, to uncover a past that has redemptive powers, is frustrated. Like the classic detective story, both of these works are built on the overlay of—to use Peter Brooks's phrase—"two temporal orders, the time of the crime . . . and the time of the inquest" (*Design*, 244). While the time of the inquest differs in each work, the time (and place) of the "crime" is exactly the same: the period between the 1916 Rising and the Irish Civil War (Pierce, "Politics," 246). A crucial difference between O'Faolain's work and the work it sets out to rewrite lies in the gender of the dreamer. Whereas Joyce presents a man as a model for the split psyche of history, O'Faolain uses a woman. The counterpart image of Joyce's fallen hero, Finnegan, in O'Faolain's work is Judith Clancy, a child/nun named after an Old Testament patriot, "the sacrificial Judith" (O'Faolain, *Young Men,* 258). Judith leads the most schizophrenic of existences: a "girl imprisoned in an aged body" (182), she exists in a fold in time. While one of her aspects inhabits the neoimperialistic Dublin of the 1970s, her other aspect inhabits Joyce's Dublin, a city where the Phoenix Park murders are still the subject of heated debate in the pubs. Straddling, as it were, the aporia or gap between the two sides of her story is James Duffy, a Californian detective/historian who bears the name of Joyce's Tristan *manque* in "A Painful Case." Duffy, a signifying monkey[1] of a sort, is the pivot on which O'Faolain's "book of Doublends" (FW 20.15–16) turns. As Robert Alter notes, "the double is a reflection or imitation, and often a covertly parodistic imitation that exposes hidden aspects of the original" (*Magic,* 23).

"THE BOOK OF DOUBLENDS JINED"

As Joyce himself points out, there are no characters in *Finnegans Wake:* its central consciousness, the dreaming mind of history, is "a family all to himself" (392.23–24). This dreamer envisages himself in a wide variety of guises, among them Freud's Wolf Man, a tombstone mason, and an envelope haunted by a buried letter. "Closer inspection of the *bordereau,*" we are informed, "would reveal a multiplicity of personalities inflicted on the . . . document" (107.23–25). These multiple personalities include Anna Livia (s/he coalesces with figures like Issy/Isolde and the Prankquean: Granuaile, or Grainne Ui Mhaille); the warring twins, Shem and Shaun; the four Elders, the authoritative custodians of history; and a detective/interpreter called, among other things, Sigerson (a pseudonym of Sherlock Holmes).

The principal actors in Joyce's dream-drama are all, in one form or another, present in O'Faolain's work. As I mentioned earlier, Judith plays the part of the haunted dreamer, and Duffy is cast as the detective who sets out to uncover her story. The chief Elders are Owen O'Malley, the patriarch of the O'Malley family and the founder of the Irish Free State, and his son Owen Roe, an IRA gunrunner. In O'Faolain's work, as in the *Wake,* history repeats itself. Just as the story of Joyce's dreamer is retold in the story of his warring sons (their struggle serves, on one level, as an analogue for the Hegelian dialectic), the story of Judith is retold in the story of her grandniece, Grainne O'Malley, a woman who bears the name of Joyce's Prankquean. In O'Faolain's work, as in the work of Joyce, Grainne is linked with the Brunonian theme of the coincidence of contraries. O'Faolain purloins not only Joyce's cast of characters but also the over-all rhythms of the murder/resurrection tale he created by fusing the plots of Sheridan Le Fanu's *The House by the Churchyard* and the Tristan and Isolde myth.

In the *Wake*, as Joyce explained to his friend Jolas, he was "trying to tell the story of this Chapelizod family in a new way" (Atherton, *Allusions*, 17). He first wove the Isolde theme into his writing in "A Painful Case." The Tristan figure here, as I noted earlier, is James Duffy, a resident of Chapelizod. Whereas O'Faolain's Duffy is infused with what Mikhail Bakhtin terms the "carnival spirit" (*Rabelais*, 4), Joyce's Duffy is a joyless creature, a timid, friendless man who is attracted to the nihilistic philosophy of Nietzsche. His story revolves around his relationship with Mrs. Sinico, a married woman he met at a concert in the Rotunda. When she offers him love, he rejects her. Years later, when he reads in a newspaper that she had committed suicide, he is horrified, not because she is dead, but because *he* had been associated with such a "fallen" woman.

Joyce takes up this theme of the betrayal of love again in *Exiles*, and again in *Ulysses* and *Finnegans Wake*. In the *Wake*, as Guy Davenport notes in his foreword to *James Joyce: The Critical Edition*, he rewrote "A Painful Case," combining it with Le Fanu's Chapelizod murder mystery. Davenport's comments warrant quoting at length:

> Joyce the imaginative reader had several points of entry into this tangled novel: its setting in Chapelizod (Isolde's chapel), the locale of *Finnegans Wake*. . . . But what Joyce focused on was a gruesome twist in the plot: a murder victim lingers on in a coma. If . . . the victim can be made conscious momentarily, [he] can be asked to name his murderer, and then can die. . . . Joyce saw in it an analogue of Finnegan coming alive at his wake. He saw in it his metaphysics of literature. . . . The writer is the irresponsible, virtuoso surgeon who can bring back the dead, momentarily. . . . The future cannot be born until the sins of the past are brought to the bar. (5–6)

O'Faolain's version of this tangled murder/resurrection story simultaneously inscribes and revises key tropes in Joyce's work. Her heroine, Judith, suffers from the kind of posttraumatic stress disorder most familiarly associated with veterans of Vietnam—men whose memories uncontrollably and suddenly reel back to encounters with enemy soldiers who had to be killed, men who struggled to convince themselves that theirs was a good and necessary war for humanity's future. Judith's story unfolds as a kind of Hamletic ghost story. Something happened during the civil war period, something that threatened the security of Judith's brother-in-law, the nationalist hero Owen O'Malley, so much that he had the seventeen-year-old Judith—as she puts it—"buried alive" (191) in a convent, informing her that if she ever tried to leave, he would have her committed to a lunatic asylum or jailed.

Like the *Wake*'s dreamer, the aged Judith is a creature of cracks and absences; she struggles endlessly to "track down [her] buried trauma" (O'Faolain, *Young Men*, 10). But her story differs from his in that her act of forgetting is totally involuntary. O'Faolain attributes Judith's condition not so much to repression and denial but to a series of shock treatments administered to her in the convent on Owen's instructions. Judith's comically painful attempts to exhume her buried past supply the book's initial comic situation. She gets "a fizzle" in her "extremities" whenever she watches "an axe or sword murder" on the television (10–11). An image of children playing with a dog evokes terrifying memories of her own dog, Bran: "Dog? Digging? That was it. A hole. . . . Judith was seventeen and the country in a perilous state. . . . She was seventy-five and wanted to see what happened next but the image had gone jumpy and her seventeen-year-old self pulled the dog from the hole. She was sweating. Both Judiths were clammy and terrified inside their clothes" (8–9).

The imagery here recalls the dog that disturbs Stephen Dedalus's train of thought as he walks along Sandymount Strand in *Ulysses*. This image links up with the image of the fox burying its grandmother in the "Proteus" episode of *Ulysses* (2.115). All of these images of encryptment/digging suggest a mind under severe repression. As if to underscore this point, a voice on the television warns Judith that she will be dead shortly and asks, "How can you make an act of perfect contrition if you're busy brushing your memories under the carpet?" (330). Even as one of her aspects tries to uncover her story, her other aspect would bury it. "It might be as well not to dig [memories] up? One can get nasty surprises. Not everything buried is treasure" (92), she observes. Judith's fear of the other encrypted within is shared by Owen Roe O'Malley, Owen's son. He knows that his demented aunt is—as one character puts it—"a live source for which any [revisionist] historian should be ready to give his eye teeth" (63). Just as the *Wake's* Elders bury the "bogey" that haunts the dreamer, Owen Roe would bury her story. Enter James Duffy.

"Sir Tristram . . . rearrived from North Armorica"

If the *Wake* opens—in medias res—with the rearrival of "Sir Tristram" from "North Armorica," O'Faolain's work begins with the arrival of James Duffy from Los Angeles. Duffy's official task in his "ancestral isle" (144) is to make a promotional film about "American intervention in the fight for Irish freedom" (39). His sponsor, Larry O'Toole—a man who bears the name of the *Wake's* masterbuilder, Laurence O'Toole or "larrons o'toolers"—wants a straightforward propaganda film to use in his fund-raising efforts on behalf of the IRA. "We don't give a goddamn about truth," he informs Duffy. "It does not set you free. It dissipates energies. Myths unify. They animate. . . . They don't want an ambiguous fucking message, right?" (320). Larry's father, a fanatic whose conversation ironically echoes that of the Anglophilic Mr. Deasy in *Ulysses*, has a very different notion about how Duffy's investigation should proceed: he wants him to investigate the suspicious death of Sparky Driscoll, a young American sent to Ireland in 1921 to report on the republican movement and trace missing funds meant to aid the nationalist cause. O'Toole is convinced that the nationalists who represented Sparky's death as part of "a last-ditch try by the old usurper [Britain] to strangle the new Free State at birth" were lying (7).

"Time pleated like a fan" (14), Duffy notes, appropriately enough, as his plane taxies down the runway at Dublin airport. Driving through "Molly Bloom's city" (14), he "imagined frugal lives of the sort portrayed in *Dubliners*. Repressed, genteel" (38). Whereas Joyce's Ur-Duffy is a disciple of Nietzsche, O'Faolain's Californian Duffy is, it seems, a Joycean. Readers familiar with Joyce's work will recognize the cast of characters here: bewildered characters in search of a spiritual center, an energizing force in their lives. The "old man in a macintosh" (328) who eavesdrops on conversations in O'Faolain's Dublin recalls the mysterious "Macintosh" who haunts *Ulysses*. The malicious gossip in the bar where Duffy meets Larry's friend Corny Kinlen echoes the gossip in Barney Kiernan's pub in "The Cyclops" episode of *Ulysses*. Here, as in Joyce's Dublin, women are underrepresented and harangued. Dubliners, Duffy notes, are "noisy like clever children: sly, devious in an obvious way, often parodying themselves and each other" (217).

What Duffy finds in O'Faolain's Dublin is precisely what Zack Bowen found in Joyce's Dublin: a "constant, ever-changing, comic chorus of trivia and comic debate all day long" (*Comic Novel*, 23). Drawing on the work of comic theorist Francis Cornford, Bowen compares this comic debate to the agon in Greek comedies: the duel of the adversaries "most frequently expressed by the opinions of a divided chorus, as in the choruses of men and women in *Lysistrata*" (22). He goes on to link Cornford's argument with Suzanne K. Langer's view of comedy as something that "celebrate[s] the bringing of life into balance." According to Langer, the conflict between men and women is "the greatest and perhaps sole subject of comedy because it is the most universal, human, civilized, primitive, and joyful challenge to our existence—self preservation and self-assertion, whose progress is the comic rhythm" (*Feeling*, 2). This comment is vitally important to my discussion here; it helps us to understand the relationship between gender, comedy, and *history* in both the *Wake* and O'Faolain's novel. At the center of both works is a Janus-faced historian who strives to introduce what Langer calls "the comic rhythm" into history: he sets out to dialogize the "official" historicist narrative by confronting it with that which it has buried: the voice of the female.

Like Joyce, O'Faolain frames her comic philosophy of history in a doubled mythic frame: the story of the journey toward "otherness" encoded in the Egyptian *Book of the Dead*, "the bog of the depths" (FW 516.25), and the seventh-century *Immram Brain* [The Voyage of Bran], the prototype for the story of the young Finn and later for the Grail myth. Duffy is cast here as at once a detective and a Grail knight: he searches for both meaning and mystery. His first act of chivalry in Dublin is to escort the drunken Michael O'Malley to his home—an Otherworld, of a sort. The O'Malley house reminds Duffy of "a house painted by Soutine, with verticals out of true, bruised shadows, surfaces fuzzy with the bloom of use" (105). He wonders if he is "Outside time?" (105). In *Immram Brain* the hero is guided to the Otherworld, a land of apples where time has no meaning and all the binary oppositions that govern conventional Western thinking collapse, by a visionary woman bearing an apple bough. The apple imagery that appears in almost all of the early voyage tales is a signifier of *jouissance*, of spiritual/sexual freedom.

What is at stake in these stories is precisely what is at stake in the Perceval tale and in contemporary works like Kafka's "Before the Law." Kafka's tale, as Cixous notes, revolves around a struggle between "presence and absence," between the "law which is absolute, verbal, invisible, negative" and the apple which, quite simply, is ("Fidelity," 16). The hero who moves beyond the "door" of the law and enters the realm of the "apple" gains access to a psychic realm that comes very close to the utopian ideal put forward by Derrida in "Choreographies." In that work Derrida envisages a world where "the relationship [to the other] would not be a-sexual, far from it, but would be sexual otherwise: beyond the binary difference that governs the decorum of all codes, beyond the opposition feminine/masculine, beyond homosexuality and heterosexuality which come to the same thing" (76).

What O'Faolain's questing knight/detective finds in the O'Malley home is no fairy-tale world "beyond binary difference" but a kind of wasteland inhabited by wounded women: Sister Judith, the reluctant bride of Christ who was finally expelled from her convent/prison by New Age nuns on the day of Duffy's arrival in Dublin, and Grainne, a woman who has just returned from her self-imposed exile in a home for battered wives. Grainne feels as "useless and used up like a ruff of an old blossom drying in the dimple of an apple" (57). The apple imagery here recalls the apple that lies rotting and forgotten in James Duffy's desk in "A Painful Case." It is as if, in casting Duffy—a eulogist, like Joyce and his early Celtic forefathers, of the physical—as the double of Joyce's repressed antihero, O'Faolain is giving him a second chance to move beyond the "door" of the law, to redeem the wasteland within. She is rewriting, once again, the narrative of the Irish nation.

"WILD OLD GRANNEWWAIL"

The story of Tristan and Isolde has its earliest roots in the story of Isis and the story of Diarmuid and Grainne—or, as Joyce puts it, "Dammad and Groany" (FW 291.24)—one of the central tales in the Matter of Ireland. Like the visionary woman who guides Bran to the Otherworld in *Immram Brain*, Grainne is an ambiguous figure, at once virginal and seductive, at once feminine and masculine: s/he is the expression of the spirit of her race. The legends in which s/he figures survived and were subsumed into the European versions of the Grail myth that emerged in the twelfth century: the *Tristan and Isolde* of the French poet Thomas and that of the German poet Gottfried von Strassburg. The mysticism of love is Strassburg's theme. In his work, the Otherworld is represented as a crystalline bed in a cave of lovers; for those who dwell there, life and death, sexuality and spirituality, self and other, are one.

In eighteenth-century Ireland, in the *Aisling* or dream-vision poems of the dispossessed bards, the visionary woman of the early Irish voyage tales, the spirit of Gaelic Ireland, appears once again. Disguised as Grainne Wael (Grainne O'Malley), Cathleen Ni Houlihan, or Dark Rosaleen, she comes to comfort the bards with prophecies of a Jacobite restoration. In the literature of the nineteenth and early twentieth century, she appears again, utterly transformed. In the work of Mangan and the young Yeats, Ireland is represented not as the dual-gendered spirit of poetry but as a feminine harbinger of blood sacrifice. "So many male Irish poets . . . have feminized the national and nationalized the feminine," Eavan Boland observes in *Object Lessons,* "that from time to time it has seemed there is no other option. But an Irish writer who turned away from such usages suggests that there was, in fact, another and more subversive choice" (144). Boland is referring to Joyce. In the opening passages of *Ulysses,* Ireland is represented in Francis Ledwidge's phrase as the poor old woman, but, as Boland rightly points out, "Joyce dazzles it with irony. By reference and inference, he shows himself to be intent on breaking the traditional association of Ireland with ideas of womanhood and tragic motherhood" (144). In the *Wake,* Joyce goes further; the spirit of the nation is at once a buried letter, an "aisling vision" (179.31), and a masculine/feminine ghost: the Prankquean, "wild old grannewwail" (22.11–12). The irony is palpable. This dual-gendered ghost, this "bog of the depths" (FW 516.25), pulls a "rosy one" (an apple) and guides the dreamer's split (male/female) selves to the "other" world, "Woeman's Land," where they are reunited with their opposites (21.15–16; 22.8). Framed in Bruno's (African) theory of the coincidence of contraries, the story of the Prankquean provides a paradigm for Joyce's revisionist theory of history. Her/his story supplies the key to the modus operandi not only of the *Wake* but of O'Faolain's work as well.

O'Faolain traces the lineaments of her revisionist Grail myth with ironic flatness. Grainne O'Malley, like Joyce's "grannewwail," exists "between worlds" (96); she struggles endlessly to assert her dual (masculine/feminine) nature, "to reamalgamate herself" (FW 575.27). She remembers a lost world where sexual identity was fluid: she "was reminded of being thirteen and in love with the principal boy in the Christmas panto, who, of course, was not a boy but a girl. . . . 'He' was a she, yet fought the wicked ogre with a convincing male flourish" (163). Bound up with the notion of a fluid gender identity, this carnivalesque pantomime motif runs like a red thread through the work of both Joyce and O'Faolain. Both Grainne's memory of the "panto" and, indeed, Judith's reference to her as "the Principal Girl" (201) recall Joyce's reference to Anna Livia as "A *princeable* girl" in the "panty*mammy's*" (FW 626.27–28; my emphasis). But like Anna Livia (and, indeed, Bloom), Grainne is forced to play a single-gendered role; she is forced to repress one part of herself. The forces of containment responsible for her split condition are not only colonialism and its aftermath but paternalistic society in general.

In the neoimperialistic Ireland of the 1970s, the lines between the genders are as rigid as battle lines in wartime. Here, woman occupies the position of the subaltern: "Men talked. Other men listened and what was said could decide a girl's future" (101). The ideology of combat, an ideology based on the opposition between self and other, Gael and Gall (foreigner), male and female shapes the cultural and social life of the country. Its architectural monuments are fortresses; its convents are governed by "guerilla-fighter[s]," nuns who saw themselves as "the shock troops of the Lord" (25). The apparatus of power set in place to control women extends from the Church, to the medical establishment, to the outlawed Irish Republican Army. The pathology of nationalism, its intense hatred of the flesh, is readily apparent in the misogyny of the IRA. Not only do they have "a romper room where they beat up women who slept with married IRA men and undermined their morals" (181), but they shoot "bullets through the kneecaps of their own men for sexual offenses" (235). In the new Irish Republic, "oddities"— women who fail to live up to the ideal of the pure, sexless woman—are marginalized or banished; England serves as a sort of underworld sewer for all the abortions, mental breakdowns, and battered wives it would repress. Duffy attributes the hypocrisy of the Irish to their colonial past: "British hypocrisy—which *they've* shed, by the way—got dumped here as part of their colonial cast-offs and you preen in their old cast-offs and think you've liberated yourselves" (229–30).

But O'Faolain does not offer the more liberal British system as an antidote for Ireland's repressive piety, nor, indeed, does she suggest that separatist feminism is a viable alternative to patriarchy. During the five months she spent working in England in the Halfway House for Battered Wives run by her friend Jane, a staunch feminist, Grainne found no healing vision; she found closed ideological viewpoints. The women, their humanity wounded, had retreated from life into a kind of silent hysteria. Casualties of marriages that conformed to the law of the battlefield, they "laughed at the drop of a hat" (61). On her return to Ireland, Grainne's quest for wholeness, her search for a love rooted in mutual respect between the genders, continues.

The two men in Grainne's life, Michael and Owen Roe, are in many ways mirror images of Jane: they view the opposite sex as the root of all evil. While this pair of misogynists undoubtedly owes much to the warring twins in the *Wake,* they also owe much to Yeats's two warring personae: the wild dreamer Michael Robartes and the worldly Owen Aherne, the public man who sets about the task of building a new Ireland. Together, Michael and Owen mirror the split psyche of the Irish nation. Like Yeats, Grainne wishes that she could combine the two men into one well-balanced individual. Michael, an ex–opera singer, personifies the mythic response to the very complex reality of postcolonial independence; he has, as it were, retreated from history into a kind of underworld: a dead-end job in the Dublin Heraldry Commission. Grainne finds that "if she didn't manipulate [him] he flopped like one of those life-size Japanese puppets which have to be held up by black-clothed puppeteers" (84). She is attracted to Owen Roe's vitality, yet she rejects his pragmatism. She still searches for "a knight who could deliver her from the dragon of her lower nature" (165).

Like a deus ex machina, James Duffy appears in her home in the early dawn hours. Not long after meeting Grainne, he finds himself groping toward a new vision of life, "for some change in his way of being, such as old Celtic ladies had had a way of offering men who let themselves be lured on strange trips. In Celtic tales, it was the woman who rode by on a white horse and bade the man leap up behind her" (170–71). In the old Celtic voyage tales, the boon offered by the female is not instant physical intimacy—"a necessity," according to Duffy, "in a town like Los Angeles" (175)—but a new way of being, a new concept of identity in which the opposition between man and woman is dissolved. This Grail is offered only to the hero who proves himself worthy. If Duffy, a man who compares himself to Yeats—the poet who had, as he puts it, "managed to get a remarkable high out of his failures with women" (144)—is to redeem the wasteland and heal the wound of history, he must resurrect the other in the self. He must deconstruct hierarchies of identity based on the opposition between masculinity and femininity. Duffy's self-begetting—a begetting that is mirrored in his efforts to exhume Judith's buried memory—is met with stringent opposition by the censoring Elders.

The struggle of O'Faolain's Tristan and Isolde, Duffy and Grainne, to escape from the forces of Owen Roe mirrors at once the struggle of Diarmuid and Grainne in the Fenian cycle of Celtic myth to escape from the army of the aged Finn and the struggle of the lovers/the Prankquean/ buried letter to evade the censoring forces of the Elders in the *Wake*. Joyce's authoritative historians censor Ireland's "gynecollege histories," recasting the Matter of Ireland as the "matther of Erryn" (FW 389.6): stories of feminine erring and "whorship" (FW 547.28). As Adaline Glasheen points out, these four cantankerous old men (who are modeled on the spies that report to Mark of Cornwall in Bedier's version of the Tristan and Isolde story) "make a good equivalent for the impotent, dithering historian in quest of truth" (*Census*, 97). "By their peevish, lunatic flux of memory," she notes, they "shrink historical discipline into something monstrous, small, creeping. We have seen them as judges, censors, law-givers, as Repression. . . . The Four are the voyeur, the poisoned imagination of *Finnegans Wake*" (lvi).

Glasheen might have been describing the Elders in O'Faolain's work. Like Joyce's "arid annalists," Owen, the young Judith, Owen Roe, and his lackey Patsy are obsessed with sexual sin. Their version of history is, to use Joyce's phrase, a tale of "woman squelch" (FW 392.36); it revolves around the question of "Has he hegemony and shall she submit" (FW 573.32). In their view, Ireland's Grail maiden is a wholly physical being, as Joyce puts it, a "strapping modern old ancient Irish prisscess" with "nothing under her hat but red hair and solid ivory" and a "firstclass pair of 'bedroom eyes'" (FW 396.7–11). For all of them, the love-death of Grainne/Isolde and her "sexfutter" is "palpably wrong and bulbubly improper" (FW 384.28–29).

The burial mound over which the Elders preside in the *Wake* is described as the "sound seemetery which iz leebez luv" (FW 17.35–36). The reference here is to the Wagnerian *Liebestod*. Although the young Joyce who wrote "Drama and Life" admired Wagner's work, in particular his use of Celtic mythic themes, the more mature Joyce seems to have viewed Wagner's treatment of these themes as contemptible. Sexual sin, as Jacques Barzun points out, is a major concern of Wagner's in successive legends from *Tannhäuser* and *Lohengrin* to *Tristan*, the *Ring*, and *Parsifal*. In Wagner's *Tristan*, he states, the love-death is "spiritually a narcotic, scenically a verbose rendezvous, and musically a sexual encounter" (*Darwin*, 236). Anything more remote from the ideal of mystical love portrayed in the old Celtic legends would be hard to imagine.

If Joyce links the *Wake*'s Elders with Wagner he also links them with Yeats (an avid Wagnerian). The Dublin they preside over "recalls Byzantium" (FW 294.27). The reference here is to Yeats's "Sailing to Byzantium" (1926), a poem in which the poet laments the fact that Ireland, a country teeming with young life, is "no country for old men." It is likely that Joyce saw Yeats's poem, a voyage tale of a sort, as a betrayal of the worldview of Gaelic Ireland. Whereas the old Irish voyage tales are a celebration of man's life in time, reflecting Gaelic culture's joyous acceptance of life and death, the speaker in Yeats's poem would control the forces of life, would conquer death. O'Faolain's *No Country for Young Men*, as its title implies, also recalls Yeats's poem. Indeed, what we find in this work is precisely what we find in the work of Joyce: a dark parody of the young Yeats's repressive "country for old men." Let us consider now the Viconian historicist narrative in which the (hi)story of the Elders is framed in O'Faolain's work.

"They were the big four"

Like Joyce, O'Faolain uses the theory of history propounded by Vico in his *Scienza Nuova* (1744) as a kind of scaffolding for her comic history of history. According to Vico, history moves through three ages: an age of gods, an age of heroes, and an age of men. The progression from one age to another, as Klaus Reichert points out, can be interpreted in many ways: "within the framework of the rises of the classes, it becomes military class, merchant class, ruling class of a democracy" ("Vico's Method," 49). In O'Faolain's novel, Owen and Judith belong to the first phase of history, Owen Roe and Patsy Flynn to the second. Grainne and James Duffy belong to the third age, an age whose characterizing institution is the funeral.

O'Faolain's portrait of Owen conforms closely with Vico's description of the first age of history as an age when man abandons the freedom of the wilderness and enters human society: Owen abandons the wilderness—a Jesuit seminary in the middle of a bog—joins the nationalist movement, and, in spite of the fact that "femininity repelled him" (190), he marries Judith's sister, Kathleen. Owen's vision of history accords closely with that of Eamon de Valera, the politician Joyce links with Shaun in the *Wake*. "What distressed Joyce about de Valera," David Pierce notes, "was his moral uprightness, his dogmatic insistence on a formula of words, his narrow view of Ireland, and his willingness to plunge his country into civil war" ("Politics," 246). Owen's and, indeed, de Valera's metaphysics of nationalism is well illustrated in the extracts from the political speeches of Padraig Pearse (the Sinn Fein leader who fought with de Valera in the Easter Week Rising of 1916) quoted in O'Faolain's work: "One man can free a people," wrote Pearse, "as one Man redeemed the world. . . . I will go into battle with bare hands. I will stand before the *Gall* as Christ hung before men on the tree" (66; my emphasis). The speaker goes on to note that Pearse, the great champion of the Gael, was, in fact, the son of a "Gall": his father was an English funeral monument maker. The imagery here recalls the Gael/Gall (self/other) imagery that reverberates throughout the *Wake*. If it is the first principle of de Valera's brand of Irish nationalism that there be an absolute, hierarchical distinction between Gael and Gall, it is the first principle of the works of Joyce and O'Faolain that this distinction be eroded: according to their comic gospel, life is—to use Joyce's phrase—"a gael galled by sheme of scorn Nock? Sangnifying nothing." (FW 515.07–8).

Like almost all the characters in O'Faolain's work, Owen has a double: the seventeen-year-old Judith. Socialized in a culture that values blood and brutality, a culture that demeans and represses any potential power in women, Judith, a die-hard republican, aligns herself with Owen's masculine ethical world of law, justice, and authority. Her response to a world in which the prototypical paradigm of the Other is the female is to cast the feminine in the self as other. In her convent school—as in Deasy's school in *Ulysses*—"History pupils were reminded that it was an Irishwoman's frail morals which led to the English first coming here in 1169. Women bore inherited guilt" (34). In spite of the efforts of her sister Kathleen, Judith's home "was male territory" (20). In her portrait of Kathleen, a member of *Cumann na mBan*, O'Faolain offers us a poignant image of an Ireland trapped in a masculinist cultural script. Kathleen is expected to bear children and bury the dead but not to intrude into the overwhelmingly male militaristic realm. According to one woman, these "girls [*Cumann na mBan*] is what gets the young fellas to take to the gun. . . . Throwing their comehither on more poor innocents. Vampires!" (129). Even her brother Seamus regards the idea of a woman warrior as comic. "It was a pity women weren't being armed," he jokes, noting Judith's skill with a bayonet. "It might calm them down to do a bit of real fighting" (81).

Like Owen, Judith represses her own sexuality: she "carefully kept herself from knowing about soppy things like love and courting" (232).

Sparky Driscoll, a Tristan figure who doubles with James Duffy, introduces her to a world of sensuality that she does not fully comprehend or care to comprehend. She sees him as a temptation "towards concupiscence" (332); when he kisses her "she felt as if a warm current of water or some unknown, insidious element had taken hold of her" (260). Her ideological commitment to Owen's absolutist vision and her rejection of Sparky's humane realism is at the emotional heart of O'Faolain's novel. While Owen speaks of submission to authority and the need for obedience, Sparky speaks of "self-assertion" and the need to think for oneself (332). In contrast to Owen's Hegelian view of history, his belief that might is right, Sparky believes that "the means justify the end" (140). Terrified of doubt, Judith rejects Sparky's vision; she holds fast to the sense of "purposefulness" Owen offered. In her old age, the young American is remembered only in haunted recall: she buries his story.

If the young Judith aligns herself with the Elders, the aged Sister Judith oscillates nervously between Owen's vision of history and the "other" world where her story (and the story of Sparky) is buried. As I noted earlier, there is a gap in her memory; she remembers very little about the Irish Civil War. The authoritative version of this period in Irish history is well known. The Rising scheduled for Easter Sunday, 23 April 1916, resulted in the execution of Pearse and fourteen other captured insurgent leaders (de Valera escaped execution because he was born in the United States). After the Anglo-Irish Treaty was signed in 1921, the country split into pro- and anti-treaty factions. In O'Faolain's work, Owen—a leader of the anti-treaty faction—turns against those moderates who support the treaty. He leads the country into civil war. Like de Valera, he manages to emerge from the war as a hero. Later on, at the head of a new political party, Fianna Fail, he enters the Dail, taking the oath of allegiance to the British Crown (the oath his anti-treaty party has so bitterly denounced). When Sister Judith discovers that he has betrayed the revolutionary ideals of Pearse for a comfortable nationalism, she denounces him as a Judas figure.

Although she rejects Owen's vision of history, for some reason she cannot free herself from his power. He sits placidly in the convent parlor eating "fairy cakes" while she pleads with him to set her free (194). "You look well," he tells Judith. "I'm going mad," she informs him (188). The reason for her internment is not discussed. Judith herself is not fully aware of why she is buried alive. Long after Owen's death and her release from her prison, she remains guilt-ridden, haunted by doubt; her dreams, like those of the *Wake*'s dreamer, are agonizingly painful.

She is terrified of the tape recorder used by Duffy and Grainne to record her story: "Clear, lucid memories beckoned and why should she resist them? Only she'd tell nothing to this pair. . . . Tricksters, shysters and offenders against the second commandment" (331). Because Judith censors her own story, it must be pieced together from the chance utterances that escape her internal censors: "'They said we were . . . No,' she corrected herself, 'they, *they* were fighting for a new Ireland. For the future. . . . There were to be no false distinctions. Oh, they had high hopes. In fifty years' time'" (140). Some incident that occurred early in 1922, something bound up with the distinction Judith makes between "we" and "*they*," proved so devastating that she was buried alive. Her fate mirrors that of the buried letter in the *Wake*.

"THE SEIM ANEW"

In the neoimperialist Ireland of the 1970s, the military class has given place to the merchant class, the mute language of symbol has given place to the heroic language of heraldry, and Owen Roe has taken the place of Owen as Ireland's chief Elder. A former government minister, he had been forced out of office for funneling funds to the Provisional IRA. He justifies his involvement with the terrorist organization by insisting that "access to power and privilege has always been won by violence." "The violence, later, has to be controlled," he adds, "in order to set up a new *status quo*" (162). Owen Roe fully expects to be "the conciliatory figure" who would "head up the new government" (162). Just as Judith was attracted by Owen's "purposefulness," Grainne finds in his son's supreme self-assurance "something antique and almost gone from the world." (160). Like his father, Owen Roe can accommodate no ambiguity; he "wanted the goodies and baddies as distinct as in a Kojak episode" (320). He too is repelled by femininity; he mocks Grainne, suggesting that her convent education has given her the notion that she has "the Holy Grail between [her] legs and that some knight is going to come and find it" (151). He warns her repeatedly to finish her affair with Duffy. Through his association with the Grateful Patriot's Youth Club—a recruiting ground for the IRA—Owen Roe influences a new generation of children, including Grainne's son, Cormac. Cormac "dreams of being a gunman" (236). People of her generation, he tells his mother, "make jokes because [they] never want to take sides on anything" (86).

Like his father, Owen Roe officially subscribes to good taste, political correctness, and fair play, all of which inhibit comedy's defiant spirit.

Through Patsy Flynn, his carnivalesque double, O'Faolain chronicles the ravages of his absolutism with ebullient joy. What is perhaps most amusing about Patsy is the fact that he takes himself very seriously: "The people I represent," he states, "have no time for humour" (221). Patriotism is mocked in his injunction to the teapot which has lost one of its legs to "Stand ye now for Erin's glory" (183). In her portrait of Patsy the would-be Celtic scholar, O'Faolain gives us Irish cultural nationalism as high comedy. There is irony in the fact that this fervent nationalist knows no Irish. It seems he tried to learn the language once but he abandoned his effort because the class was taught by a woman. Like Joyce, O'Faolain mocks the nationalist view that the Irish could exhume an ancient cultural identity that belonged to themselves alone. Although he insists that he knows no British verse, Patsy's mind—like the mind of the dreamer in the *Wake*—is saturated with snippets of poetry from the work of Shakespeare and Tennyson. He is under the impression that the line he quotes from Tennyson's "Charge of the Light Brigade"—"Ours not to reason why, Ours but to do and die" (185)—a line that reverberates throughout the *Wake*—is a "Christmas-cracker motto" (186). When he learns that he is quoting British verse, he is incredulous: "Sure they colonized our thoughts and minds," he says, "the buggers!" (186).

Patsy's reactions to sex are amongst the most mirth-producing episodes in the book. It seems he "had never touched a female" (265). His "knowledge of [sex] had been gleaned in farmyards and from watching stray dogs in alleys" (360). When a local policeman suggests that girls should be allowed to join the Grateful Patriot's Youth Club, Patsy is aghast: "To be ignored, denied, told to bring in *girls*. Trivialization, he thought. Sex. The threat to him was dark. He felt as though the laughter in the street were wiping him out" (266). His antagonism toward women is bound up with their proclivity, as he puts it, to "mix public and private" (365). Patsy is a hilariously funny petty dictator. Disguised in a scarf from Belvedere College (the Jesuit school Joyce attended) and a macintosh, he issues a dark warning to Duffy, "a foreigner, who may not realize the standards of morality we aim for in this country" (220). "The said parties," he states, "do not approve of adultery, consorting with married women or poking your nose into private concerns. . . . They're referring to your interest in the old nun and in the wedded wife. Leave the two alone and no harm will come to you. Is that clear?" (220).

Like the demented Elders who spy on Tristan and Isolde in the *Wake*,

Patsy takes it upon himself to spy on Duffy and Grainne. "What right had that gurrier above," he asks from his perch beneath Grainne's bedroom, "to intrude in other people's cunts or countries?" (361). Patsy, the self-described "Man in the Gap" (357), is the clown, the mimic father figure, who introduces folk carnival humor into the dour world of the "Elders" in O'Faolain's work. Yet he is not just a flat, two-dimensional figure. As he listens to the lovers, he realizes that "the [sexual] act . . . could be a way of escaping the mean limits of the self." He has a fleeting vision of another world where opposites dissolve, but this vision is quickly repressed (360). His "sickness," O'Faolain notes, "was of the soul" (360); it fed on other people's unhappiness. Love is something Patsy hates because it was denied to him; he had been rejected and brutalized as both a child and an adult. His tragicomic history mirrors that of Judith; both are scapegoats who bear the burden of the Father's sins; both are objects of curiosity, condescension, and cruel abuse; both are reduced to less than human status by those whose monolithic vision they so faithfully serve. Their very idealism makes them at once piteous and dangerous.

In her portraits of Owen, Owen Roe, Judith, and Patsy, O'Faolain offers us a vision of a world gone insane for lack of balance, a world that has lost its soul. The Elders would bury everything—laughter, love, compassion, sex—that might blur the rigid boundaries they have erected between the self and other. But there are cracks in their authoritative facade. Hybrid, carnivalesque forms surface everywhere in their petrified world. Indeed, the plot in which they figure is itself a hybrid form, built as it is on the work of Joyce. The bog, O'Faolain's chief metaphor for hybridity, is also purloined from Joyce's work. In the *Wake,* the bog (and its inverse mirror image, dog) is inextricably intertwined with the "bogey" that haunts the dreamer (34). This "bogey" is, on one level, a way of seeing: the kind of dialogic double vision that informs the *Immram Brain* and the Egyptian *Book of the Dead.*

On one occasion, the dreamer is informed that he is "about to be bagged in the bog again. Bugge" (FW 58.16–17). Elsewhere, a voice states, "big the dog the dig the bog the bagger the dugger" (186.20–21). Later on, in the phrase "Buy bran biscuits and you'll never say dog" (376.29), the dog is linked to Bran. This phrase can be read on a number of different levels simultaneously: it might refer to bran biscuits, to Bran, Finn's dog in the Fenian cycle of myth, or to Bran, the god/hero of *Immram Brain.* In between is the idea of God in nature and nature in God that permeates early Irish literature. Toward the end of the *Wake,* a voice asks that "that Boggey Godde, be airwaked" (560.14–15). The point Joyce seeks to establish is a philosophical one: he asks that the spirit of early Gaelic culture, a culture that has at its center the kind of dialogic or doubled worldview championed by Joyce's great hero, Giordano Bruno of Nola, be waked. In O'Faolain's novel, this "Boggey Godde" speaks, as it were, in the form of endless cross-references and ever-recurring parallels with Joyce's work. This doubled text, this hybrid narrative, is the subaltern "historian" that leads the reader to the "bogey" interred in nationalist history. As Grainne explains to Duffy, "the thing ricochets up. . . . the old bogey returns. You start to laugh and then, Jesus, the damn thing turns out to be real" (208).

"THAT BOGGEY GODDE, BE AIRWAKED"

Much of the comedy in the work of both Joyce and O'Faolain lies in the relentless way they expose the "bogey" at the heart of patriarchy and patriotism. In the work of both, this "bogey" is linked with the Devereux estate near Chapelizod in the Phoenix Park. Consider the story of Demi Devereux, the Anglo-Irish owner of the estate, and his—to use O'Faolain's term—"bum lover," Timmy (an IRA supporter). Devereux, we are told, "came of a rapacious breed who had themselves preyed on the natives, stolen the land in their time and so forth" (338). Timmy is his (Irish) mirror image. Timmy, it seems, willingly prostituted himself and several generations of the boys in his family in an attempt to gain control of the Devereux estate. What we have here is an allegory of the parasitic relationship between colonizer and colonized. In her portrait of these avaricious men, O'Faolain attacks once again the root cause of war: the construction of an Other, a "Gall," who bears no resemblance to oneself and who must be crushed.

O'Faolain mocks the notoriously homophobic IRA by linking them repeatedly with the *Sidhe* (fairies). Larry O'Toole compares the old IRA of the twenties to the "Tuatha De Danaan": "They wrapped themselves in a cloud and withdrew into the hills. Not a bad move: protoguerrilla tactics. Unfortunately, they never came out. They lost the key to reality and turned into fairies" (41). This association between terrorists and fairies is underscored again in the unseemly appetite of Owen, a founder of the Provisional IRA, for "fairy cakes" (194). Joyce uses the same metaphor to suggest the hesitancies and irresolution, the cracks, as it were, in the gender identity of the *Wake*'s dreamer: *Sidhe* (pronounced "she") haunt this Everyman. Words like "feyrieglenn" (553.22), "Shee, shee, shee!" (9.7), "buckshee" (52.21), "man Shee" (409.2), and "sheeshea" (92.31) punctuate his dreams. What we have here is a kind of intralingual joke. In the early Gaelic tradition in which the *Immram Brain* is rooted, the realm of the *Sidhe*, the Otherworld where gender differences collapse, is the realm of Brigid, the patroness of poetry. The *Sidhe* are, on at least one level, signifiers for the creative imagination. In English slang, the word *fairy* is used in a pejorative sense to represent the feminine man. Viewed from the perspective of the English language (and Freudian dream theory), the "man Shee" that haunts the *Wake*'s dreamer suggests some kind of repressed sexual desire. Viewed from the perspective of the Gaelic language and Gaelic culture, it suggests something very different: repressed creativity or spirituality.

In her hilarious portrait of Mucklea, the (decidedly phallic) "Victorian" fortress whose battlements Judith patrolled like a demented Hamlet for more than fifty years, O'Faolain takes aim once again at the sacred truths on which the Elders' power rests:

> It was run by nuns and housed in a sharp-angled, Gothic structure. . . . Topiaried trees and slices of lawn contrasted with the surrounding landscape which was a bog. . . . "Bog" was the Gaelic word for "soft" and this one had places into which a sheep or a man could be sucked without trace.
>
> The bog was pagan and the nuns saw in it an image of fallen nature. It signified mortality, they said, and the sadness of the flesh, for it had once been the hunting ground of pre-Christian warriors, a forest which had fallen, become fossilized and was now dug for fuel.
>
> Sometimes, in later life, Judith would say "my memory is a bog," referring as much to its power of suction as to its unfathomable layers. (12)

The point O'Faolain is making here, the notion that the "rock" of certainty, of truth, is rooted in indeterminacy, in the void, is precisely the same point Joyce makes in his comic rewriting of the gospel of St. John, "In the buginning is the woid" (FW 378.29), and in his mocking reference to the Hegelian concept of history as the coming to consciousness of the *Geist*: "In the beginning was the gest" (FW 468.5–6). Suspended, as it were, between fixity and stasis, between tree and stone, the bog—like the *Wake*'s Tristan (tree/stone)—is an image of the coincidence of opposites. The repressive Christian worldview in which this "Boggey Godde" of indeterminacy is framed in the passage quoted above is turned on its head in O'Faolain's portrayal of the love-death, the *Liebestod*, of

Duffy and Grainne. As representatives of what Vico calls the democratic age of men, they strive to overthrow the forces of repression, to retrieve all that the Elders had buried. Their quest for wholeness, their struggle to circumvent the sexual straitjacketing of neocolonial Ireland, is framed in the story of Bran.

In O'Faolain's version of the myth, it is Duffy who lures Grainne to the Otherworld. Like the loathly lady in the Celtic Grail myth, this "frog turned prince" (198) is transformed by love; he is also the instrument of Grainne's transformation. He sets out to teach her "the word from California": "Therapy teaches us to live with ourselves. Gym improves the God-given body. Love helps us to live with others. Now sex, combining all three, must be the healthiest activity" (226). Here, the Christian gospel of spiritual love is dialogized by Duffy's comic gospel of physicality. He protests when Grainne tries to keep their love hidden; he refuses to be treated like "a nineteenth-century whore" (228). "You divide yourself into the decent and the improper," he tells her, "Sex—me—kept out of sight" (228). Before she met Duffy, Grainne anesthetized her feelings, "taking communion under two species: brown bread and whiskey" (99). For her, the bread with its *boggy* texture is "the substance of Ireland" (99; my emphasis). Ultimately, Duffy becomes for her the regenerative equivalent of this bog/Eucharist: his "name became flesh in her mouth" (358). In *this* Duffy the "woid" is made flesh. The language the lovers use as they try to define the boundaries of their emotional and spiritual life and their potential for mystical experience is deeply concerned with the indeterminate, the unexpressed, and the inexpressible. In Duffy's view, their love belongs to a realm "outside time": "Like that Irish myth. The one about the timeless land, *Tir na n'óg*" (254–55).

In their struggle to translate this timeless world into the world of time, into history, to live irreducible difference *now,* they find themselves "clawing" after "the next to impossible" (360). Their struggle mirrors the struggle of the *Wake*'s dreamer to "introduce a notion of time . . . by punct! ingh oles in iSpace?" (124.3–12). We are reminded too of Judith's struggle to fill in the "hole" in her story. But whereas Grainne and Duffy view the realm "outside time" as a paradise, Judith views it as a hell; for her, the lost world of her youth—a "*Tir na n'óg*" of a sort—is a nightmare world inhabited by ogres. Like Joyce's dreamer, she would "never ask to see sight or light of this world or the other world or any either world, of Tyre nan-Og" (FW 91.24–25). In O'Faolain's work, as in the work of Joyce, the Otherworld is given a geographical location: the Devereux house in the Phoenix Park. The mind of Joyce's dreamer circles endlessly about the question of "What Gipsy Devereux vowed to Lylian and *why the elm and how the stone?*" (563.20–21; my emphasis). Judith too is haunted by shadowy memories of an encounter in the Devereux house. In an attempt to unravel the mystery, to exhume her story, Duffy and Grainne set out on a journey to the famous house in Chapelizod in the Phoenix Park.

"What Gipsy Devereux vowed to Lylian"

Judith hears the story of the May ball held in the deserted Devereux house just before the Civil War from her sister Kathleen. It seems Timmy hosted a ball in the house for his IRA cronies while the Devereux family was enjoying the London season. The *Cumann na mBan* transformed the ballroom of the house with yards of green bunting: for a brief time, they made of a war zone a kind of otherworldly garden. But the revelers were betrayed. Shortly after the fairy-tale ball began two lorry-loads of Black and Tan soldiers entered the ballroom shooting. As Judith puts it, "It was like a Last Judgement" (23). Judith's memories of her own story are less vivid. As she sits in Grainne's house, an aged sentinel gazing out at the river flowing by, jumbled memories come flooding back, guilty reconstructions that link her dog, Bran, with Sparky Driscoll: "Mindless as the red setter, the prancing Sparky could destroy her sister" (332). Sparky, it seems, had "a way of summoning the worst, most buried filth" (300). We are reminded again of the many images of encryptment in Joyce's work. We are reminded too of the god/hero of *Immram Brain*, the hero who sets out in quest of the mystical. Dark, funny, and frightful, the story of Judith's fall unfolds like a surreal horror story.

In the early months of 1922, the Irish-American organization that sponsored Sparky Driscoll's journey summon him home to America. They are curious about rumors of splits in the Sinn Fein movement. On the eve of his departure, he appears at Judith's home in search of Kathleen "all dressed up in a celluloid wing collar and ulster cape" (333). His Sherlockian costume recalls the Sherlock Holmes figure, Sigerson, who searches for the buried letter in the *Wake*. Before leaving Ireland, it seems, Sparky wants to take some photographs of the Devereux ballroom, the scene of the famous May ball. Since Kathleen is not available, he asks Judith to join him on his walk to the park. A storm is blowing up as they reach the gates of the house, so they take shelter in the gun room. The ballroom is barricaded.

As they wait for the storm to pass, Sparky tells Judith of his plan to help Kathleen escape from Owen. He tells her of Kathleen's fear that Owen "may be afraid that he really is like Timmy" (340). Judith's reaction to Sparky's tale is one of utter disbelief and denial: she links his story with the Christian story of the Fall. She feels that she understands for the first time the meaning of the "apple of knowledge" (300). Unaware of the fact that Judith sees herself as a soldier in Owen's revolutionary army, Sparky goes on to tell her that Owen is a fanatic who "must be stopped. He, Sparky, had no choice but to denounce him" (341). Her knowledge of war is all in her head, he tells her, as he hands her a bayonet from the wall.

Judith's response is instinctive. Like a robotic soldier, a puppet, she begins to go through the military drill that her brother Seamus laughingly taught her: she plunges the bayonet first into a feather cushion, and then as Sparky bends to examine the holes she had made, she plunges it through the pit of his stomach, pinning him like a butterfly to the green silk of the divan. Judith proves herself as able a warrior as her namesake, the biblical Judith who beheaded the Assyrian general Holofernes as he slept. As she sits in the darkness watching the goose down feathers from the torn cushion mingle with Sparky's blood, thunder rings out overhead (343).

Here, as in the work of Vico and Joyce, thunder signals the birth of a new age. The imagery here recalls not only Vico's philosophy of history but also Yeats's theory of history in "Leda and the Swan." In representing Judith as a Zeus-like warrior who impails a (feather-covered) lover, O'Faolain subverts the patriarchal representation of woman as passive victim and man as the violent conqueror who initiates historical change in Yeats's poem. In representing the aged Judith as a brainwashed prisoner, she makes us aware of the complicity between repressive sexual politics and nationalist politics. Because she is a female, Judith pays a terrible price for her act of equal-opportunity terrorism. Her action is viewed as heinous by the IRA not because it violates any moral law but because it violates the social order, an order based on the binary opposition between man and woman. Just as the story of the biblical Judith was considered apocryphal by Protestants and Jews, the story of Judith Clancy is regarded as apocryphal by the Irish nationalists and buried in the national memory, in (his)story.

Duffy shares Judith's fate: he never reaches the otherworldly ballroom in the Devereux estate. As he sits in his car on the canal bank opposite the O'Malley house waiting for Grainne to join him, Patsy

Flynn heaves the car into the canal and drowns him (366). The impotent rage that motivates this crime is shadowed forth in Patsy's reference to Duffy as "the Californicator" (363). The only witness to the tragic scene is Judith. Her story is presented as a kind of—to use Joyce's term—"funferal" (fun/funeral) tale (FW 111.15). "He's dead," she tells Owen Roe. "Killed. I saw it" (366). Under the impression that the old woman was at last going to reveal her buried secret, "Owen Roe got very excited" (366). When Judith tells him that the incident occurred "just now," Owen Roe dismisses her as "Bonkers!" "If Duffy got no more than that," he tells Grainne, "we needn't worry" (367). The irony is palpable.

"A LONE A LAST . . . A LONG THE RIVERRUN"

"That neither Yeats nor Fanon offers a prescription for undertaking the transition from direct force to a period *after* decolonization when a new political order achieves moral hegemony," Edward Said observes, "is part of the difficulty we live with today in Ireland, Asia, Africa, the Caribbean, Latin America and the Middle East" ("Nationalism," 22). But how to forge a new vision of history in which the voice of the subaltern is not silenced or buried? Postcolonial writers and theorists offer no easy answers to this question. In *Midnight's Children*, as Fawzia Afzal-Khan points out, Salman Rushdie "constantly refers to the 'pickling' or 'chutneyfication' of history as one of the processes whereby the painfulness of history can be transmuted into something else, making it bearable" (156). As Rushdie himself states, "*Melange*, hotch-potch, a bit of this and a bit of that is how *newness enters the world*" ("Pen," 482).

O'Faolain's work too is a celebration of hybridity. Indeed, Beckett's comment on the *Wake* might be applied to O'Faolain's work: "Here form *is* content, content *is* form. . . . His writing is not *about* something; *it is that something itself*" ("Dante," 14). How effective or desirable is this hybridity in the political arena? In the view of David Pierce, the political message outlined in *Wake* "amounts to very little." In comparison to the "insightfulness about war everywhere apparent in Brecht's *Mother Courage and Her Children* (1939)," he argues, "the discourse on peace in *Finnegans Wake*" is "too generalized and bland, too lacking in the necessary edge and focus, to ultimately challenge us" ("Politics," 251).

But this very lack of "edge," this resistance to binary classifications, *is* Joyce's political message: indeterminacy is his "Boggey Godde"/Grail, his "*pharmakon.*" Joyce offers a unique and highly efficacious solution to the problem of self-Other relations in the *Wake*. Drawing on the old Celtic voyage tales, he calls for nothing less than a reconstruction of consciousness: a change in the prevalent constructions of masculinity and femininity in Western culture (a construction that breeds combat between nations and lovers alike). The *Wake*'s most profound political message is found in its injunction to "let his be exasperated, letters be blowed! I is a femaline person. O, of provocative gender. U unisingular case" (251.30–32).

The political message in O'Faolain's work is encoded, as it were, in her dialogic encounter with the work of Joyce, one of the foremost male feminist writers of the twentieth century. O'Faolain's work is a "funferal" tale told by *two genders:* it is a comedy of shifting perspectives that demands of its readers a new double optic, a dual-gendered vision of history. There is no grand telos in O'Faolain's work; rather, there is a kind of cyclical order, a "comic rhythm," a Brunonian coincidence of opposites. Joyce's "Tobecontinued's tale" (626.18) ends with the return of Anna Livia to the paternal sea; O'Faolain's version of his story ends with the drowning of James Duffy in the maternal waters of the Liffey. We are left at the end of *No Country for Young Men* with an image of a new quester walking alone along the river bank. What we have here is an image of a nation in the process of reconstructing its identity. All that is required of the reader who would interpret her/history is a dialogic vision, "The doubleviewed seeds" (FW 296.01).

NOTE

1. See Henry Louis Gates, Jr., *The Signifying Monkey: A Theory of African-American Literary Criticism* (Oxford: Oxford University Press, 1988), 1–50.

WORKS CITED

Afzal-Khan, Fawzia. *Cultural Imperialism and the Indo-English Novel.* University Park: Pennsylvania State University Press, 1993.

Alter, Robert. *Partial Magic: The Novel as a Self-Conscious Genre.* Berkeley: University of California, 1975.

Atherton, James S. *The Books at the Wake: A Study of Literary Allusions in James Joyce's Finnegans Wake.* 1959. Reprint, Mamaroneck, N.Y.: Paul P. Appel, 1974.

Bakhtin, Mikhail. *Rabelais and His World.* Translated by Hélène Iswolsky. Cambridge, Mass.: MIT Press, 1968.

Barzun, Jacques. *Darwin, Marx, Wagner.* New York: Doubleday Anchor Books, 1985.

Beckett, Samuel. "Dante . . . Bruno . . . Vico . . . Joyce." In *Our Examination Round His Factification For Incamination of Work in Progress.* 1929. Reprint, London: Faber and Faber, 1961.

Bhabha, Homi K. "DissemiNation." In *Nation and Narration,* edited by Homi K. Bhabha. London: Routledge, 1990.

Boland, Eavan. *Object Lessons: The Life of the Woman and the Poet in Our Time.* Manchester: Carcanet Press, 1995.

Bowen, Zack. *Ulysses as a Comic Novel.* Syracuse, N.Y.: Syracuse University Press, 1989.

Brooks, Peter. *Reading For the Plot: Design and Intention in Narrative.* Cambridge: Harvard University Press, 1992.

Cixous, Hélène. "Extreme Fidelity." Translated by Ann Liddle and Susan Sellers. In *Writing Differences: Readings From the Seminars of Hélene Cixous,* edited by Susan Sellers. New York: St. Martin's Press, 1988.

Davenport, Guy. Foreword to *James Joyce: The Critical Edition,* edited by Ellsworth Mason and Richard Ellmann. New York: Viking Press, 1959.

Derrida, Jacques. "Choreographies." Interview by Christie V. McDonald. *Diacritics* 2 (1982): 12.

Glasheen, Adaline. *Third Census of Finnegans Wake.* Berkeley: University of California Press, 1977.

Joyce, James. *Finnegans Wake.* New York: Viking Press, 1939.

———. *Ulysses.* Edited by Hans Walter Gabler. New York: Garland Publishing, 1984.

Langer, Suzanne K. *Feeling and Form.* New York: Scribner's, 1953.

Meyer, Kuno, and Alfred Nutt. *The Voyage of Bran.* 2 vols. Grimm Library Series. London: Nutt, 1995–97.

O'Faolain, Julia. *No Country for Young Men.* New York: Carroll and Graf, 1980.

Pierce, David. "The Politics of *Finnegans Wake.*" In *Critical Essays on James Joyce's Finnegans Wake,* edited by Patrick A. McCarthy. New York: G. L. Hall; Canada: Maxwell Macmillan, 1992.

Reichert, Klaus. "Vico's Method and Its Relation to Joyce's." In *Finnegans Wake Fifty Years,* vol. 2, edited by Geert Lernout. European Joyce Studies. Amsterdam and Atlanta: Rodopi, 1990.

Rushdie, Salman. "A Pen Against the Sword." In *One World, Many Cultures,* edited by Stuart Hirschberg. New York: Macmillan, 1992.

Said, Edward. "Nationalism, Colonialism and Literature: Yeats and Decolonization." *Field Day Pamphlet* 15 (1988).

Lashings of the Mother Tongue
Nuala Ní Dhomhnaill's Anarchic Laughter

MARY O'CONNOR

Ach fogra do na	*But a warning to furriers.*
fionnadóiri;	*Let ye be careful.*
bígí curamach.	*This is no meek hare*
Ní haon giorra	*that you have here*
í seo agaibh	*but a red fox*
ach sionnach rua	*down from the mountain*
anuas ón gcnoc.	*I bite*
Bainim snap	*at the hand that feeds me.*
as láimh mo chothaithe.	

NUALA NÍ DHOMHNAILL, "THE FOX,"
TRANS. HARTNETT

It is no accident that the work of a woman writing in Gaelic in contemporary Irish society would manifest a radical comic vision. Doubly entitled to marginal status by her position as a woman and by her choice of a minority language, and this on the margin of a culture that has itself been dominated by colonial control into a forgetting of its own identity, Nuala Ní Dhomhnaill chooses one of the most effective options open to her to confront the forces keeping her submerged. The sheer vitality and iconoclastic humor of her poetry resists subjection by the dominant language and master narrative of the colonizers, questions the hegemony of the patriarchal powers, and deconstructs the very tradition on which is it based.

The subversive force of her poetry, challenging the prohibitions and restrictions of the patriarchy, may be usefully read in terms of the carnival. But where Mikhail Bakhtin, associating under the general heading of carnivalistic logic a number of "familiar contacts, mesalliances, disguises and mystifications, contrasting paired images, scandals, crownings/decrownings" (*Dostoevsky*, 137), sees carnival as celebrating a temporary liberation, Ní Dhomhnaill's lively employment of these same elements works for more permanent effect. Her language use, her celebration of the body, her masking and unmasking disrupt the imprisoning conventions not just for their temporary suspension but to model the actual struggle she and the women in her audience have faced. While carnivalesque play among the dominant class in a metropolitan or dominant society actually reaffirms and reinforces norms from which the participants are encouraged to take temporary respite,[1] Ní Dhomhnaill comes from a position of powerlessness to unsettle the powerful. Her poetry, founded on an older oral tradition, carries still that tradition's communal purposes: even while her readers are laughing, her poetry works toward the creation of a critical awareness in them that is the seedbed of change.

First, her choice of language. Ní Dhomhnaill is at the center of a contemporary flowering of Irish language poets that is often dated from the establishment of *Innti*, a broadsheet representing the new movement, in 1970. We must of course recognize that such movements do not spring forth without ancestry and recognize that the language, though commonly thought of as dying, has flickered on through the last hundred and fifty years of its decline, sometimes because of government interventions, sometimes in spite of them. Having been made a hurdle for high-schoolers, the Leaving Certificate examination in Irish, instead of acting as the practical spur to a nationwide revival of the language, became just another kind of oppression, and the policy caused thousands of children in each generation to hate the language and in effect to renounce Irish as part of their heritage. As Donal Flynn informs us, now that passing Irish is no longer compulsory, about one-third of the young people who finish their secondary education either do not take Irish or fail it, though the Irish language still occupies 21 percent of the curriculum in primary schools in the Republic ("Irish," 79). Grassroots efforts at language revival sometimes flourish, as in, for example, the prisons of Her Majesty's government and the Catholic ghettos of the North, and in the recent enthusiasm of small communities in both Northern Ireland and the Republic to establish Gaelic-language schools—more than 80 percent of the Gaelic language schools in operation in Ireland today have been founded within the past ten years. And other govenment policies support the language by economic bolstering of employment schemes, schools, and radio and TV broadcasts in the few remaining Gaeltacht areas, and, nationwide, by providing generous grants for publication of Irish prose and poetry.

Ní Dhomhnaill's entry into the ranks of poets thus enabled and recognized was far from being a straight path. The daughter of physicians who worked for many of their active years in England, Ní Dhomhnaill's first language was English; her fluency in Irish came from her childhood lodging and boarding-school holidays with her grandmother in a West Kerry Gaeltacht. This hybrid formation, which, as David Lloyd observes, is not merely the normal lot of the postcolonized but especially that of the postcolonized intellectual, was further complicated by Ní Dhomhnaill's marriage to a Turk, Dogan Leflef, and a chosen or inevitable exile in Turkey for eight years thereafter. Certain lines from her poem "Oriental Morning" seem to comment on this move: "I chose / the big loaf and my mother's curse, / not the small loaf and her love" (*Pharaoh's*, 83). The couple, with their four children, now live happily in Ireland, where Ní Dhomhnaill has published three collections of poetry in Irish and three selections in dual-language editions since 1981.

The mixture of backgrounds, societies, and languages has, in the long run, been useful for the poet. She has been enriched by the freedom to absorb outside influences, theoretical and creative: for example, as Proinsias Ó Drisceoil informs us, her often-quoted "We Are Damned, My Sisters" is based on a poem by Marina Tsvetayeva ("Irish," 8). She does not shy from talking about the contemporary world in this ancient tongue, incorporating the machines that run our lives, such as the car and the *dípfríos,* into the melodic lines of accentual, highly assonantal verse. Most important, she has been freed to make the choices she does: to cut through the iconic and stylized use of the folk tradition that supported a certain romanticized native identity and to reimagine and authenticate a wider range of roles for Irish women.

Ní Dhomhnaill's advocacy of her chosen language has been extremely effective in keeping the reality of a native language alive for the ordinary citizen, though her enthusiasm sometimes paints her into corners. While English is certainly a supple instrument of analysis and explanation, to imply as she does that it is more suitable for analysis than for poetry ("Filíocht," 175) is to ignore the glories of a far vaster body of work than one finds in all the Celtic languages together. I have reservations, too, about Ní Dhomhnaill's promotion of the Irish language as a specifically feminist tool, though it is not irrelevant that, as Seamus Deane writes in his introduction to *The Field Day Anthology of Irish Writing*, "it is in the two languages of Ireland that the history of power and powerlessness is most deeply inscribed" (6). Ní Dhomhnaill, however, plays with the phrase "mother tongue," advising women writers that the use of Irish will help them break out of the patriarchal mindset, from which English, "intellectualized out of experience," is impotent to free itself ("Filíocht," 168). As she tells Rebecca Wilson, "The Irish language wasn't . . . patriarchalized. And many things, including this idea of a deeper quality, this negative femininity, this Hag energy, which is so painful to mankind, hasn't been wiped from our consciousness, as it has in most cultures. Irish in the Irish context is the language of the Mothers, because everything that has been done to women has been done to Irish" (*Conversations*, 154).

Ní Dhomhnaill's postrational line of talk in interviews, insofar as it includes an anti-intellectual stance, is partly a pose: she is well versed in the works of Freud and Jung, reads broadly and analytically in American, European, and Middle Eastern literature, and stays au courant with the contemporary critical theorists, especially the French feminists. And it cannot be denied that no matter what leaps she takes in her explication of a philosophy, Ní Dhomhnaill has been consistent in thought and poetic action for the whole of her creative life. In her hands, Irish does become a feminist tool. She exemplifies, in her choices both of language and of subject matter, effective resistance to cultural and gender subjection. Her talk about it is an additional way of controlling and directing her work's effect on the reader.

A second act of resistance within Ní Dhomhnaill's poetic practice challenges the native patriarchal hold on the Irish language. It was natural for the cultural nationalists who took on the task of reviving the language to want to preserve it in its purest form. It followed, therefore, that writers in Irish, to be part of such an educational project, had a particular responsibility to write a noble and graceful and most comprehensible version of the language, uncorrupted by sloppy pronunciation and its attendant misspelling, by English loan words or syntax, by obscure local dialect usages. Words and phrases from English in Ní Dhomhnaill, such as *dípfríos* and *diet*, would have been anathema to the cultural nationalists, as evincing an adulteration not only of language and of syntax but even of culture: as when the speaker in "An Tonn" says "[tá] mo *nerves* ag cur go h-olc orm" [my nerves are bad]

(*Astrakhan*, 96), or when the hero Cúchulainn is made to say to his mother, "bain an *feaig* as do bhéal neoimint" [take the fag out of your mouth a minute], the standard Irish for cigarette being *toitín* (*Féar*, 91).

Less objectionable, but still not quite standard, are Ní Dhomhnaill's numerous dialect usages and spelling variations from Irish itself. Bakhtin's notion of polyphony within the carnival is exemplified in this contemporary practice: Ní Dhomhnaill's transgressive use of language springs from her knowledge of a living spoken language, which, because it is used in a relatively small and sheltered community, has developed its own character; and which indeed carries within it the effects of colonization and the consequent muddying of the linguistic waters. Ní Dhomhnaill places these extrusions of the living language very deliberately, and each instance of the natural polyphony brings a smile, a laugh, a shock of recognition, a feeling of at-homeness or discomfort depending on the reader's stance. In one poem's sedate and declamatory opening lines, we read "thangas i mo ríon álainn, mar *phósae phinc* ar chrann" [I came (to you) as a gorgeous queen, like a pink blossom on a tree] (*Selected*, 122). The bold, irreverent, and slightly tacky "pink posy," spelled and lenited as if it were Gaelic, pulls readers up short and delivers them (with a surprised laugh) from the distant world of myth into their own lives.

Language play has also been central to the Gaelic Irish comic tradition, a tradition in which Ní Dhomhnaill may be comfortably situated: she has a satirical eye and a keen sense of the absurd, and her mockery of people in high places and coopting of the grotesque and the fantastic into her comic vision, all expressed in the most lively and playful combination of glorious sound and vernacular argot, mark her as heir to and transmitter of the earliest (oral) comic tradition. We shall look at these qualities more closely in the section on rewritten myths.

Ní Dhomhnaill's decision to write openly and in the first-person singular about women's lives, women's struggles, women's sex drives, makes her more than Barra Ó Séaghdha's description of her as the "unofficial President to the Gaelic side of Irish culture" ("Review," 144); it makes her a catalyst for women's renewed understanding of their identity and meaning within the culture. Her freedom of expression with regard to the body has represented a liberating movement from suppression of body talk to its celebratory expression, a change in positioning from sexual object or even victim, to that of Chooser, Initiator, autonomous Subject-who-desires.

In the sheer exuberance of her bawdiest early poems there lies an open challenge to several taboos: as June Sochen recognizes, "bawdy women comics . . . [are] satirists, both self and social mockers of society's role expectations about women" ("Slapsticks," 154). Ní Dhomhnaill's heroines contravene the unspoken rule of silence about the body, a rule even more stringently enforced by their society with regard to women's own compelling drives. As in "Dúil" (Desire): "An fear / lena mhealbhóg / ag cur ocras orm; / a torthaí úra / fém shúile / ag tarrac súlach / óm' cheathrúna" [This man / with his pouch / makes me hungry; / his fresh fruits / under my eyes / drawing juice / from my thighs] (*Droighin*, 15).[2]

Even in the 1990s, a poem about enjoyed adultery, no matter how ironically cast, is unprecedented in Ireland. Here, for example, is the fifth verse of "An Bhean Mhídhílis" (The Unfaithful Wife) in the Paul Muldoon translation, which replicates effectively the rollicking, off-beat rhythms of the original:

> For his body was every bit as sweet
> as a garden after a shower
> and his skin was as sheer-delicate as my own—
> which is saying rather a lot—
> while the way he looked me straight in the eye
> as he took such great delight
> gave me a sense of power and the kind of insight
> I'd not had since I'd been married.
> (*Pharaoh's*, 107)

The poem is a subversive one. Though the man is the initiator and an old hand at the game—*cleachtaithe deaslámhach* (practiced, dexterous)—the woman is happy to cooperate. Interestingly, in terms of the guilt issue, the speaker decides to bear the specific guilt of adultery alone, either to maintain control or in a spirit of noblesse oblige: if she meets the man at a party in future, she will "keep faith and not betray his trust / by letting on I was married." But guilt is complicated. Ní Dhomhnaill allows the readers to wonder if the speaker's motives are quite so pure as she would have herself believe: perhaps the less she spreads the guilt, the better time she'll have. There is even the possibility that the poet is laughing at a woman caught up in the feminine ethic of putting others first, in this case to spare the men grief. To her ambiguous stance, as well as to the whole petty adventure, the last line of the poem asks, "An ndéanfása?" [Wouldn't you do the same?], which slyly attempts to implicate even the most offended readers who have read the tale to the end.

A more serious mood characterizes the poem "Welcome of the Shannon's Mouth to the Fish." The speaker views the phallic object (the salmon) with some erotic delight; however, it is obvious that her encompassing presence, represented metonymically in the title by the longest Irish river, need not fear its domination: "Léim an bradáin / Sa doircheacht / Lann lom / . . . / Mise atá fáiltúil, líontach" [The salmon jumped / in the darkness / a bare blade / . . . / And I am full welcoming, ready to catch it] (*Droighin*, 88).

Ní Dhomhnaill's salmon, while strong and tenacious, is wholly subsumed by the river in which it lives and mates. And yet "power" is not the essence of the river: the poet does not simply reinscribe the heirarchy of patriarchal power so that women are now dominant in the social structure. Although Ní Dhomhnaill recognizes the strength of Witch and Crone, the individual journeying toward selfhood is her recurrent theme; and such journeys are essentially made alone, by those willing to experience vulnerability.

Even in lyrical expositions of sweet romance, humor breaks in to wake the reader from compulsive fantasy. In "Blodewedd," for example, the speaker begins: "At the least touch of your fingertips / I break into blossom . . . / I sprawl like a grassy meadow / fragrant in the sun;" (*Pharaoh's*, 117). In Welsh mythology, Blodewedd is a woman made from flowers, as her name implies. Her story here, however, is not romantic fluff, but a human mixture of love and lust, of blood and clay: Ní Dhomhnaill's final stanza has the heroine "Hours later," lingering "in the ladies' toilet, / a sweet scent wafting / from all my pores" as she muses on the events of the evening. Ní Dhomhnaill does not have to dig far to get inside a woman's mind, and when there, she is less concerned with the work of art than with the woman. No transcendent parer of fingernails, this creator is down scrubbing floors in the heart of her creation; a woman writing about woman's body; a female taking the male for erotic Object; a divided Self trying to remain open to the sometimes terrifying personified elements of her unconscious.

Ní Dhomhnaill's language is sometimes a weapon, a violent instrument, and her laughter is harsh, reminding us perhaps of the laughter of the women in Monique Wittig's *Les Guérillères*, who "incite with their laughs and shouts those who fight" (84) and whose "laughter does not lessen" as, pulling down the patriarchal edifice, they "pick up the bricks and using them as missiles . . . bombard the statues that remain standing" (92). We shall see the violence of this anarchic laughter in action as we move to examine the new myths being created by Ní Dhomhnaill out of the stones of the past.

Ní Dhomhnaill's Women

Masks and disguises—vital elements of the carnival—are to be found in abundance and with serious purpose in Ní Dhomhnaill's work: queens and goddesses, clowns and hags populate her poems in continuous play around the self-object function. In Bakhtin's charting of carnival logic, such masking is simply a temporary suspension of law; Peter Stallybrass and Allon White, even less sure of carnival's political potential than Bakhtin, call transgression a "counter-sublimation" that has the end result of reinforcing the status quo (*Transgression*, 201). But when Ní Dhomhnaill uses Irish folklore and tradition in this way to explore the topic of female identity, she subverts the traditional dichotomies of bad/ good, virgin/temptress, queen/hag, housewife/changeling wife: dominant images of women in Irish literature.

The function of masks is ambiguous both in a patriarchal culture and in a postcolonial society, "where the colonizer," as David Lloyd writes, has sought to "reduce the colonized to a surveyable surface whose meaning is always the same." He cautions that "demarcations of the borderline between damage and creative strategies for resistance are hard to fix" ("Adulteration," 99). For the colonizer, one may wear the mask of the pleasant, if less than rational, charmer; for the cultural nationalists, the mask of the macho patriot, the pure *cailín*, or the ideal mother.

Ní Dhomhnaill seems to escape, perhaps by her very lack of stereotypical upbringing and influence, the need to submit to either the patriarchal or the colonial order in her choice of masks. Instead, the poet provides an access for the imagination to a wide range of possibilities of being female and a fresh, affirmative look at the available models in folklore and tradition. This is not to say that her journeys, or "strategies for creative resistance," have been without danger or "damage." But each successive poem and book is a victorious homecoming.

The Complete Woman

The most basic of Ní Dhomhnaill's female protagonists is the contemporary woman who is sensually alive and aware of the male body, whether the situation is one that produces joy, guilt, humor, loneliness, consciousness of her own beauty, or a combination of any of these. In a further affirmation of womanhood, this mask, lavishly decorated, is brought forth again and again as an apotheosized or idealized female persona. Mothers, lovers, queens are transparently godlike; the "Toirceas" series from Ní Dhomhnaill's latest collection, *Feis*, sees women's experience of pregnancy as the Creation in small. Since earliest times, women's grotesque lower parts—the ones which bled, opened for intercourse, produced life—were a cause of their being excluded from the sanctuary. Ní Dhomhnaill's use of the goddess/creator mask reflects not a narcissistic need but an attempt to heal patriarchally caused wounds to the psyche. "A feminine deity allows women to experience themselves as truly 'like the Goddess,' as imaging divinity in their very life-giving powers," says feminist theologian Sandra Schneiders. "Rather than being unclean because of their bodily capacity to give life, they are divine because of it" (*Faith*, 42).

The other side of the coin is that grotesqueries brandished without shame become part of carnival iconoclasm; the poet evokes quite as much laughter by her references to bodily needs and functions as she does admiration at the body's perfect and godlike mechanism. Though such wonderful love-poems as "Angel of the Lord" and "Rainbow" show the speaker capable of enjoying the unsettling delights of romance, Ní Dhomhnaill's sarcastic, funny glances at "Masculus Giganticus Hibernicus" in his many guises win her "soft" victories over his age-old dominance. The speaker in these humorously cynical poems does not present herself as a moral lamppost in the light of which men may see their own mistakes; she mocks pomposity while freely donning the mask of the clown herself.

From the Nonresponsive Mother to the Great Mother

It is clear that Ní Dhomhnaill's mask-wearing, though comedic, is not really play, that is, suspension of reality. At carnival, after having fun with the cross-dressing, one goes back to one's ordinary life and expected behaviors. Ní Dhomhnaill's witch/cailleach/hag masks, by contrast, seem inspired by a vital need: to find an explanation and a mirroring for the horrible/uncontrollable Self so that her self-cohesion is not threatened. "Once the inexpressible is brought within the scope of human imagination, then you don't have to be acting out," she says.[3] Thus, one result of assuming these rather fearsome personae is a greater wholeness, a greater ability not to reject parts of the personality. Barbara Walker tells us that "unlike later patriarchal societies, which [admitted a goddess figure] only as the passive, humble, ever-benevolent

Mother . . . like Mary, prepatriarchal societies frankly envisioned her actively sexual and destructive sides. In nature, they reasoned, destruction is as necessary to cosmic balance as creation" (*Crone*, 27). In Ní Dhomhnaill's poetry, the bitch-woman, the rival who has somehow got her claws in the lover's flesh; the hag who gives cryptic advice at the ford; Persephone, quite bewildered and naive, writing a letter to her mother from Hades; the Snow Queen whose icy grip causes the death of the heart; the *Sean Bhean Bhocht*, witchlike, calling for the death of her loving sons; "Madame," ruler/brothel owner of the kingdom of death: all are aspects of the Goddess, who, if she has the power to create, has also the power to destroy.

A recurring presence in Ní Dhomhnaill's poetry is the mother who doesn't live up to expectations. In "Máthair," we hear a residual fear and bitter anger at the nonempathic mother, emotions that are so often buried with the suppressed fears of childhood. Ní Dhomhnaill, however, manages to give these feelings their full play: "Do thugais dom gúna / is do thógais arís é; / do thugais dom capall / a dhíolais i m'éagmais; / do tugais dom cláirseach / is d'iarrais thar n-ais é; / do thugais dom beatha" [You gave me dress / And you took it again; / You gave me a house / That you sold in my absence; / You gave me a harp / And demanded it back; / You gave me life] (*Droighin*, 28). The form of the poem is the classic *rosc*, with its strong dimeters, particularly suitable for the accusatory tone: its regularity here mimics the anguished rocking of a person in pain. When the final line of the first stanza suddenly stops the pattern ("you gave me life"), the reader experiences a forced intake of breath, which becomes a gasp at the implication of the unsaid line.

The faithless mother in "Mathair" is not the shadow side of the Mother goddess, but an altogether more petty tyrant: she is a patriarchal mouthpiece whose adherence to the expectations of a repressive society make her part of the prison for her daughters. But she is also the beginning of understanding for the poet, who faces the tension of the struggle with adversarial women first in this poem and pushes forward until she comes to an awareness of the Adversary within.

In "Poem for Melissa" (Ní Dhomhnaill's eldest daughter), the poet takes on the awful burden of motherhood herself, wanting only joys for her child but knowing she will have suffering. In "The Broken Doll," the poet extends her concern beyond the family to the wider circle of women as potential casualties of a careless world and their own frangibility. The poet has begun to "see your pallor staring starkly back at me

/ from every swimming hole, from every pool, Ophelia" (*Pharaoh's*, 58–59). This is the movement that characterizes Ní Dhomhnaill's poetic growth: from inner reflection and awareness of the emotions, needs, and drives to empathy, to broader concern for a wide group or class. She is ever on a journey, sometimes in darkness and unconsciousness, via dreams—the "night-sea-journey" referred to in *Feis*—from human, fallible motherhood, in which she confronts both her powerlessness and her destructive power, to the Great Mother or Terrible Mother, by means of whose dark, encompassing womb the persona achieves a transformed self, joining the conscious and unconscious parts of the psyche.[4] Ní Dhomhnaill spells out the longing and anxiety of this female quest at the end of "The Race": "and thou, dark mother, cave of wonders, / since it's to you that we spin on our violent course, / is it true what they say that your kiss is sweeter / than Spanish wine, Greek honey, or the golden mead of the Norse?" (*Pharaoh's*, 95).

By the publication of *Feis* in 1991, it is clear that the poet has internalized the world of myth as her worldview optic; the objectified female who triumphs, suffers, or causes suffering can be managed while still being allowed vulnerability. In this collection, Ní Dhomhnaill recovers irony as one of her management strategies for the "mother": Mother Ireland, in a hilarious blow to romantic nostalgia for the ideal Mother, is depicted in "Cathleen" as: "Old Gummy Granny, / [taking] none of this on board because of her uncanny / knack of hearing only what confirms / her own sense of herself, her honey-nubile form / and the red rose, proud rose or canker / tucked behind her ear, in the headband of her blinkers" (*Astrakhan*, 38–41).

The *Bean an Leasa* Changeling

Another woman who doesn't quite fit the mold of proper housewife/ mother appears in Irish folktale and myth as a woman of the Lios, or fairy-fort, a *Bean an Leasa*. This term is Ní Dhomhnaill's own shorthand for a number of related folk-legend figures of off-kilter housewives, the use of which shows the poet working through perceived failures to some forgiveness and equilibrium. A *Bean an Leasa* myth becomes also, in Ní Dhomhnaill's hands, paradigmatic of the experience of life on the margin for her sex.

Countless folktales, currrent in Ireland even into the middle of this century, show ordinary housewives "replaced" by women with special powers, often willful and capricious, if not exactly evil. Sometimes the woman dies and is "replaced" by her transmuted self, which eventually must be freed. Often, the focus of the stories is the husband's bewilderment, loss, or ongoing efforts to deal with the difficult, changed woman. Ní Dhomhnaill's poem "Abduction" shows the confusion of the wife herself at the appearance of this strange and unwelcome persona.

Sean O'Sullivan, in his valuable collection *Folktales of Ireland*, tells us that the *sí* (*sidhe* in the older orthography, often translated "fairies") and the dead "seemed to be part of the same milieu" (xxxix). An example of how the worlds of the dead and the *sí* are interchangeable can be seen in the folktale "The Children of the Dead Woman." A dead wife comes back to her home every night, eats heartily, and feeds, washes, and puts to sleep the child of her deathbed. She belongs to the *sí* now. However, when the husband, with the help of his brothers and the priest, rescues her by holding on until morning, she is released, and the story ends: "So she stayed with her husband and child, much the same as she had been before, except that she had a wild look in her eyes till the day she died. She bore nine sons to her husband after her rescue, and they came to be known as the children of the dead woman." The last phrase brings the story ingenuously into daily life: "'My grandfather saw one of the dead woman's children,' said the storyteller" (176). The editor explains: "It was a common belief in Irish oral tradition that the fairies were continually trying to abduct newborn children (usually males) to replenish their own fairy population, and that they also took young mothers into fairyland to suckle such abducted children. The Irish Folklore Commission [which began work in 1935 as an official body] has thousands of tales illustrating this belief. In many of them, attempts to rescue the abducted woman failed at the last moment through lack of courage. More rarely, the attempt succeeded, as in this version, but the rescued woman was dumb" (273).

What does the presence of changeling-wife stories suggest about the tenets of the society that produced them? Allowing yourself to put one foot over the border of a tightly knit society brings its own lasting damages. The marginalized—which includes anybody out of the power loop: the poor, the homeless, the mad, single mothers, dreamers, those living on the borders of society—are also people made dumb, because their voices are not listened to. But Ní Dhomhnaill has been to the world of the unconscious and back, and she refuses to be dumb. In fact, her willed living out of this not uncommon female experience becomes her base for critique. Suspicion is leveled at the changed woman, the woman who will not obey, who has needs not understood by the conventional husband from the conventionally patriarchal society. Such woman is represented in Ní Dhomhnaill with harsh realism, but with all of her rights streaming like banners.

THE WARRIOR QUEEN

Finally, as we move to a detailed look at Ní Dhomhnaill's treatment of a single mythological self-object, let us ask what she is doing with myth. I suggest she is creating and becoming part of what Frantz Fanon calls "a national literature." This is, in Ketu Katrak's summary, accomplished not by "simply using the past or using oral traditions nostalgically, but using, for example, traditional, oral storytelling methods for contemporary . . . problems. The writer's imagination will refashion the past, use legend and myth, and make them relevant to postcolonial society" ("Decolonizing," 172). Too commonly, Irish writers' use of the old myths is misinterpreted as nostalgia when in fact it forms part of the large work of creating/discovering an identity. Further, as Ashis Nandy reminds us, speaking of the work of Gandhi, "for those seeking liberation, history can sometimes be made to follow from myth" (*Colonialism*, 63). But first it may be necessary for women to retell the myth.

Readers who remember the Irish pound note may recall that it featured Queen Maeve, one of the main protagonists of the *Táin Bó Cuailnge*—hence of Ní Dhomhnaill's revision of the *Tain*, a poem sequence called *Atáin*. Maeve seems to have been such an important part of the Irish cultural self-image that she was acceptable for the job of icon on a twentieth-century economic symbol, joining Duns Scotus, Swift, and Yeats to cover Irish history.

It appears that the Irish are proud of their warrior women: of Maeve and other goddesses of her era; of Emer, whose name means "granite"; of Scathac, the wise woman who trained Cúchulainn in the arts of war; of Grace O'Malley, the pirate whose exploits have passed over into myth; and, in modern times, of Constance Gore-Booth, the rebel leader, and Eva Gore-Booth, the militant pacifist; of Grace Gifford and Dora Maguire, Charlotte Despard and Mother Jones—fighters for independence, suffrage, and women's rights. The inevitable backlash of promoting the continuance of the myth of strong matriarchs was that Irish society (unswervingly patriarchal from the sixth or seventh century onward, at least, and probably from the invasion of the Celts) thereby set women up to be regarded with suspicion and strong women to be feared.

Maeve's story, then, has come down to us through men's eyes. A human version of the sovereignty goddess, she is catalyst rather than

heroine of the *Táin Bó Cuailnge*, the famous battle between her and
Ailill, her husband, for economic sovereignty and prestige. Fergus, army
commander and Maeve's erstwhile lover, says, after the final battle: "We
followed the rump of a misguiding woman. . . . It is the usual thing for
a herd led by a mare to be strayed and destroyed" (251). Proinsias
MacCana describes Maeve as "an unscrupulous and masterful virago
[catch the implications of "master" and "vir" in those words] who domi-
nates her husband, king Ailill and cuckolds him with . . . Ferghus" ("Mythology," 522). Maeve's womanliness also causes trouble in the sim-
plest physical ways: when, in the heat of battle, she "[gets] her gush of
blood," she must abandon her post to relieve herself. We are spared no
graphic detail as the patriarchal tradition shows its disgust at women's
weakness and uncleanliness: "it [her flow] dug three great channels,
each big enough to take a household. The place is called Fual Medba,
Medb's Foul Place, ever since" (*Tain*, 250). The very maleness of the
men in the Ulster Cycle is compromised by womanly weakness: the
armies are cursed with the punishment of menstrual cramps (some
translators read this affliction as labor pains) at times convenient to their
enemies.

So we can see in this case, as in many others, what Alicia Ostriker
observes: myth can be "inhospitable terrain for a woman writer" ("Revisionist," 316) even in the women-strong Celtic tradition. When a
woman rewrites a myth, therefore, one thing we must not miss is the
way in which, as Ostriker says, "the old stories are changed, changed
utterly, by female knowledge of female experience, so that they can no
longer stand as foundations of collective male fantasy. Instead, they are
corrections; they are representations of what women find divine and
demonic in themselves; they are retrieved images of what women have
collectively and historically suffered; in some cases they are instructions for survival" (318). In the *Atáin* poems, Ní Dhomhnaill's interaction with the traditional material reclaims the image of the strong
woman and demystifies and humanizes patriarchal constructions of supreme womanhood at its most awe-ful. Ní Dhomhnaill accomplishes
this chiefly by giving us the stories from the woman's point of view.
The Maeve we find in *Atáin* (which means "*The Tain* revisited/re-writ-
ten") is a strange and compelling mixture of that strong queen and victimized modern woman. Maeve's name means "she who intoxicates,"
which probably connects her with the Goddess of Sovereignty, who, as
Muireann Ní Bhrolcháin tells us, "is frequently associated with the dis-
pensing of a drink. . . . many sagas refer to the cup of liquid which the

woman, in the role of goddess, brings to the king, her prospective husband" ("Myths," 527), representing the power the king is being given. "The goddess is a symbol of the land, whose union with the prospective king ensures his sovereignty," and in her turn she needs a true king, for "without her rightful ruler she is lost, old and occasionally deranged" (525).

The contemporary narrator of *Atáin* has simply put on the cloak of Maeve to wage war for what she says is a thousand times more valuable than cattle: her dignity. "Maeve Speaks," the first poem of the group, declares war and gives due cause: "I give notice of battle without pity / . . . / for heroes of twenty pints / who would sit on a bench beside me / who would put a sly hand under my skirt / without an excuse me or a reason / but looking for a chance / to dominate my body / and I announce merciless war on them" (11–19). The rage evident in these lines suggests that the poet is seeing Queen Maeve's victimhood in that of the common woman; in Maeve's name she renounces it. Subtly the picture of the "masterful virago" has shifted. In fact, destructiveness in women is more commonly experienced as self-destructiveness, in silence or in-turned anger at abuse by others, or even in abusive behavior toward their own bodies: thus, the shout of this first poem is not a cry of power but a rising up from powerlessness.

Reappropriating male tools, war and language, the poet has turned them in the form of threat on those who have stolen a woman's human dignity. Though Ní Dhomhnaill, through the Maeve persona, threatens only imagined battle, there are many ways of waging war and in the process sublimating violent responses to oppression.[5] And as for language as Weapon, we have noted in the first section of this essay the poet's festive license in the wielding of this instrument. Let us now see it as Ní Dhomhnaill uses it more aggressively to topple some monuments.

In the following section from "The High Queen Berates the Badb to Cúchulainn," the poet employs the concept of the toothed vagina, a symbol of female power and male fear of such. Ní Dhomhnaill refuses to capitalize on, or to be intimidated by, the structures of patriarchal angst about loss of power. Instead, the poet takes up the concept, only to make pointed fun of it; she waves it before the cowering partner (may we not imagine him so?) with a belly laugh of scornful amusement: "Afraid, certainly, that you'd be lost / that I'd have a set of teeth on my cunt, / that I'd crush you between my two jaws / like corn in a mill. / And I had a good set of teeth to grind you, / you brat of the devil, you pale sickly man, you stump of a fool!" (6–11). Here we have a lively example of what Bakhtin identifies as "billingsgate," a discourse of carnival, which can be recognized also in Ní Dhomhnaill's use of slang, jokes, and curses.

What is the effect of the language used here? First of all, the humor of the whole deflates the extreme and puffed-up seriousness of male paranoid fantasies. Second, the shock of the vulgar term for "vagina" creates a multiplicity of reactions in the reader, from distaste at a woman's use of a term connoting disrespect and violence toward her sex, to a releasing laughter. On the subject of the subversive uses of vulgarity, Shirley Ardener, in "The Cultural Construction of Sexuality," argues that "it is precisely the irreverence and vulgarity of feminist vagina imagery which is most effective in specific contexts. . . . Impudence is always contextual and relies heavily on the unexpected" (quoted in Mullin, "Representations," 37–38). In this case the vagina imagery is so successfully subversive, not to say off-putting, for one male translator that, after a brave start, he renders line 10 ("is cíor mhaith agam chun do mheilte,") as: "me having a good comb to tease you."

And of course the main joke for Irish readers, if they can afford to laugh at it, is in the iconoclasm; for the words are directed to an unassailable hero of Irish patriotic myth. But Ní Dhomhnaill rewrites the princely role of Cúchulainn. The most familiar image of this superhuman hero is the famous Oliver Sheppard sculpture in the General Post Office in Dublin, headquarters of the 1916 rebellion: the dying warrior faces his foes, sword in hand, through the expedient of being tied to a post, while on his shoulder sits an ominous bird, avatar of the death-bringing goddess. He is there to commemorate the tiny band who in 1916 set themselves up against the might of British imperialism; and in both roles, the Iron Age legendary and the symbolic, he's a perfectly unshakeable idol. One hundred percent bronze. No clay feet.

With a swift twitch of the rug, Ní Dhomhnaill pulls everything away from Cúchulainn: in her rewriting, the hero, the superior man, needs more than just the customary libation from the sovereignty goddess to keep him going. Already in an oppositional role to Maeve as the star of the opposing army, his new and more subtly antagonistic role in *Atáin* seems to be that of loutish lover. His extraordinary birth—the customary extraordinary birth of the hero, complete with multiple fathers, one of whom appears as a fly in a wine goblet—is presented satirically in "Cú Chulainn II" as a scene from a soap opera: "put away your knitting / and take the fag out of your mouth a minute; / tell me one thing / and tell me no more—just this: / who is my father?" (15–19). His amazing childhood, filled with mighty feats of strength and courage, is reduced to a fairly meaningless existence in which his single mother leaves him, a bored delinquent throwing stones at trains, when she goes to the pub. The contrast between Ní Dhomhnaill's Cúchulainn and the hero of the Ulster Cycle may be highlighted by the following example from *The Táin*, which indicates the magnificent, surreal quality of Cúchulainn's heroic warp-spasm: "On his head the temple-sinews stretched to the nape of his neck, each mighty, immense, measureless knob as big as the head of a month-old child. His face and features became a red bowl. . . . Then tall and thick, steady and strong, high as the mast of a noble ship, rose up from the center of his skull a straight spout of black blood darkly and magically smoking" (152–53). By contrast, Ní Dhomhnaill's Cúchulainn is "a rigid/tight dark little man" who never achieves greater dimensions in any way. But this is all done very lightly: though the icons toppling are massive, the weapons used here are humor and a deadpan tone in which the reader catches an ironic awareness of the contrast between heroic boasting and life's muddy realities and more complex requirements.

Though the traditional stories of Cúchulainn's heroic birth and early feats are portrayed in this satirical contemporary version as mere lures to catch the women, nevertheless, the speaker is caught: in a relationship marked by jealousy and present and potential hurt. The anger we heard at the beginning in that declaration of war returns for the two "dialogues" of the High Queen with Cúchulainn: "I wasn't the worst woman for you by a / long shot. Another woman is with you. / She is the proto-harlot. She is dark / and she has no pity, fear, or faith" ("Cú Chulainn I" 14–16). The stinging soreness evident in the emotions of this poem is "caused" by an evil woman, identified by the speaker as the Badb. You remember the crow that came to perch on Cúchulainn's shoulder as he hung dying? That's one of those trios of goddesses all representing the same force—in this case the force of war/death, and their names are Badb, Morrigan, and Nemain. In *The Táin*, Cúchulainn is the Badb's ally, doing her work of death dealing: "Builder of the Badb's fold with walls of human bodies" (148). In "Cú Chulainn I," he is her wimpish lover, jealously warned about her by the angry protagonist. Badb's depiction as the speaker's rival here poses some problem for a feminist reading: death-dealing goddesses may be creations of the burgeoning patriarchal culture, which, at the dawn of history, decided to replace the overwhelming majority of female deities with male counterparts, demonizing some of the female deities and robbing others of their power.

But what is the Badb's function as antagonist in a series of poems that attempts to extend the range of permitted emotions for women to include rage, that attends to the woman's own needs over those of her sovereign consort? The flip, sardonic tone turns deadly serious as her "portrait" is painted: "She is the Badb / hovering over the crowd / she pricks the eyes /_from babies in their cradles. / She is the shrike / the butcher-bird / your blood / will be in lakes under your feet / your flesh / will be hanging / in frozen joints / from steel crooks" (37–48). At this point the reader starts to become aware of an anomaly.

In the companion poem to this, "Agallamh na Mór-Riona le Cú Chulainn," which Hartnett translates as "The Great Queen Speaks. Cú Chulainn Listens," the ending is just as violent, as the speaker promises vengeance on the man for rejecting her sexually. The poem opens with an almost liturgical solemnity: "I came to you / in the form of a queen / clothes of many colors on me / and the appearance of a speirbhean, / that I might bestow power upon you / and sovereignty over the land" (1–6). The brief dimeter (in the original) lines of the opening litany, full of long assonant vowel sounds, rock the reader into a respectful trance; but the poet is preparing a surprise. Juxtaposing the dignity of the royal woman's approach with the response of the hero, Ní Dhomhnaill finishes the scene with brutal swiftness: when the queen slips into bed with him for the ritual coition of sovereignty, Cúchulainn snaps, "Get off! / This is no time to play / Not for women's arses was I brought to earth!" (20–23).

Cúchulainn's reply here is very close to the original, certainly as translated by Thomas Kinsella (*Tain*, 133); the change occurs for the reader because of the point of view from which Ní Dhomhnaill presents it. Suddenly identification is possible, and the reader feels that slap in the face that is the hero's crass denial of the woman's inherent dignity (admittedly here imaged by consumer goods—her lengthy dowry list—as much as by the formal voice). At this, the Mór Rion draws up all her strength and all her self-esteem into one ball and excoriates him.

What are we to make of the cursing of one woman's wrath and the privileging of another's? The question is further complicated by the discovery that the two women in question are two aspects of the same goddess. *Mór Rion*, or *Mór Rioghan*, in its older orthography, is the same as Mórrigan, the goddess of death. Kinsella does, in fact, give as alternative translations for Morrigan: "Great Queen" and "Queen of Demons"(263). It is possible that Ní Dhomhnaill herself collapses the two, Maeve and Morrigan, in her version of *The Táin*. If so, an interesting degree of complexity is added. Máire Breathnach and Kim McCone have both written at greater length, and disagreed, about the appearance of the sovereignty goddess as a goddess of death.[6] But whether Ní Dhomhnaill makes room for this possibility or not, we must still try to address the problem of the Badb and Morrigan, aspects of the same goddess of death, placed in awkward rivalry.

A closer look preserves the consistency of the feminist stance. The Badb, here, instead of announcing war in a statesmanlike way or trading open curses for bad behavior, is manipulative. She strews her way with corpses of people who died surprised. She is also seen as very alluring, in the mode of the stereotypical anima woman.[7] Does she have dignity to be guarded? Not quite: she has power, and it is unassailable. Against such impermeability, violence must be used by the powerless. I want to rescue her from being a mere reproduction of male hatred or fear of woman by suggesting that she is the shadow side of the speaker, pushed to the unconscious and all the more violent and subversive for being suppressed. The speaker must hate and fear this other side of herself, precisely because she recognizes her so well.

Finally, we have the "libation" poem. The sovereignty motif of a drink offered to the prospective king is again given (here, as in *The Tain*) to Morrigan to administer. Allied with that, we have the very common motif of transformation, where hero sees beneath a repulsive exterior to some essential quality, responds to that with a kiss or a drink proffered, and reveals both the real beauty of the prospective spouse and his own nobility.

By taking the point of view of the ugly, damaged woman, Ní Dhomhnaill again siphons off the nobility, the romance, the altruism, with an ironic awareness. In "The Great Queen Speaks," we first meet the queen in her old hag form: half-witted, half-blind, half-lame. Cúchulainn asks a drink of milk of her, from her similarly maimed and decrepit cow. He blesses her for the drink, and she, by his blessing, is healed, made whole. All quite unintentional on his part, for, as we discover: "it was you / who wounded me in the beginning." The queen explains: "You give up your sovereignty / because of a thirst, / I come whole from your wound / because of your healing balm" (17–18, 23–26). The tightly whorled ironies of the ending, emphasized in the original by multiple assonances and the balanced verbs *de dheasca* and *de bhithin* spotlight a tit-for-tat economy of good deeds: you pay your debts, let go of your personal sovereignty or independence, because of a thirst; I come whole from a wound you gave, because of a balm which it is in your unique power to apply. The conclusion about sovereignty is this: it is a goal that must inevitably be relinquished in favor of an active acceptance of interconnectedness.

That last concept is central to the meaning of women's struggle to establish themselves as active agents on the world's stage. Says Sandra Schneiders: "The word which has progressively come to serve as a cipher for feminist spirituality is 'interconnectedness.' [Many feminists seek] ways to reunify [that which] has been divided by the all-pervasive dichotomous dualism of the patriarchal system, to replace the win-lose, either-or, we-they, in-out, right-wrong bases of mutual destruction with a both-and inclusiveness which will both achieve and be achieved by reconnecting that which has been separated" (*Faith*, 89). What the hero and heroine of *Atáin* want from each other is fundamentally in line with the traditions of the sovereignty myth: he wants legitimation through union with the powerful sovereignty goddess; she, physical transformation and renewal of life as a result of his acceptance of her and their subsequent union. But the trouble with the woman-in-need of protection theme is that even while the woman is safeguarded, her image is reduced to that of a dependent on the more powerful male. Ní Dhomhnaill's conclusion is more hard-edged and respectful of women: yes, they can be healed—men can repair the damage done—but that will happen when the outcome is seen to have clear advantage for the human son or suitor.

Ní Dhomhnaill's warrior queen carries the qualities needed by women breaking free of oppressive and centuries-old traditional expectations of them; breaking through, not to the masculinist ideal of self-sufficiency and personal sovereignty, but to a transformation, both interior and inter-relational, that springs from the empowering knowledge of shared human dignity.

The poet positions herself amid the discourse of contemporary Irish literature as a catalyst for rebellion: a site where critical awareness can begin. In this she corresponds to Kristeva's analysis of the function of carnival. In the freedom with which Ní Dhomhnaill breaks the rules (both the literary codes of language and those that repress women's speech in the name of propriety), owns without shame her body and all its drives, and takes up the masks of goddess and hag to access the energy of a complete and complex female identity, her audience observes "a game, but also a daily undertaking" (*Desire,* 78). The next steps are their own.

NOTES

1. See also Stallybrass and White's discussion of Dollimore in *The Politics and Poetics of Transgression,* 201.

2. For this and other translations from poems published without translation, I use my own line-by-line prose translation. See Works Cited for the collections that have attributed translators.

3. Nuala Ní Dhomhnaill, personal interview, April 1991.

4. In Erich Neumann's summary: "The underworld, the earth womb, as the perilous land of the dead through which the deceased must pass, either to be judged there and to arrive at a chthonic realm of salvation or doom, or to pass through that territory to a new and higher existence, is one of the archetypal symbols of the Terrible Mother. It is experienced in the archetypal nocturnal sea voyage of the sun or hero" (*Great Mother,* 157).

5. See Julia Kristeva, *Kristeva Reader,* 203.

6. See chapter 5 of *Pagan Past and Christian Present in Early Irish Literature,* in which McCone responds to Bhreathnach's exploratory "The Sovereignty Goddess as Goddess of Death?"

7. The term is taken from M. E. Harding.

WORKS CITED

Bakhtin, Mikhail. *Problems of Dostoevsky's Poetics.* Translated by Caryl Emerson. Minneapolis: University of Minneapolis Press, 1984.

Bhreathnach, Máire. "The Sovereignty Goddess as Goddess of Death?" *Zeitschrift für Celtische Philologie* (1982): 242–60.

Flynn, Donal. "Irish in the School Curriculum: A Matter of Politics." *The Irish Review* (Summer 1993): 79.

Katrak, Ketu. "Decolonizing Culture: Toward a Theory for Postcolonial Women's Texts." *Modern Fiction Studies* 35, no.1 (1989): 159–79.

Kinsella, Thomas. *The Táin.* Oxford: Oxford University Press, 1969.

Kristeva, Julia. *Desire in Language.* New York: Columbia University Press, 1980.

———. *Kristeva Reader.* New York: Columbia University Press, 1986.

Lloyd, David. *Anomalous States.* Durham, N.C.: Duke University Press, 1993.

MacCana, Proinsias. "Women in Irish Mythology." In *The Crane Bag Book of Irish Studies, 1977–1981,* 520–24. Dublin: Blackwater Press, 1982.

McCone, Kim. *Pagan Past and Christian Present in Early Irish Literature.* Maynooth: An Sagart, 1990.

Mullin, Molly. "Representations of History, Irish Feminism, and the Politics of Difference." *Feminist Studies* 17, no.1 (1991): 29–50.

Nandy, Ashis. *The Intimate Enemy: Loss and Recovery of Self under Colonialism.* Delhi: Oxford University Press, 1983.

Neumann, Erich. *The Great Mother.* Princeton: Princeton University Press, 1972.

Ní Bhrolcháin, Muireann. "Women in Early Irish Myths and Sagas." In *The Crane Bag Book of Irish Studies, 1977–1981,* 525–32. Dublin, Blackwater Press, 1982.

Ní Dhomhnaill, Nuala. *An Dealg Droighin.* Dublin: Cló Mercier, 1981.

———. "An Filíocht á Cumadh" [Writing poetry]. *Léachtaí Cholm Cille* 17 (1986): 147–79.

———. *The Astrakhan Cloak.* Translated by Paul Muldoon. Loughcrew: Gallery Press, 1990.

———. *Féar Suaithinseach.* Maynooth: An Sagart, 1984.

———. *Feis.* Maynooth: An Sagart, 1991.

———. Personal interview. April 1991.

———. *Pharaoh's Daughter.* Translated by Ciaran Carson et al. Loughcrew: Gallery Press, 1990.

———. *Selected Poems* [*Rogha Dánta*]. Translated by Michael Hartnett. Dublin: Raven Arts Press, 1988.

Ó Drisceoil, Proinsias. "Irish as Seen through Other Words." *Irish Times,* 22 January 1994: 8.

Ó Séaghdha, Barra. "Review of *The Astrakhan Cloak.*" *Irish Review* (Autumn 1993): 144.

Ostriker, Alicia. "The Thieves of Language: Women Poets and Revisionist Mythmaking." In *The New Feminist Criticism,* edited by Elaine Showalter, 314–38. New York: Pantheon, 1985.

O'Sullivan, Sean. *Folktales of Ireland.* London: Routledge, Kegan Paul, 1966.

Schneiders, Sandra. *Beyond Patching: Faith and Feminism in the Catholic Church.* New York: Paulist Press, 1991.

Sochen, June. "Slapsticks, Screwballs, and Bawds." In *Women's Comic Visions,* edited by June Sochen, 141–57. Detroit: Wayne State University Press, 1991.

Stallybrass, Peter, and Allon White. *The Politics and Poetics of Transgression.* Ithaca, N.Y.: Cornell University Press, 1986.

Walker, Barbara G. *The Crone.* San Francisco: Harper and Row, 1985.

Wilson, Rebecca. *Sleeping With Monsters: Conversations with Scottish and Irish Women Poets.* Edinburgh: Polygon, 1990.

Wittig, Monique. *Les Guérillères.* Boston: Beacon Press, 1969.

10

Joyce and Boylan's *Black Baby*
"Swiftly and Silently"

Jean-Louis Giovannangeli

She had decided something about the shape of memory. It grew differently in different climates. In these parts people . . . employed the gift of forgetting for things that were still relevant to their active lives. They forgot about joy. They cast out the dread so big that it found its own form and crept back into their nightmares.
CLARE BOYLAN, *Black Baby*

The Irish had always had an intense sentimental preoccupation with distant pagans. . . . it was the dusky heathen who stirred the infant imagination, sleeping his soulless sleep until awakened by God's love and the magic of His holy wizards.
CLARE BOYLAN, *Black Baby*

"keep black!"
JAMES JOYCE, *Finnegans Wake*

What we find in Clare Boylan's *Black Baby* is a kind of philosophical comedy that is strikingly reminiscent of the work of Joyce. Like *Finnegans Wake,* Boylan's *Black Baby* is structured around the idea of comatic hallucination; in both works the central character is language, a father tongue which has lost or buried an aspect of itself, "which had thrown away its own key" (23). In both works this lost or repressed something is linked with memory and desire, with indeterminacy and wit. In Joyce's work Ireland's father tongue is personified as a traumatized Everyman; in Boylan's work it is personified as a woman (Alice) in a coma, a virgin in search of a black baby called Dinah.

The setting of Boylan's novel is Ireland, an Ireland which is a victim of itself and keeps playing again and again the game of its own inevitable loss. Dublin, which has become today entirely part of the Ulyssean cosmography, is the limited and insurmountable horizon of her novels. With *Black Baby*, the sudden intrusion of otherhood in the guise of a stranger within the confined world of the capital city will trigger a story in which our (dis)belief will always be put into question. The code of reading emerges slowly and is suddenly revealed: the structure of the comatic hallucination is one where the characters are shown in their dimension of pure onomastic creations, appearing and disappearing in an illimited self-engendering process where situations rebound on the words themselves.

An Unstable Narrative

In *Black Baby*, the narrative is always destabilized by the way the events are staged and the words used. The novel can be read as a procession of unknown people. The story is marked by a series of appearances and disappearances, brutal displacements and violent changes in focus. The first chapter is set in the African jungle, in a lost tribe in the process of being taught the word of God. We are then taken to the cozy house of Alice, an old woman in Dublin. Here, the second chapter uses as an echo the expression "all forgotten" to introduce us to the central figure of the mother/daughter couple: "It seems they have all forgotten" (7). "'All forgotten,' echoed a burly stranger as she labored along the strange suburban streets" (8). The stranger, "foreigner" (8), alluded to here is Dinah, a young black woman, stranded in Dublin without any clear reason. This sudden and unexpected appearance is at the heart of a novel based on permanent partings: "And, without a by-your-leave, she left" (62). "I had a life, you know," Alice informs Dinah, "before you came along." In response Dinah "stamped off out of the room." "Why was she always doing that?" (88), Alice wondered. Near this mother/daughter couple so difficult to hold together, characters fill the narrative space, without anybody knowing where they come from. Everyone in the novel comes on the scene, tells his/her story, and disappears into nothingness without leaving any sign behind.

The necessary need for a story that makes a novel exist in its printed form is transformed here into a wish for a story inside the story itself. To Alice's "nothing ever happens," meditating on her empty, snowy television screen, her neighbor Mrs. Willoughby answers, "Do you know what?" (90), to which Alice says in return: "No, tell me!" (90). The answer that comes then is the following: "Between ourselves, he was a bit too fond of you-know-what" (91). The "what" that Alice does not understand, the "what" that is the always-desired but constantly-refused object of the story, is the omission around which the novel revolves. *Black Baby* is the story of this hole, this lack, this repressed desire that nothing could fill but words.

All the random characters in *Black Baby* meet through newspaper ads or by buying information. Dinah buys Alice's address and Alice finds Dinah through a personal message in the local newspaper: "Mother remembers. Dinah, please contact Alice" (44). Other kinds of messages are mentioned, such as: "Farmer, aged fifty, own car, wishes to meet lady, thirty-five" (48). Or "Wash yourself in Christ's Blood," followed by an address to which Alice goes, only for the sake of meeting people: "In recent months she had been to a gathering of Edgar Cayce Legacy and a talk on molecules" (69). The isolation and loneliness of Boylan's characters mirror that of Joyce's Dubliners.

The staging of encounters in Boylan's novel is part of a scheme which structures the novel as a whole: Dinah is looking for a mother and Alice for a baby she has never seen. But even with the completion of this literary topos, a feeling of incompleteness prevails, and the partitioning and dispersal of lives results in an itinerary that goes from void to death for Alice and from nothing to nothingness for Dinah. The very pattern itself, being all the time stretched in an extensible manner, breaks upon the rock of reality—a reality that is shown exclusively in its most sordid aspects.

This swarming world is also a world where identities are dissimulated. Alice, who gives names to clocks (191), is also good at naming people according to her whims. Dinah's name is the result of a story that Alice told to herself. As a child she had given half a crown to buy a little black baby and name her:

> "Penny for the black baby," was one of the first phrases learnt. . . . The privilege of buying a black baby was reserved for older children who had partaken of the fleshy feast of First Communion. Decked out as miniature brides and at the peak of financial solvency due to the bounty of relatives who filled their little white handbags, they queued to purchase a savage soul. . . . Few could resist this early placation of maternity. (50)

Alice called her (spiritual) child Dinah "After her black doll with the plaster face" (51). To this phantasmal maternity corresponds the wish to recover the lost child whom she recognizes in a heart-rending recognition scene—as the laws of the genre want it—while Dinah is totally stunned. In a mocking reference to the imperialist impulse at the heart of this mercantile exchange in human relations—a reference that is totally lost on Alice—Dinah asks her if they sent the babies "parcel post or did they pack them in with a vanload of bananas?" (49). Elsewhere, musing on her own experience as a child in a convent school in Africa, she wonders, "What had the child been to them [the white nuns]? Not quite a person, for people were white" (24).

Everyone in the novel is caught in a web of projections of hidden desires and impulses. Names are used to condense imaginary stories and to shed an oblique light on the scene of action. Here, as in the *Wake*, much information is buried at the core of the text, information that might easily pass unnoticed. The words "coffin" and "will"—the last, with its Shakespearean double-entendre—seem to rule the relationship between Alice and her nephews and nieces: "The children had brought Alice a coffin for her birthday" (10). "They gave me a coffin," Alice tells Dinah, her voice quavering. "It's useful" (16). "As you know, I had intended to remember you in my will" (187). In fact, the coffin turns out to be a gramophone—a well-known Joycean instrument—on which she can hear the voice of her deceased father, who will come back to life in order to become a character in the novel: "He hauled himself up and began to swing his legs over the edge of his box" (201). The "coffin" is precisely where the nephews and nieces would like to send her when the doctor in the hospital asks to unplug the machine that ties her to life: "Since her seizure a month before, when she stole the limelight from some other old lady's funeral, she had lived in a world of her own. . . . All the same, she seemed happy. Now and then the nurses heard her laughing. . . . and, before her final collapse, she seemed to imagine she had a baby" (197).

On Christmas morning, the doctor had called on her nieces and nephews to tell them that Alice was "technically dead": "the long sleep that followed her stroke had become the final stage of a coma" (197). It is only from this moment onward and by rebuilding everything from this episode in a sort of backward reading that we can understand the allusion more than a hundred pages earlier: "She appeared to exist in some atmosphere heavier than air and the people around her did not seem real" (99). At that moment, and without the reader being aware of it, the novel had imperceptibly entered a coma—i.e., followed Alice's vagaries. Any event that Alice lived in her coma is linked to this authorial and doctoral commentary, which is exterior to Alice's narrative but totally part of the story. The coma will give its vagrant and delirious structure to the novel. In other words, the coma is not just a narrative event, but the very structure of the second half of the novel—which does not look, by contrast, more delirious than the first half.

The construction that could have led us to believe that, after meeting Alice, Dinah had consented to Catholic values and that Alice had adopted some of Dinah's good humor, is in fact a debunked chiasmic construction. Although it is true that the novel starts with Alice (before it introduces us to Dinah) and finishes with Dinah (preceded by a scene with Alice), it must be read as a sort of flat line, like the monotonous line on the control screen showing that Alice's brain has ceased to live precisely at the moment when the story was the center of an incredible number of unexpected actions and filled with so many characters. Nothing has happened then, except in the words and to the words, and the story leaves everything unturned, as it was before it started.

"She herself supplied that story" (155), Dinah tells us when she explains that her biography has been totally invented by Alice. The novel foregrounds the fact that its texture is primarily an invention of biographies and stories, stories that give to it a retrospective coherence, close to the Joycean idea of "retrospective arrangement."

The ultimate explanation that is supposed to give an overall coherence to the story by providing a final clue is but one more lure hidden behind the alluring features of an authorial presence. Dinah, in the course of the whole novel, is supposed to have been looking for a mother figure: "Swiftly and silently through the frozen park she began to stalk after her mother" (210). This last reversal imposes a closure on the novel that seems all the more arbitrary since the reader's gullibility has been under strain throughout two hundred pages—just to be taught the novel resists closure. Resting on the anguish produced by the novel, the language of laughter rechannels the reader toward the words taken in all their extensions. Many procedures are working to trigger laughter.

Alice's repetitions of formulas such as "I have neither chick nor child" (16), which her relatives are used to, are gradually replaced by a surprising leitmotif: "She's my daughter" (31), pointing to Dinah—stunning for all those who have known her for a long time. She is thus transformed into a farcical character. The bringing together of various levels of languages is quite usual. Dublin's old ladies know everything about technocratic jargon and are very much at ease with it: "There can be no margin for doubt" (31); "only patterns of education and economic necessity" (165). At the same time, the novel is full of familiar phrases and proverbial expressions: "Marriage is like drinking gin—a little buzz and a long hangover" (15); "there are no pockets in a shroud" (111). The newly converted African tribes practice play-on-words, transforming God into a local divinity of the African cosmogony: "In the name of the Fadda and the Sun." Dinah herself evokes the following alternative: "Hell and Havana" (129). It is easy to suspect some trap hiding behind the name of the main character—as a matter of fact, we are finally told: "I had a very dim eye as a child. I used to feel like Alice in Wonderland, too large for everything around me, one foot in the chimney and the other in my mouth" (162).

In the narrative, many words are taken at their face value and their meaning overturned: "I have not enjoyed the married state"—"It's not a question of enjoy" (32). This exchange is echoed later in a scene where Dinah reads Alice's Bible in her room: "Dinah scanned the book idly, as if it were a thriller. 'Abraham begat Isaac . . . . And Aram begat A-min-a-dab!' . . . . 'And?' Alice pursued her through the keyhole. 'And they enjoyed it!' Dinah shouted back" (117). Around the verb "enjoy" a dead language is shown, fossilized in its abstraction ("I have not enjoyed"). Further on we find another mode of demolition of time-honored figurative meanings with the use of a dictionary to go back to the first meaning: "A life lived to the hilt? *Hilt. n.—the handle of a sword*; that was what the dictionary said. A life lived to the handle of a sword; she did not think she was up to it" (68).

The dominant tendency in the novel consists in bringing about comparisons through the use of an implicit or explicit locution that plays the part of an arouser and makes us await the witticism: "like," "as," "the same," and comparison verbs are among the devices most commonly used. Consider, for instance, such expressions as "You are like this house, ice to the foundation" (116), and "The door had gone from green to yellow. Its mildewed brasses sparkled bold as cliché would have it" (185). On the whole, those various procedures of unveiling clichés, always playing on two levels of meaning, operate a constant movement that might lead to a classical vision of language, with an originary stage where the separation between the word and its secondary meanings has not yet happened, where the verbal expression is a figure of speech of what had once a literal meaning.

The playful intertextuality of Boylan's novel drops hints followed by a confirmation of a humoristic nature, underlining the game it entails. The alternation of forms destabilizing the mimesis and creating at the same time a self-referential entity of language likely to translate Ireland in this very empty space left by the absence of a master language, a mother tongue, recognized as such, transforms the display of writing procedures in the greatest expectation of the novel.

In some aspects we can think of a Beckettian filiation, particularly the Beckett of *Murphy*, with its mechanical characters, its delirious situations, and its hidden, playful references. But, more clearly, the Joycean lineage seems to be obvious. I have already outlined the parallels between Boylan's work and the *Wake*. But *Black Baby* also reworks several other key Joycean themes. The Christmas Eve spent around the aunt's deathbed (161), which makes the nephew recall his past, reminds us of a similar scene in "The Dead" where Gabriel Conroy comes face to face with his, as it were, other—his buried self. The "boarding house" where Alice spent her summers as a child (138) recalls the story bearing that title in *Dubliners*, and Alice's romantic musings recall Eveline's. When Dinah decides to leave town, her point of departure is precisely Stephen's Green, where Stephen himself decides he will leave Ireland. The character of "the old Jew who ran a small business in loans and securities" (24) seems to portray an aged but still suspicious Bloom. "A bad girl, Brigid Mulvey," whom Alice knew in school, might be a descendant of the Mulvey Molly loved in Gibraltar and whom she remembers in her monologue (118), all the more so as the reference to the liberated Miss Mulvey is followed closely by a doubled reference to blooming. A room that had previously been described as "Blooming freezing!" (105) is now described as blooming: "The room bloomed. 'Ah, yes'" (120). The play with the word "bloom" here followed by the fatidic "Yes" are indisputable references to *Ulysses*. A few details—such as the ads in the newspapers like those Bloom used to get in touch with Martha, the songs in the pubs like those in the "Sirens" chapter, the prostitutes who are ready to prostitute their grandmothers, like Bloom in "Circe"—act as reminders of a recognizable voice. Similarly, those characters with undefined fluctuating identities and this insecure onomastics recall the Joycean tendency toward a generalized epistemological uncertainty as exemplified by the example of the figure of "Mac Intosh" in *Ulysses*. At a structural level, just as *Ulysses* is built on the narrative pattern of the father/son motif, largely used as a pretext, *Black Baby* bearing on the theme of the lost parental link plays on the mother/daughter relationship, similarly impossible and unaccomplished. Finally, something of the mode of writing of "Circe" and, of course, the *Wake* pervades the writing of the whole novel, where the series of appearances and disappearances is structured on the hallucination of the coma not as a theme but as the very structure of the narrative pattern.

If Boylan's novel reworks the *Wake* theme of cultural amnesia, it also shares the strategies Joyce uses to overcome censorship, to awaken a dead culture and a dead language—specifically, his use of laughter, a kind of Swiftian tragicomic wit. In *Black Baby*, as in Joyce's work, laughter becomes an essential component, if not one of the main characters in the novel. It tries to overcome the anguish by giving a joyful point of view whose foundation stone is sadness.

All the procedures used by Boylan in *Black Baby*, among them disguise, mystification, the transformation of surnames into nicknames, are defined by Bakhtin as being those of the "realistic grotesque." Conditioned by their link with the forms of popular rejoicing, these procedures, according to Bakhtin, restore the "authentic laugh" of the people. Many of the procedures described by Bakhtin in *Rabelais and His World* and elsewhere can be found in the following passage:

> Christmas mass was lovely, the children in their woolens, clutching giant dolls and mechanical monsters which had been brought by Santa. Even the adults enjoyed a temporary suspension of disbelief. They wore eccentric additions to their clothing, Noddy hats and fur gloves like bears' paws and, when they shook hands for the gesture of friendship, there were conspiratorial grins as if to say that even friendship was acceptable because it was a children's day. . . . Alice, steered by Dinah's loyal arm, beamed at everyone. She didn't usually do so. It is an offense to catch the eye of others when you are lonely. (182–83)

At this stage, another Bakhtinian concern makes the link with the Joycean subtext which is always present: the consciousness of a lack of a unique language of reference, authoritarian and irrefutable. We enter here a world outside literature; we reach the margin or the threshold of the text, like an invisible line that is precisely the equilibrium point on which it rests.

OF WIT AND WORDS

Black Baby makes laughter explode in the middle of the page. In terms of narrative events, the occurrences of laughter in the novel are easy to trace; they correspond to moments when inhibitions are suspended. These moments are sometimes linked to alcohol (61), but more frequently they are linked to Dinah, who is seen throughout the novel as a conveyor of laughter; she uses wit to break up the psychic crypt in which Alice has entombed herself.

The desecration of Alice's past follows when the prostitute Ferrety wears Alice's mother's dress on Christmas Eve: Alice was "awed by life's capacity for transformation, swift and unpredictable as the seasons. . . . From time to time, in the midst of her drinking and singing, Alice would catch her mother looking at her from a corner of the room and for an instant she would feel fraudulent and abashed" (189). Here laughing is a way of overcoming censorship.

In Joyce's work the censoring force is represented by four old men. In Boylan's work it is represented by a woman, Alice's mother. Her mother, Alice admits, "was a bit of a termagant" (165). The ferocious repression exercised by the mother on the daughter when she came of age is described in a scene in the boardinghouse where she forces Alice to eat an incredible amount of food (139) and promises decay if she disobeys and, above all, if she copulates someday: "She told me horrible things that would happen to me night after night, and my parents, under the same roof, would be unable to answer my cries because he would be married to me and it would be his right to use me as he wished. Of course I knew about the married act, but I had no idea, until poor Mother told me, that it would be so painful, so brutal" (141–42).

It is this oppressive vision that is transgressed by laughter. The "wit" is based on an empty blank whose traces are numerous: it becomes then the essential element which rebuilds an interpersonal link where it had been refused. Alice, a soul in search of light, is a kind of Cyclops figure: "'My eye is single!' she protested" (119). Through Dinah's wit, "intimacy invaded [Alice's] life, not with the fabled braggadocio of sanctified virile lust, but in the ancient dependencies of her own, good, fastidious parents—not just night after night, but day after day and night after night. Not, after all, so terrible or shocking; menial, helpless, unimportant, sour" (142). The process of the resocialization of Alice through the sharing of "wit," once she has overcome a first facade of refusal, is linked to the void she feels in herself—the absence of any form of sexual life: "Sex—she had read everything on the subject on which she could lay hands, yet still she could not understand" (35). Hence, a sublimation into an imaginary maternity and an incapacity to inhabit her female body otherwise than as a sort of punishment: "As a warning I was visited by the illness every month and each month I prayed and was healed. As a penance I ate all that was put before me. It was a year before I learnt that this . . . thing . . . happens to all women with or without milk puddings" (139).

Beyond this game, even on literary purple patches and rhetorical stock topics which at times recall the hectic rhythm and the turnover of males in *Moll Flanders,* the staging of laughter based on "wit" requires the presence of a third person; it is necessary for Dinah to be here in order to make laughter explode and for the reader to be part of the reading process in order to relay it. Such is the architecture of the "wit"—both included in the narrative and springing out of the page, but always linked to an implied third person.

It is Dinah who creates the social link, thanks to her witticisms. This means that the "wit" does not belong in particular either to the first or to the third person; laughing means being together, in an impersonal and neutral way. No person could ever be an autonomous narcissus: the "wit" passes from mouth to mouth, and it is political in the sense that it creates socialization beyond a community of language. Just for the time of a celebration, the space of "wit" enables the recreation of the original "socius," that is to say a relationship prior to the distinction between subjects and to the constitution of a first or a "third" person.

What Dinah brings to Alice is the phallus she was missing and which satisfies her completely, through an immersion in her past and a surging up of what she calls her "nature," and which a constant denying had prevented her from seeing: "My father wasn't a saint either. I can see that now—and something else. I take after him. I always knew I hankered after a bit of cheer but it's more than that. I'm attracted by vulgarity. Mother used to say he was a vulgar little man. She wanted me to despise him too, but the nearest I could get was to dent his nature: my nature" (165–66).

"You have taught me not to fear the truth," Alice tells Dinah. For Dinah, "The impulse of creation is closely allied to the spirit" (122). The word "spirit," with its multiple meanings, is clearly linked to sex: "I have always believed that those who are indifferent to sex are poorly endowed with spirit" (122). The "wit" is the "last laugh," the final success after previous defeats: "The man in the moon had the last laugh" (43). The "wit" is a means of overcoming the various censorships erected by Catholic Ireland, of plunging into the unconscious of a country via the characters, since the "wit" is a double-faced Janus (as Freud has it [803], looking at both on the side of meaning and on the side of nonsense), a critical function and a premium of pleasure, which enables the expression of suppressed unconscious tendencies. Here, as in the *Wake,* the "wit" wakes the buried mother tongue: it has a topical value, and the presence of a third person is what makes it get out of the unconscious. The techniques of "wit" bring pleasure because they make us find something known where we expected to find something new: unification, assonance, multiple use, modification of current locutions, allusions to quotations. Freud adds that it is not something already known which rejoyces but the apparition of something known where something new was expected.

But the "wit" is something impossible to translate; it can only be savored: "[She] savoured the sister's wit with a splurt of joy that sprayed neat gin upon the counterpane" (85). Like those works of art whose silence triggers a critical response, translating a "wit" is a Pyrrhus-like victory. The "wit" is "membra disjecta," nonsense talk with no logical lineage, and to reconstitute the "wit" under the shape of a "corpus," to unify in one body what is separate, is to be afraid of its import and to restrain it. Always playing as she does on two levels of meaning and disclosing the artifact of the secondary meanings by putting forward their supposedly primary meaning, Clare Boylan builds the "wit" at the same time that she deconstructs it, to the real meaning of the word, that is to say she places it in a moment that defies its appearance, uncovering the multiple layers that made it signify. The "wit" in *Black Baby,* then, is on the side of translation. An intra-linguistic translation of the "wit"—to say the same thing with different words—means the complete dissolution of the "wit." The "wit" is already the translation of another text of which it keeps a trace like a vestige. It plays on indirect representation, on representation by correlation. This strange language establishes connections between what is said and what is not said, connections that no translation could supply except by reducing it to the translation of a contents. Contrary to the comic which tries to avoid pain, the "wit" aches and does not look for a narcissistic satisfaction. It destroys in advance the critical function and imposes the law of silence.

"Swiftly and silently" (210), then, are the two key words that conclude the novel, circulate through it, and place it between Swift and silence—silence being another Joycean modality to express the ideas of the missing language.

Protean as it is, this text with no firm ground on which it can stabilize itself draws attention to words and keeps wavering between many levels: a game on literary clichés, even in their up-to-date psychoanalytic version of family conflicts, a world of puppets, and, behind, an apparent linearity, the coherence of reading put into question.

This novel by Clare Boylan is a constant exploration of the main resource of the Irish: language. In the absence of a unique and global language assumed as such, it is only thanks to "wit" that she can escape from a language she deconstructs.

WORKS CITED

Bakhtin, Mikhail. *Rabelais and His World.* Translated by Hélène Iswolsky. Cambridge, Mass.: MIT Press, 1968.
Boylan, Clare. *Black Baby.* London: Penguin, 1989.
Freud, Sigmund. *The Basic Writings of Sigmund Freud.* Edited by A. A. Brill. New York: Random House, 1938.

Contributors

Nuala Ní Dhomhnaill is a poet whose books include *An Dealg Droighinn, Féar Suaithinseach, Feis, Selected Poems/Rogha Danta, The Astrakhan Cloak* (in Irish, with translations by Paul Muldoon), and *Pharaoh's Daughter* (in Irish, with translations by thirteen of Ireland's leading poets). She is currently working on a translation from Turkish into Irish of Nazim Hikmet's book-length poem "Memliketinden Insan Manzaralari."

Eiléan Ní Chuilleanáin is a poet and professor of English at Trinity College, Dublin. Her books include *Acts and Monuments, The Rose Geranium, Site of Ambush, The Second Voyage, The Magdalene Sermon and Earlier Poems,* and *The Brazen Serpent.*

Mary Lowe-Evans is dean of arts and sciences at the University of West Florida. She is the author of *Crimes Against Fecundity: Joyce and Population Control* and has contributed articles to *Studies in the Novel,* the *James Joyce Quarterly,* the *Journal of Modern Literature,* and the *Encyclopedic Handbook of American Women's History.*

James M. Cahalan is professor of English at Indiana University of Pennsylvania, where he formerly directed the doctoral program in literature and criticism and the IUP Ireland program at Trinity College, Dublin. He was also director of the Irish studies program at the University of Massachusetts, Boston. He is the author of many articles—including "Forging a Tradition: Emily Lawless and the Irish

Literary Canon"—and five books: *Great Hatred, Little Room: the Irish Historical Novel, Liam O'Flaherty: A Study of the Short Fiction, Practicing Theory in Introductory College Literature Courses,* and *Modern Irish Literature and Culture: A Chronology.*

RACHAEL JANE LYNCH is assistant professor of English at the University of Connecticut, Waterbury. She has published articles on nineteenth-century literature and Anglo-Irish literature, and has completed a book on Thackeray.

FLORA ALEXANDER is senior lecturer in English at the University of Aberdeen, Scotland. She is the author of *Contemporary Women Novelists* and numerous articles on Scottish and English medieval literature and is a regular contributor to *Bibliographical Bulletin of the International Arthurian Society.* She is currently working on a study of recent fiction in English by Canadian women.

MICHAEL PATRICK GILLESPIE is professor of English at Marquette University, Milwaukee. He is the author of *Inverted Volumes Improperly Arranged* and *James Joyce's Trieste Library: Reading the Book of Himself* and coauthor of *Joycean Occasions.* His books *The Picture of Dorian Gray: "As The World Sees Me"* and *James Joyce A to Z* are forthcoming.

THERESA O'CONNOR teaches postcolonial literature at Knox College, Galesburg, Illinois. She is a founder of the Graduate Student Conference in Irish Studies. She has published articles on Joyce and nationalism and is currently working on a book on Joyce's African philosophy of history.

MARY O'CONNOR is assistant professor of English at the State University of South Dakota, Brookings. She has written about the Irish language poet Nuala Ní Dhomhnaill and translated much of her poetry. Her own poetry and fiction has been published in *Contemplative Review, Footprints, Columbia,* and *New Irish Writing.*

JEAN-LOUIS GIOVANNANGELI is a lecturer in English at the University of Paris. A member of the French Joyce group at the Centre de Recherché sur James Joyce (Institut des Textes et Manuscrits Modernes) in Paris, he has published numerous works on Joyce, including a study of *Ulysses, Detours et Retours.*

Index